D0169386

Teaching Faulkner's
The Sound and the Fury

Approaches to Teaching World Literature

Joseph Gibaldi, series editor

For a complete listing of titles,
see the last pages of this book.

Approaches to Teaching Faulkner's *The Sound and the Fury*

Edited by
Stephen Hahn
and
Arthur F. Kinney

The Modern Language Association of America
New York   1996

PS3511
.A86
S77
1996

©1996 by The Modern Language Association of America
All rights reserved. Printed in the United States of America

For information about obtaining permission to reprint material from
MLA book publications, send your request by mail (see address below),
e-mail (permissions@mla.org), or fax (212 533-0680).

Library of Congress Cataloging-in-Publication Data

Approaches to teaching Faulkner's The sound and the fury / edited by
 Stephen Hahn and Arthur F. Kinney.
    p.   cm. — (Approaches to teaching world literature : 57)
  Includes bibliographical references and index.
  ISBN 0-87352-737-2. — ISBN 0-87352-738-0 (pbk.)
  1. Faulkner, William, 1897–1962. Sound and the fury.
  2. Faulkner, William, 1897–1962—Study and teaching. I. Hahn,
  Stephen, 1950– . II. Kinney, Arthur F., 1933– . III. Series.
  PS3511.A86S77   1996
  813'.54—dc20   96-7601

ISSN 1059-1133

Cover illustration for the paperback edition: *Oxford on the Hill*, 1939, by
John McCrady (1911–68). Oil on canvas. Collection of the City of Oxford.
Print for the reproduction provided by the University of Mississippi's Center
for the Study of Southern Culture.

Set in Caledonia and Bodoni. Printed on recycled paper

Published by The Modern Language Association of America
10 Astor Place, New York, New York 10003-6981

CONTENTS

DEC 1 7 1998

PREFACE TO THE SERIES

In *The Art of Teaching* Gilbert Highet wrote, "Bad teaching wastes a great deal of effort, and spoils many lives which might have been full of energy and happiness." All too many teachers have failed in their work, Highet argued, simply "because they have not thought about it." We hope that the Approaches to Teaching World Literature series, sponsored by the Modern Language Association's Publications Committee, will not only improve the craft—as well as the art—of teaching but also encourage serious and continuing discussion of the aims and methods of teaching literature.

The principal objective of the series is to collect within each volume different points of view on teaching a specific literary work, a literary tradition, or a writer widely taught at the undergraduate level. The preparation of each volume begins with a wide-ranging survey of instructors, thus enabling us to include in the volume the philosophies and approaches, thoughts and methods of scores of experienced teachers. The result is a sourcebook of material, information, and ideas on teaching the subject of the volume to undergradates.

The series is intended to serve nonspecialists as well as specialists, inexperienced as well as experienced teachers, graduate students who wish to learn effective ways of teaching as well as senior professors who wish to compare their own approaches with the approaches of colleagues in other schools. Of course, no volume in the series can ever substitute for erudition, intelligence, creativity, and sensitivity in teaching. We hope merely that each book will point readers in useful directions; at most each will offer only a first step in the long journey to successful teaching.

Joseph Gibaldi
Series Editor

PREFACE TO THE VOLUME

In this volume we bring together essays on teaching William Faulkner's *The Sound and the Fury* from a variety of approaches and in a variety of contexts that represent, we believe, as broad an array of curricular, theoretical, and practical concerns as is feasible in a book of this length. Like most editors, and authors, we have often wished that we had both pages enough and time to encompass more—in this case, more of the Faulkner canon. Early in the project, we established *The Sound and the Fury* as our focal text, although other Faulkner novels and stories have their claims to similar status in the teaching canon. Throughout the development of the book we were guided by others: first, by the respondents to our questionnaire on teaching Faulkner and, subsequently, by our contributors, consulting readers, the editorial staff at the MLA, and the MLA Publications Committee. Along the way, several changes of focus in the project occurred, and some proposed essays that seemed to fit at an earlier stage had to find their homes elsewhere—not without our regret. We are grateful to all who have contributed to the final product—those whom we know and those who remain anonymous. The names of respondents to our early questionnaire appear at the end of the volume. We would like to make special note here of the contribution of Robert Dale Parker, who allowed his essay to be used as a model as we developed the book and who supplied us with several references we were unable to locate. Participants in the annual Faulkner and Yoknapatawpha Conference and in the work of the Center for the Study of Southern Culture at the University of Mississippi have been especially helpful, and we have benefited from joining in the discussions at the Teaching Faulkner sessions of the conference over the last several years.

We hope that this volume contributes to conversations among teachers and students about a broad range of Faulkner's writing—since each of the essays presents an approach that can be extended to other works by Faulkner—and about Faulkner's place and significance in the literary canon. As that canon has grown more diverse over the last several decades, so has the community of readers and teachers who spend at least some of their time thinking and writing about Faulkner. As a result, this volume looks different from what a similar volume would have looked like in previous decades, as it will look different from what a similar volume might look like some decades hence, but we hope that in our endeavor we have struck a balance between the timely and the more or less permanent and that we will stimulate critical discourse within the community of Faulkner's readers.

Stephen Hahn, *William Paterson College*
Arthur F. Kinney, *University of Massachusetts, Amherst*

Introduction

The Sound and the Fury emerged with other works by William Faulkner as part of the undergraduate teaching canon of American and world literature in the 1950s, following the publication in 1946 of *The Portable Faulkner*, edited by Malcolm Cowley, and the award to Faulkner in 1950 of the Nobel Prize for literature. In January 1957, *College English* published what appears to be the first pedagogical essay devoted exclusively to this novel, "Teaching *The Sound and the Fury*," by Martha Winburn England—an essay that had been preceded in the same journal in 1955 by a more inclusive essay on Faulkner, Ilse Dusoir Lind's "The Teachable Faulkner." Both essays outline approaches to teaching the novel in the then current mode of humanistic appreciation, to an audience that England calls "unselected freshmen" (221) and that Lind describes as "a mixed group" including both "the connoisseurs of Kafka and Carson McCullers" and "those who can count on the fingers of one hand all the poems or novels they have ever read" (284). In retrospect, these mid-century essays suggest a unanimity of opinion about the purposes of teaching literature and a confidence about the status of the literary work—in contrast to the broader spectrum of teaching concerns in the latter part of the century. But they also speak to the issue of difficulty and accessibility in approaching Faulkner's writing in high school, college, and university classrooms.

Today, as in the 1950s, *The Sound and the Fury* challenges teachers and students at a variety of academic levels and in a variety of contexts. We chose this novel as the focus of the volume because studying it is especially rewarding, bringing before us the central issues of teaching any work by Faulkner. While *The Sound and the Fury* may not be the most commonly assigned novel by Faulkner, it is the novel people associate most frequently with the author, and it is the novel the author seems to have regarded most highly, calling it his "most splendid failure" (Gwynn and Blotner 76). Within its compass, the novel presents through unusual perspectives a range of interior and social life, invoking themes of race, clan, and class; adolescence and identity; virtue and weakness of will; generativity and despair; honesty, deception, and self-deception; and belief and unbelief in the traditions and values of a culture. In addition, at the primary level of aesthetic response, reading any passage of the novel aloud is an experience teachers and students can relish. *The Sound and the Fury* is representative of the best of Faulkner's writing, and it is accessible, whatever its immediate difficulties, to many levels of teaching and learning.

For the high school student and teacher, Faulkner's novel is often viewed foremost as an opportunity to reflect on family and the difficult and awkward relationships between parents and children, brothers and sisters, those who stay home and those who go away. For college students, it can be a novel of adolescence and coming of age, of daring experimentation with language, or of the problems of psychology and consciousness, as well as of the relation of individuals to social and historical circumstances. At all levels, in ways that academic critics are still discovering, it is a novel that asks us to reflect on our habits of understanding and reading, on the assumptions we hold about literature and about the function of stories in our lives and the life of our culture.

For teachers who approach literature from the perspective of the transmutation of biography into fiction, *The Sound and the Fury* offers many avenues to explore. Much of Faulkner's own adolescent confusion and angst is reflected in Quentin III's troubled thoughts and tortured relationships. Much of the malaise of Faulkner's father, Murry, is reflected in the depiction of Jason IV. The Faulkner family servant Caroline Barr resembles Dilsey, while Caroline Compson shares with the historical Estelle Oldham Franklin Faulkner a dependency and a tendency to illness and melancholy that (combined with William's own problems, which are not unlike those of Jason III) disturbed the Faulkner's marriage. Other, more specific, biographical and local antecedents can be discovered. Near Faulkner's childhood home, the Chandler family lived in the antebellum Thompson house—the combination of the names appears to have produced the name Compson. There, on his daily walk to school as a young boy, Faulkner saw Edwin Chandler, a victim of Down's syndrome, whose demeanor and behavior may have later suggested the characterization of Benjy. Moreover, Faulkner knew of, and purchased with the money he earned from sales of *The Sound and the Fury*, an antebellum house with a rotting portico like that of the Compsons' house—a house called the Shegog place after a historically significant Oxford, Mississippi, entrepreneur, whose name perhaps ironically suggested that of the black Saint Louis preacher who turns the Easter sermon on redemption into a pentecostal speaking in tongues in the last section of the novel.

In the most traditional critical reading of the novel as a study in the decline of the Old South and the rise of the New South, *The Sound and the Fury* provides a historical perspective on how these transitions affect individuals and a family for whom history turns from romance to nightmare. Recent historians substantiate what Faulkner probably knew from his own experience, that the supposed glories of the antebellum South were never fully established in northern Mississippi and that the lineage of white families with aristocratic pretensions was never as pure and singular as the public record would overtly tell. Read from this angle, *The Sound and the Fury* represents not only a sense of the loss of social and economic prerogative but also the need to preserve or invent cultural values regardless of circumstance and historical fact—a theme implicit in the novel and rather explicit in Faulkner's 1946 "Appendix: Compson." The sharing of the names across generations—Jason (father and son) and Quentin (uncle and niece)—and the renaming of Benjy (originally Maurice, after his maternal uncle) invite us to consider what the names themselves allude to and to consider as well the claims that cross-generational naming makes on later generations and on the community in which individuals are to take their place.

The presence in this novel of an affiliated African American family, the Gibsons, both within and outside the Compson household—equally present through their participation in dialogue and absent through their lack of a representative narrator—introduces issues of race as well as of class. While early readings of the novel tended to see Dilsey Gibson as symbolic of redemptive Christian values in the novel, more recent readings stress the ambiguities and ambivalences of the relationships between the Gibsons and the Compsons; the Gibsons function somewhat like a "shadow family" for the Compsons, and, in contrast to them or in sufferance of them, as Faulkner says in his later appendix to the novel, the Gibsons "endure" (Faulkner, *Sound* [Norton] 215). If the characterization of Dilsey has seemed to some critics and readers perilously close to a stereotypical depiction of a mammy, there is a lively if less obviously foregrounded depiction of resistance to and subversion of the presumptions of white advantage played out in the characterizations of Luster, T. P., Roskus, Frony, and Jason's coworker, Job.

The novel also highlights issues of gender. Much of the second and third sections focuses on attempts by Quentin III and Jason IV to achieve a sense of manliness—though what this means differs for each. Jasons III and IV and Quentin III give voice in different registers, in the apt words of the feminist theorist Judith Butler, to "the notion that being female is a natural indisposition" (viii), while Caddy and her daughter Quentin (sometimes called Quentin IV), as well as Caroline Compson, seem determined in different ways to embody the same notion. But if this notion is being voiced, it is voiced in so blatant and troubled a way that one cannot help but conclude that Faulkner, whatever his views and feelings, drew these characters to bring into question the categories of gender, whose boundaries some seem to cross (the two Quentins, for instance) while others are busy reifying them (Caroline and Jason IV, for example).

The sounds of the novel and the fury of its actions—which include putative if not actual incest, suicide, self-mutilation, legal castration, embezzlement, robbery, adultery, sexual assault, and statutory rape—do indeed signify, though what they signify is not contained in the words on the page alone; it is contained also in the readers and communities of readers who interact with those words. In its most inclusive sense, the novel is about signifying and perhaps also about what Faulkner in an early and now seldom read novel had his narrator call "the utter and heartbreaking stupidity of words" (*Mosquitoes* 186). *The Sound and the Fury* draws us into the rhythms of its signification and yet delivers us abruptly to silence and to reflection at the end of each of its four, nonsequential narrative sections. Its status as a classic derives not simply because it appears frequently on course syllabi but because it brings us to the borders of the ineffable—as in the depiction of Benjy's reveries—at the same time that it remains teachable and readable in the classroom. Like other classic works of world literature, *The Sound and the Fury* reflects the exorbitant aspiration to transform the reader's experience of what it means to read a book and to participate in a literary tradition.

Following our comments on teaching materials, the essays by our contributors are organized in groups. In the first group, "Beginnings," Robert Dale Parker, Arnold Weinstein, and Anthony Barthelemy suggest how instructors might begin to think about teaching this novel. Parker describes a pedagogical protocol and provides supporting material to guide them through their initial classes on *The Sound and the Fury*; Weinstein discusses an approach that highlights the effect—sensuous, emotive, intellectual—of the poetic language of the novel; and Barthelemy addresses the question of how instructors might contextualize the issues of race, the racially charged language and racially motivated thoughts and actions of the characters and narrators. Together, these essays provide an overview.

The essays in the second group, "Exploring the Novel and Its Related Texts," treat the use of Faulkner's personal, private, and fugitive writings, as well as his "Appendix: Compson," focusing on issues of authorial intention. Philip Cohen and Doreen Fowler discuss the relevance of the now much cited introduction to the novel that Faulkner wrote in the early 1930s for a proposed but never realized reprinting of *The Sound and the Fury*. Their essay especially addresses using the introduction to understand the novel as an expression and elaboration of authorial desires and anxieties. James G. Watson approaches issues of authorial intention by outlining the development of elements in Faulkner's personal writing—themes, characteristic symbols, and stylistic techniques—that are subsequently deployed in his novel. Walter Taylor's essay on what has casually come to be known as "the Compson appendix" warns instructors against using this later work as a key to the meanings of the novel; Taylor provides information that instructors will find useful in discussing the origin and genesis of the appendix. In contrast, Charles Peek suggests ways of using the appendix to help students overcome their initial estrangement from the narrative dislocations and cultural differences embodied in the novel.

Our third section, "Psychological and Philosophical Approaches," and fourth section, "Contextual and Comparative Approaches," illustrate how teachers may relate *The Sound and the Fury* to the dominant intellectual and literary trends that preceded and followed the writing and publication of the novel, and to historical and cultural contexts. In "Psychological and Philosophical Approaches," Judith Bryant Wittenberg discusses classroom presentation of information on Faulkner's probable knowledge of Freud's writing, the perspectives of major Freudian critics of the novel, and applications of Freudian theory to the analysis of the major characters. Terrell L. Tebbetts outlines how a teacher can use the Jungian analysis of individuation—specifically, the failure of individuation in dysfunctional families—to guide students to a richer understanding of the human drama of the novel. John F. Desmond addresses some religious issues peculiar to the literary tradition of the American South—specifically, the treatment of problems of despair in relation to the writings of Kierkegaard. Desmond's essay is particularly useful in showing students how despair—often considered simply an inexplicable psychological disposition allied to depression—is a historically and intellectually important issue allied to our quest for meaning and significance. Jun Liu analyzes varieties of nihilism in the novel, suggesting how the writings of Nietzsche can be employed in exploring the failure of characters to overcome their weakness of will. Like Desmond, Liu addresses the problem of despair. He suggests that students consider the resonance between the novel's title and one of the novel's most important intertexts, Shakespeare's *Macbeth*. The essays in this section obviously go beyond the scope of a typical period course, indicating ways that *The Sound and the Fury* can be taught in the context of broader humanities courses, although the essays also contain important insights for teachers who work in specifically literary contexts.

The essays in "Contextual and Comparative Approaches" concern teaching the novel in relation to historical, cultural, and literary traditions. Daniel J. Holtz approaches the novel as a product of the uniquely southern milieu—a milieu in which the trajectory of history, the relation between classes and races, and the structures of preferment, recognition, and acceptance differ from those codified in the broader national culture of the United States. John N. Duvall connects to that perspective even as he discusses how the novel is located in issues general to the national culture and to the cultural ferment of the 1920s. Duvall's suggestions for assignments are especially useful to those teaching period or survey courses in American literature. He explores the relation of Faulkner's writing to that of other American writers, such as Willa Cather, T. S. Eliot, Ernest Hemingway, Zora Neale Hurston, and Tennessee Williams. (These two essays and Gail L. Mortimer's essay on "Barn Burning" in the next section speak especially to issues of teaching Faulkner in the context of an American tradition.) Broadening the aesthetic and geographical range of reference, Philip M. Weinstein discusses teaching the novel in a course on modernist literature, against the background of nineteenth-century realism and in the company of the major European novelists of the twentieth century. Weinstein comments specifically on ways to help students address the stylistic eccentricity of Faulkner's narrative. Approaching the novel through a concern with stylistic technique is also the focus of Panthea Reid's essay, which discusses Faulkner's awareness of developments in the visual arts and their probable influence on his stylistic development. Reid indicates how instructors can develop stylistic analogies for students to explore this aspect of Faulkner's writing, even as she cautions us about the limitations of such analogies. And John T. Matthews discusses ways to encourage advanced students to read "against the grain," with attention to Faulkner's stylistic procedures and to the cultural and historical implications of varieties of representation. He develops an approach for teaching the novel "after theory."

The essays in the last group, "Teaching *The Sound and the Fury* in the Faulkner Canon," outline ways in which thematic and stylistic aspects of Faulkner's short fiction can be illuminated and used as a preparation for approaching his longer work. Gail L. Mortimer suggests approaches instructors can adopt with "Barn Burning" to explore the familiar American themes of family life and economic struggle in Faulkner's work and to analyze his shifts in narrative perspective. Mortimer relates Faulkner's writing to the broader American tradition, thereby amplifying on material presented in the previous essays by Holtz and Duvall and supplying further insights about how a teacher can incorporate Faulkner's texts into a survey course in American literature. Louise K. Barnett discusses how the use of the concept of a "gender paradigm" and the differential application of gender-role ascriptions on the basis of race can be used to teach Faulkner's short story "That Evening Sun" and to prepare students for their reading of the novel. She shows how Caddy Compson's role as interrogator in the short story can provide a counterperspective to the depiction of the same character in the novel. Barnett's essay complements particularly Barthelemy's essay on race. Arthur F. Kinney uses an analysis of "narrative as meaning"—our understanding of the effects of the layering and segmenting of narrative lines—to connect the short story "A Justice" to the novel and to assist students in exploring connections (and disconnections) between the character of Quentin III in the short story and in the novel. Claudia Clausius discusses teaching "A Rose for Emily" as a story in which different understandings of the narrative are simultaneously evoked and deferred, while the reader shuttles between different constructions of the significance of action produced by the layering of narrative and what is inferred as being narrated. This approach, she argues, can help prepare students to work with the larger, multiple units of narration in *The Sound and the Fury*. And Stephen Hahn describes ways in which raising key questions about the relation between words and actions—and between words and words as they constitute actions—in "Dry September" can help students develop a better understanding of such complexities, which will enable them to encounter the novel more successfully and more resonantly. These five essays—on the relation of the five most widely anthologized Faulkner stories to one of his most frequently taught novels—open up possibilities for teaching in a number of different contexts.

Teachers will find common themes weaving these essays together. They will hear from a variety of perspectives about Faulkner's treatment of subjectivity and language as he portrays characters like Benjy "trying to say"; about Faulkner's engagement with the particular history and culture of the South in relation to that of the nation; about his engagement with the texts of the literary traditions of the United States and Europe; and about other recurrent topics. The result is a confirmation of our ability to communicate from a range of positions and concerns about the relevance of Faulkner's work.

Part One

MATERIALS

For teachers and students, the world of *The Sound and the Fury* centers on readily available paperback editions of the novel and expands outward through biographies and collections of letters to textual, critical, and historical studies of varying complexity and relevance. The body of critical writing on Faulkner grows at a pace daunting even to specialists. Fortunately, the way into this novel can be as simple as opening to the first page and reading: "Through the fence, between the curling flower spaces. . . ." Indeed, in response to our survey of teachers of Faulkner, some specialists indicate that they no longer assign secondary works in their initial classes on *The Sound and the Fury* or other works by Faulkner. These teachers report that they like to begin with a clean slate to provide a relatively authentic encounter with the novelty and difficulty of the work. Others, as indicated by many of the suggestions of the contributors to this volume, approach Faulkner's work in different ways, employing a variety of texts, strategies, and media.

Essential Materials

There are currently two principal teaching texts of *The Sound and the Fury*. One is the Vintage International edition, cited as the primary reference in this volume; it presents the text of the novel without the 1946 appendix and is based on the 1984 "corrected text" established under the direction of Noel Polk. This edition is adopted by instructors who want to approximate a reading of the novel as it was first published in 1929. Other teachers find that ancillary material such as the 1946 appendix and Faulkner's suppressed introductions to the novel provide useful contexts for critical reading. David Minter's Norton Critical Edition (2nd ed.), which is also based on the "corrected text," includes Faulkner's appendix and introductions, selections from his letters, interviews, and related writings; and a number of major critical and historical essays. Teachers who wish to use additional materials should consider this edition the primary alternative to the Vintage International edition. (More detailed annotations appear under "The Instructor's Library" below.)

The teacher or student who wants to develop a small library of important critical and reference works should consider at least the following. Edmond L. Volpe's *A Reader's Guide to William Faulkner* (1968) provides a chronology, a genealogy, and explication for *The Sound and the Fury*; it remains a key reference work. Among the major early studies of Faulkner, those by Cleanth Brooks (1963), Michael Millgate (1966), and Olga W. Vickery (1964) are still accessible and generally reliable resources for matters of fact and interpretation. Michel Gresset's *A Faulkner Chronology* is perhaps the handiest resource to establish a chronological context for the novel. David Minter's "Faulkner, Childhood, and the Making of *The Sound and the Fury*" provides a concise and readable psychoanalytic exploration of themes in the novel (and it is reprinted in Minter's Norton Critical Edition). For classroom presentation, the documentary video *William Faulkner: A Life on Paper* offers a remarkably comprehensive and engaging portrait of Faulkner as a person and an artist—and it makes fine use of visual imagery, including some of the author's own early drawings. Of the interviews that Faulkner gave, the widely reprinted *Paris Review* interview with Jean Stein vanden Heuvel is the most focused and accessible, and every teacher will want to be familiar with it. A useful work introducing a contemporary critical perspective is John T. Matthews, The Sound and the Fury: *Faulkner and the Lost Cause*, and a similarly useful introductory work of an earlier generation, employing a structuralist approach, is André Bleikasten's *The Most Splendid Failure*. A range of critical opinion spanning several generations is presented in the familiar Prentice Hall Twentieth Century series, edited by Robert Penn Warren (1966), Michael H. Cowan (1968), and Richard H. Brodhead (1983). Similar collections of essays include Bleikasten's *William Faulkner's* The Sound and the Fury: *A Critical Casebook* and Harold Bloom's *William Faulkner's* The Sound and the Fury: *Modern Critical Interpretations*. Collections of essays not previously published in other formats include Noel Polk's *New Essays on* The Sound and the Fury and Philip M. Weinstein's *The Cambridge Companion to William Faulkner*.

The teacher or student who elects to conduct further research will want to expand this small collection to a shelf or more. The standard biographies—those by Joseph Blotner, David Minter, Frederick R. Karl, and Richard Gray—and selections of Faulkner's letters and interviews are obvious volumes to add. In addition, studies by Edward L. Ayers, Eugene D. Genovese, Daniel J. Singal, Joel Williamson, C. Vann Woodward, and Bertram Wyatt-Brown provide a foundation for understanding Faulkner in a historical context. Charles Reagan Wilson and William Ferris's *Encyclopedia of Southern Culture* is the single most comprehensive reference work on the history and culture of the South. On the themes of race and class, Myra Jehlen's *Class and Character in Faulkner's South* and Thadious M. Davis's *Faulkner's "Negro": Art and the Southern Context* provide good starting points; they can be supplemented by later critical studies, such as Cheryl Lester's "Racial Awareness and Arrested Development: *The Sound and the Fury* and the Great Migration." Finally, a broad range of biographical, historical, critical, and interpretive materials is available in Arthur F. Kinney's *Critical Essays on William Faulkner: The Compson Family*.

Teachers who approach *The Sound and the Fury* through Faulkner's short fiction should refer to *Collected Stories* or *Selected Short Stories of William Faulkner* for accurate texts. To explore the textual history of particular stories, teachers may consult critical and interpretive studies such as Hans H. Skei's *William Faulkner: The Short Story Career*, James B. Carothers's *William Faulkner's Short Stories*, and James Ferguson's *Faulkner's Short Fiction*. In addition, Evans Harrington and Ann J. Abadie have edited a collection of essays from the 1990 Faulkner and Yoknapatawpha Conference, *Faulkner and the Short Story*. Finally, and most recently, there is Diane Brown Jones's comprehensive *A Reader's Guide to the Short Stories of William Faulkner*.

The *MLA Bibliography* provides a central tool for teachers who want to research publications on themes and topics in Faulkner studies. And the more than occasional teacher of Faulkner will want to subscribe to *Teaching Faulkner*, edited by Robert W. Hamblin and Charles Peek and published by the Center for Faulkner Studies at Southeast Missouri State University, Cape Girardeau.

The Instructor's Library

Editions

The Vintage International edition of *The Sound and the Fury*, reprinting the "corrected text" published by Random House in 1984, is "based on a comparison—under the direction of Noel Polk—of the first edition [Jonathan Cape and Harrison Smith, 1929] and Faulkner's original manuscript and carbon typescript." Polk's rationale as editorial consultant for establishing this text can be found in *An Editorial Handbook for William Faulkner's* The Sound and the Fury, xiii–xviii, a page tipped in, 1–22. Facsimiles of the materials from which Polk worked, except for the first edition, are available in *William Faulkner Manuscripts*, volume 6. Other editions of interest are the double volume in the Modern Library, a reprint of the first-edition texts of *The Sound and the Fury* and *As I Lay Dying* with the "Appendix: Compson: 1699–1945" prefacing *The Sound and the Fury*, and the Penguin edition, which has an introduction by the novelist Richard Hughes. The Norton Critical Edition of *The Sound and the Fury* (2nd ed.), reprinting the "corrected text" with ancillary textual materials, is described above.

Related Texts

In 1946 Faulkner prepared for *The Portable Faulkner*, published by Viking Press and edited by Malcolm Cowley, a text entitled "Appendix: Compson: 1699–1945," which narrates subsequent events in the fictional lives of characters belonging to the Compson and Gibson families (Gibson is the surname of Dilsey and her kin). In some later editions of *The Sound and the Fury*, the appendix was printed before the text of the novel; in some, it was printed after; and in some (including the 1984 edition), it was omitted altogether. While certain critics have treated the appendix (with the author's explicit approval) as an integral part of the novel, as a partial key to open up its meanings, it differs from the novel on some matters of fact, and most critics now consider it a separate work.

In addition, in the summer of 1933 Faulkner wrote several drafts of an introduction to a projected but never published edition of the novel. Initially, two versions of the introduction, now thought to be drafts of a single work, were edited and published by James B. Meriwether. (A longer version was published in *Mississippi Quarterly* and reprinted in Meriwether's *A Faulkner Miscellany*; a shorter version was published in the *Southern Review*. Both are reprinted in Minter's Norton Critical Edition and, along with Faulkner's prefatory note on the 1946 appendix, in Kinney's *Critical Essays*. The note, written apparently for Cowley on the reverse side of the appendix typescript, was first published by Meriwether as "A Prefatory Note by Faulkner for the Compson Appendix" in *American Literature*.) Additional portions of Faulkner's introduction and related material later discovered among the Rowan Oak papers in the Faulkner collection at the University of Mississippi Library have been published with commentary by Philip Cohen and Doreen Fowler in *American Literature*.

Three early works in which Faulkner initially explored themes and developed characters that appear in *The Sound and the Fury* are reprinted in Kinney's *Critical Essays: Mayday*, first printed by hand as a presentation gift to Helen Baird and dated by Faulkner "Oxford, Mississippi, 27 January 1926" and later published by the University of Notre Dame Press; and two 1925 newspaper columns in the New Orleans *Times-Picayune*, "The Kingdom of God" and "The Kid Learns." These columns were republished in *William Faulkner: New Orleans Sketches*, edited by Carvel Collins. Members of the Compson family also appear in these later works by Faulkner: *Absalom, Absalom!*, *The Unvanquished*, *Go Down, Moses*, *Requiem for a Nun*, *The Town*, *The Mansion*, "That Evening Sun," "A Justice," "Lion," "Skirmish at Sartoris," "My Grandmother Millard," "Vendee," "Retreat," "Raid," "A Bear Hunt," "The Old People," "The Bear," and "Delta Autumn."

References to Faulkner's short stories in this volume are to *Collected Stories*, which is readily available in a Vintage paperback edition. Another reliable source for the texts of these stories is *Selected Short Stories of William Faulkner*. Of the stories discussed as companion texts to *The Sound and the Fury*, "A Justice" was first published in Faulkner's collection *These Thirteen*; manuscript materials for the story are published in *William Faulkner Manuscripts* (9: 215–27). "A Rose for Emily" was first published in the *Forum* (83 [1930] 233–38) and collected in *These Thirteen*; a facsimile of an earlier typescript which includes unpublished material is provided in *William Faulkner Manuscripts* 9: 198–214; of special interest is a conversation between Miss Emily and Tobe that was excised from the printed story (*William Faulkner Manuscripts* 9: 210–12). "That Evening Sun" was first published as "That Evening Sun Go Down" in the *American Mercury* (Mar. 1931: 257–67); it was collected in *These Thirteen*, where the character named Jubah is renamed

Jesus; that "Jesus" was Faulkner's initial intention and that the name was changed by the magazine editors is made clear in the facsimile typescript published in *William Faulkner Manuscripts* 9: 228–56. "Barn Burning" was first published in *Harper's Magazine* (June 1939: 86–96); the holograph manuscript, with many additions and deletions, is in *William Faulkner Manuscripts* 15.1: 216–31. "Dry September" was first published in *Scribner's* (Jan. 1931: 49–56) and collected with minor revision in *These Thirteen*; portions of significant early typescripts of the story, which was entitled "Drought," are published in *William Faulkner Manuscripts* 9: 258–92. Stories that Faulkner did not publish during his lifetime and short story variants incorporated into longer works are published in *William Faulkner: Uncollected Stories*, edited by Joseph Blotner. Volume 25 of *William Faulkner Manuscripts, Unpublished Stories*, includes extant manuscripts and typescripts of stories Faulkner never published.

Biographies and Biographical Materials

The authorized biography of Faulkner remains *Faulkner: A Biography*, by Joseph Blotner, published by Random House first in two volumes and then in a condensed one-volume edition with revisions and corrections. Other major biographical studies are *William Faulkner: American Writer*, by Frederick R. Karl; *William Faulkner: His Life and Work*, by David Minter; *Faulkner: The Transfiguration of Biography*, by Judith Bryant Wittenberg; *William Faulkner and Southern History*, by Joel Williamson; and *The Life of William Faulkner*, by Richard Gray. More specialized studies include two on Faulkner's early years: *The Origins of Faulkner's Art*, by Judith L. Sensibar, and the introduction by Carvel Collins to a reprinting of the text of Faulkner's early handmade book of poems, published as *Helen: A Courtship*. A very useful summary of principal historical, literary, and biographical events relevant to Faulkner is Michel Gresset's *A Faulkner Chronology*, based on Gresset's *Faulkner: Oeuvres Romanesques*.

Members of Faulkner's family have published several books of reminiscences. Two are by Faulkner's brothers—John Faulkner's *My Brother Bill: An Affectionate Reminiscence* and Murry C. Falkner's (sic) *The Falkners of Mississippi: A Memoir*. His stepson and nephew each wrote one—Malcolm Franklin's *Bitterweeds: Life with William Faulkner at Rowan Oak* and Jim Faulkner's *Across the Creek: Faulkner Family Stories*. Faulkner's niece, Dean Faulkner Wells, has edited *The Ghosts of Rowan Oak: William Faulkner's Ghost Stories for Children*. Other documents and memoirs cast individual and helpful perspectives on Faulkner's life and artistic processes. Among them are two volumes of documents collected by Jane Isbell Haynes: *William Faulkner: His Lafayette County Heritage: Lands, Houses, and Businesses, Oxford, Mississippi* and *William Faulkner: His Tippah County Heritage: Lands, Houses, and Businesses, Ripley, Mississippi*. Additional personal recollections include *William Faulkner of Oxford*, a collection of portraits of the author by fellow townspeople, edited by James W. Webb and A. Wigfall Green; *Count No 'Count: Flashbacks to Faulkner*, by his early friend and agent Ben Wasson; and *Old Times in the Faulkner Country*, by his hunting companion John B. Cullen, as told to Floyd C. Watkins. The novelist William Styron gives a moving account of Faulkner's death and burial in *"This Quiet Dust" and Other Writings*. Finally, biographies of persons central to Faulkner's early artistic development include *Sherwood Anderson*, by Kim Townsend, and *Phil Stone of Oxford: A Vicarious Life*, by Susan Snell.

Letters, Public Statements, and Interviews

Correspondence collected in *Selected Letters of William Faulkner*, edited by Joseph Blotner, can be supplemented by *The Letters*, volume 2 of *Faulkner: A Comprehensive Guide to the Brodsky Collection*, edited by Louis Daniel Brodsky and Robert W. Hamblin, and by *Thinking of Home: William Faulkner's Letters to His Mother and Father, 1918–1925*, edited by James G. Watson. The evolution of *The Portable Faulkner*, a historically important but now superseded anthology, is outlined by Malcolm Cowley in *The Faulkner-Cowley File: Letters and Memories, 1944–1962*.

Essays, Speeches, and Public Letters by William Faulkner, edited by James B. Meriwether, contains a selection of pronouncements by the later, "public" Faulkner. Many of Faulkner's major interviews throughout his life are collected in *Lion in the Garden: Interviews with William Faulkner, 1926–1962*, edited by James Meriwether and Michael Millgate; it includes the famous *Paris Review* interview with Jean Stein vanden Heuvel, which may also be found in *Writers at Work: The* Paris Review *Interviews*, edited by Malcolm Cowley. This is the most comprehensive interview Faulkner gave. Excerpts from Faulkner's many appearances as writer in residence at the University of Virginia near the close of his career are transcribed in *Faulkner in the University: Class Conferences at the University of Virginia, 1957–1958*, edited by Frederick L. Gwynn and Joseph Blotner. And Faulkner's final public appearance and class sessions with United States Army cadets are recorded in *Faulkner at West Point*, edited by Joseph L. Fant and Robert Ashley.

Handbooks, Bibliographies, and Reference Guides

The most comprehensive handbook for teachers and students of Faulkner is Volpe's *A Reader's Guide to William Faulkner*. It includes a narrative summary of *The Sound and the Fury* (87–126), a genealogical table of the Compson family (88), and a chronology of scenes and guide to the scene shifts (353–77) discussed by various contributors in this volume. *Crowell's Handbook of Faulkner*, by Dorothy Tuck, is available in paperback as *The Apollo Handbook of Faulkner*. A directory of Faulkner's characters in *The Sound and the Fury*, with biographical synopses based on passages in the novel, is in Thomas E. Connolly, *Faulkner's World*, which also covers the Compson appendix (79–82).

The best authority on dialect and colloquial expressions in *The Sound and the Fury* is *A Glossary of Faulkner's South*, by Calvin S. Brown. In *Yoknapatawpha: Faulkner's "Little Postage Stamp of Native Soil,"* Elizabeth M. Kerr has traced the places Faulkner uses as settings and the places that provide social, racial, historical, and economic background to *The Sound and the Fury* and his short stories. Resources for such study can also be found in Arthur F. Kinney, editor, *Critical Essays on Faulkner: The Compson Family*. Books that are wholly or in part guides or indexes to the Compsons and the Gibsons are *William Faulkner's Characters: An Index to the Published and Unpublished Fiction*, by Thomas E. Dasher; *Faulkner's Art and Characters*, by Walter K. Everett; *Who's Who in Faulkner*, by Margaret Patricia Ford and Suzanne Kincaid; *Faulkner's People: A Complete Guide and Index to the Characters in the Fiction of William Faulkner*, by Robert W. Kirk and Marvin Klotz; and *A Faulkner Glossary*, by Harry Runyan.

A general resource work including a condensed biography of Faulkner and a reference guide to *The Sound and the Fury* is *William Faulkner: A Biographical and Reference Guide* (128–39), edited by Leland H. Cox. John Bassett's *William Faulkner: An Annotated Checklist of Criticism* covers book reviews, critical essays, and scholarly books on the novel through the 1960s (32–52). This bibliography is supplemented by Bassett's *Faulkner: An Annotated Checklist of Recent Criticism* (esp. 19–32) and *Faulkner in the Eighties: An Annotated Critical Bibliography* (54–67). Perhaps the most specialized Faulkner bibliography is *William Faulkner's Women Characters*, by Patricia E. Sweeney, which lists works relating to *The Sound and the Fury* (50–90). Finally, Blotner has published *William Faulkner's Library: A Catalogue*, a list of books found in Faulkner's home at the time of his death.

Regional and Historical Studies

The best general guide to the history, culture, and economics of Faulkner's region is the *Encyclopedia of Southern Culture*, edited by Charles Reagan Wilson and William Ferris. This work may be usefully supplemented by Edward N. Akin's *Mississippi: An Illustrated History*, published in cooperation with the Mississippi Historical Society, and by the irreplaceable *Mississippi: The WPA Guide to the Magnolia State*, compiled and written under the auspices of the Writer's Project of the Works Progress Administration in the 1930s and reissued with a new introduction by Robert S. McElvaine. The *Atlas of Mississippi*, edited by Ralph D. Cross, Robert W. Wales, and Charles T. Traylor, covers geography, demography, history, economics, and related fields. On specifically literary-historical matters, readers may wish to consult Louis D. Rubin, Jr., et al., *The History of Southern Literature*.

Three classic studies of the American South remain extremely rewarding and establish a context for later historians and sociologists: W. J. Cash, *The Mind of the South* (1941); John Dollard, *Caste and Class in a Southern Town* (1937); and C. Vann Woodward, *The Burden of Southern History* (1960), the latest edition of which contains a coda entitled "The Burden for William Faulkner" (265–80). All three works are available in paperback editions. More recent studies that provide fruitful contexts for teaching *The Sound and the Fury* are *The Myth of Southern History: Historical Consciousness in Twentieth-Century Southern Literature*, by F. Garvin Davenport, Jr.; *Southern Honor: Ethics and Behavior in the Old South*, by Bertram Wyatt-Brown; *Slave Religion: The "Invisible Institution" in the Antebellum South*, by Albert J. Raboteau; *Cavalier and Yankee: The Old South and American National Character*, by William R. Taylor; *A Rage for Order: Black/White Relations in the American South since Emancipation*, by Joel Williamson; *A Southern Renaissance: The Cultural Awakening of the American South, 1930–1955*, by Richard H. King; *Mississippi: The Closed Society*, by James W. Silver; and *The Promise of the New South: Life after Reconstruction*, by Edward L. Ayers, and its highly readable abridgement, *Southern Crossing: A History of the American South, 1877–1906*. "Part One: Mississippi" in *North toward Home*, by Willie Morris, contains many personal observations by this Mississippi writer that resonate with events in Faulkner's work (3–15), as does Anthony Walton's *Mississippi: An American Journey* (6–10, 163–66, 186–87).

Among historical works that treat aspects of what may be called southern exceptionalism and the relation of the region to the national culture, Eugene D. Genovese's *The Southern Tradition: The Achievement and Limitations of an American Conservatism* illuminates a tradition of political and social thought in the South. Dewey W. Grantham's *The South in Modern America: A Region at Odds* provides a comprehensive view of political, economic, and social conditions in the South since Reconstruction and emphasizes its distinctiveness as a region. Daniel J. Singal's *The War Within: From Victorian to Modernist Thought in the South, 1919–1945* chronicles and comments on manners, mores, and attitudes throughout the period of Faulkner's development and most of his career. Singal devotes a chapter of commentary to Faulkner (153–97).

The mythical Yoknapatawpha County and its county seat, Jefferson—literary analogues of the actual Lafayette County, Mississippi, and in different aspects and instances of the towns of Oxford, Ripley, Holly Springs, and Water Valley—have since 1936 been provided with several maps, including Faulkner's. The literary representation of geographical spaces is an interesting topic in its own right, and many teachers will find it useful to employ geographical-historical approaches to *The Sound and the Fury*. Several important studies of literary setting and actual place include G. T. Buckley, "Is Oxford the Original of Jefferson in William Faulkner's Novels?," three essays by the geographer Charles S. Aiken in the *Geographical Review*, and the recent book-length study by Gabriele Gutting, *Yoknapatawpha: The Function of Geographical and Historical Facts in William Faulkner's Fictional Picture of the Deep South*. The last is especially important for the information it provides about inaccuracies in the reproductions and redrawings of Faulkner's maps of his apocryphal county, which many instructors use in the classroom. It also contains theoretical discussions of literary, physical, and imaginative spaces. A brief but informative critical study of structures and places in Lafayette County and in passages of Faulkner's works appears, with photographs, in Thomas Hines, "Architecture and the Tangible Past: The Built Environment of Faulkner's Yoknapatawpha."

Additional literary and historical perspectives on Faulkner's fiction can be gathered from chapters in *The Literature of Memory: Modern Writers of the American South* and *Writing the South: Ideas of an American Region*, both by Richard Gray, and *The Brazen Face of History: Studies in the Literary Consciousness of America*, by Lewis P. Simpson. Teachers and students may also find useful Bertram Wyatt-Brown's study *The Literary Percys: Family History, Gender, and the Southern Imagination* for the insight it provides into relations between gender identification and the profession of writing and the relation of these to themes of melancholy or despair and of honor in southern writing, as focused in the works of the forebears of the memoirist William Alexander Percy and the novelist Walker Percy.

Photographic Collections and Illustrated Books

Illustrated books on Mississippi include collections of photographs taken by Eudora Welty for the Works Progress Administration and published selectively in *One Time, One Place: Mississippi in the Depression: A Snapshot Album* and more fully in *Eudora Welty: Photographs*, which has a preface by Reynolds Price and a transcript of an interview with Miss Welty conducted by Hunter Cole and Seetha Srinivasan. *Mississippi* is a remarkable collection of color photographs by Franke Keating with a full and informative text by Bern Keating. An important critical study of documentary photography of the South undertaken through the auspices of the Farm Security Administration in the 1930s—especially work by Jack Delano, Dorothea Lange, Russell Lee, and Ben Shahn—is Nicholas Nathanson's *The Black Image in the New Deal: The Politics of FSA Photography*.

In creating the settings for his fictions, Faulkner depicted many actual places in and around Oxford and Lafayette County in the northern tier of the state. Several publications capture images of those places. Besides the photographs of probable analogues in Kinney's *Critical Essays*, such images are represented in *Faulkners, Fortunes, and Flames*, by Jack Case Wilson; *Faulkner's County: Yoknapatawpha*, by Martin J. Dain; *Yoknapatawpha: The Land of William Faulkner*, with photographs by Alain Desvergnes and text by Regis Durand; *Faulkner's Mississippi*, with photographs by William Eggleston and text by Willie Morris; and "Faulkner's Mississippi," with photographs by William Albert Allard and text by Willie Morris, in *National Geographic. William Faulkner: The*

Cofield Collection is a lifelong photographic retrospective of Faulkner and his family by their official family photographer in Oxford, Jack Cofield.

Specialized Studies

Kinney's *Critical Essays on William Faulkner: The Compson Family* contains a long introduction tracing probable sources and resources for the creation of the Compson family, early versions of the Compsons, reviews of *The Sound and the Fury*, and old and new essays on the novel, including "In Defense of Caroline Compson," by Joan Williams. A comprehensive explication de texte of the novel is Gail M. Morrison's doctoral dissertation, "William Faulkner's *The Sound and the Fury*: A Critical and Textual Study." Three book-length studies of the novel of special value in preparing to teach it are Bleikasten's *The Most Splendid Failure: Faulkner's* The Sound and the Fury, which traces themes and images of absence; John T. Matthews's The Sound and the Fury: *Faulkner and the Lost Cause*, which examines structures of the novel and historical themes; and John T. Irwin's *Doubling and Incest / Repetition and Revenge: A Specula-tive Reading of Faulkner*, which reads *The Sound and the Fury* alongside *Absalom, Absalom!* to develop a psychoanalytic portrait of Quentin III. Together, these books apply to Faulkner's novel three major strands of critical theory: structuralist, new historicist, and psychoanalytic. In addition, *New Essays on Faulkner's* The Sound and the Fury, edited by Polk, contains important and original essays viewing the novel from feminist and new historicist perspec-tives. "Candace," by Alan Cheuse, is a novella that imaginatively extends the story of Caddy Compson after she leaves Jefferson.

Six books are particularly valuable for teachers who approach teaching *The Sound and the Fury* through or along with Faulkner's short stories: Hans H. Skei, *William Faulkner: The Short Story Career: An Outline of Faulkner's Short Story Writing from 1919 to 1962*; Evans Harrington and Ann J. Abadie, editors, *Faulkner and the Short Story: Faulkner and Yoknapatawpha, 1990*; James B. Carothers, *William Faulkner's Short Stories*; James Ferguson, *Faulkner's Short Fiction*, which provides the reader with an alphabetical listing of the short stories and their publishing histories; Joanne V. Creighton, *William Faulkner's Craft of Revision*; and Diane Brown Jones, *A Reader's Guide to the Short Stories of William Faulkner*.

Periodicals and General Critical Studies

Periodicals devoted to Faulkner include *The Faulkner Journal* (usually twice a year, beginning fall 1985), the summer issues of *Mississippi Quarterly* (beginning in 1971), and the more informal *Faulkner Newsletter* (quarterly, beginning 1980) and *Teaching Faulkner* (twice a year, beginning 1992). Two Faulkner journals are published in Japan: *William Faulkner: Materials, Studies, and Criticism* (beginning in 1978) and *Faulkner Studies* (twice a year, beginning 1991). One issue of *Faulkner Studies: An Annual of Research, Criticism, and Reviews*, edited by Barnett Guttenberg, was published in 1980. Among the most prominent journals in which essays on Faulkner frequently appear are *American Literature*, *Arizona Quarterly*, the *Georgia Review*, *Studies in American Fiction*, the *Southern Review*, *Southern Literary Journal*, and *Southern Quarterly*.

Several anthologies draw together major criticism from periodical publications. *William Faulkner: The Critical Heritage*, edited by John Bassett, includes criticism of *The Sound and the Fury* from 1929 to 1931. A decades of criticism series begins with *William Faulkner: Two Decades of Criticism*, edited by Frederick J. Hoffman and Olga W. Vickery, and continues with *William Faulkner: Three Decades of Criticism*, also edited by Hoffman and Vickery, and *William Faulkner: Four Decades of Criticism*, edited by Linda Welsheimer Wagner. Essays were deleted as well as added in the progress of this series, so teachers may wish to consult earlier titles even if they have a later one at hand. *Faulkner: A Collection of Critical Essays* was edited by Robert Penn Warren for the Prentice-Hall Twentieth Century Views series; a subsequent volume in this series, *Faulkner (New Perspectives)*, was edited by Richard C. Brodhead. The most recent among these collections, *On Faulkner: The Best from* American Literature, edited by Louis J. Budd and Edwin H. Cady, reprints seminal articles on Faulkner from that important journal. Other collections (ed. Bleikasten; Bloom; Polk; Weinstein) bring together commentary by a number of critics in accessible formats.

While Faulkner attracted the notice of other writers such as Evelyn Scott and Conrad Aiken almost immediately on publication of *The Sound and the Fury*, extended critical treatment of his work did not begin until after the Second World War. The earliest of these treatments, Malcolm Cowley's *Portable Faulkner* and Robert Coughlan's *The Private World of William Faulkner*, were heavily biographical in their approach. Subsequently, the dominance of New Criticism in academia can be seen in books published in the early 1960s, but critics of nearly every theoretical persuasion have addressed Faulkner's writing in succeeding generations.

Since their appearance in the early 1960s, the perennial standard works of criticism on Faulkner have been Michael Millgate, *The Achievement of William Faulkner*, which begins the discussion of each major work with its textual history; Cleanth Brooks, *William Faulkner: The Yoknapatawpha Country*, a New Critical study by a fellow southerner (see also Brooks's *William Faulkner: First Encounters*, a text that is highly accessible for students); and Olga W. Vickery, *The Novels of William Faulkner: A Critical Interpretation*. These volumes provide useful overviews of Faulkner's work for undergraduate students and other interested readers.

Other general but helpful early studies include Melvin Backman, *Faulkner: The Major Years: A Critical Study*; Harry Modean Campbell and Ruel E. Foster,

William Faulkner: A Critical Appraisal; Frederick J. Hoffman, *William Faulkner*; Irving Howe, *William Faulkner: A Critical Study*; John W. Hunt, *William Faulkner: Art in Theological Tension*; Ward L. Miner, *The World of William Faulkner*; William Van O'Connor, *The Tangled Fire of William Faulkner*; Walter Slatoff, *Quest for Failure: A Study of William Faulkner*; Lawrance Thompson, *William Faulkner: An Introduction and Interpretation*; and Hyatt H. Waggoner, *William Faulkner: From Jefferson to the World*. Among these, Howe's study remains the most important for its treatment of social and political issues in Faulkner from the perspective of an influential "New York intellectual."

Important later critical studies include Richard P. Adams, *Faulkner: Myth and Motion*; André Bleikasten, *The Ink of Melancholy: Faulkner's Novels from The Sound and the Fury to Light in August*; Panthea Reid Broughton, *William Faulkner: The Abstract and the Actual*; Michel Gresset, *Fascination: Faulkner's Fiction, 1919–1936*; Michael Grimwood, *Heart in Conflict: Faulkner's Struggles with Vocation*; Donald M. Kartiganer, *The Fragile Thread: The Meaning of Form in Faulkner's Novels*; Arthur F. Kinney, *Faulkner's Narrative Poetics: Style as Vision*; Martin Kreiswirth, *William Faulkner: The Making of a Novelist*; John T. Matthews, *The Play of Faulkner's Language*; Gail L. Mortimer, *Faulkner's Rhetoric of Loss: A Study in Perception and Meaning*; Robert Dale Parker, *Faulkner and the Novelistic Imagination*; John Pilkington, *The Heart of Yoknapatawpha*; Joseph W. Reed, Jr., *Faulkner's Narrative*; Lawrence H. Schwartz, *Creating Faulkner's Reputation: The Politics of Modern Literary Criticism*; James A. Snead, *Figures of Division: William Faulkner's Major Novels*; Walter Taylor, *Faulkner's Search for a South*; and Warwick Wadlington, *Reading Faulknerian Tragedy*. Characteristic of these studies is their emphasis on close stylistic analysis combined with sophisticated linguistic, psychoanalytic, and sociological insights. They are particularly useful in directing specialized research projects or in creating assignments for advanced students.

Beginning in the 1990s, as the topic of the 1994 Faulkner and Yoknapatawpha Conference—Faulkner and Gender—attests, there has been a particular emphasis in general studies on the role of gender in Faulkner's writing. Books with chapters or substantial thematic focus on *The Sound and the Fury* and gender issues include Deborah Clarke, *Robbing the Mother: Women in Faulkner*; John N. Duvall, *Faulkner's Marginal Couple: Invisible, Outlaw, and Unspeakable Communities*; Minrose C. Gwin, *The Feminine and Faulkner: Reading (beyond) Sexual Difference*; Judith Lockyer, *Ordered by Words: Language and Narration in the Novels of William Faulkner*; and Diane Roberts, *Faulkner and Southern Womanhood*. Perspectives on issues of gender are also the focus of a collection of essays, *Faulkner and Women: Faulkner and Yoknapatawpha, 1985*, edited by Doreen Fowler and Ann J. Abadie. In addition, a special issue of the *Faulkner Journal* (4.1–2 [1988–89]) is devoted to the topic Faulkner and Feminisms.

Finally, as mentioned above, teachers will want to be aware of important studies that deal with cultural aspects of Faulkner's South and with representations of race and social class in his fiction. An accessible general study is Myra Jehlen, *Class and Character in Faulkner's South*. Race is the central subject in the following works of criticism: *Faulkner and Race: Faulkner and Yoknapatawpha, 1986*, edited by Doreen Fowler and Ann J. Abadie; Thadious M. Davis, *Faulkner's "Negro": Art and the Southern Context*; Lee C. Jenkins, *Faulkner and Black-White Relations: A Psychoanalytic Approach*; and Eric J. Sundquist, *Faulkner: The House Divided* and the more recent *To Wake the Nations: Race in the Making of American Literature*. Multicultural issues are addressed in *Faulkner: International Perspectives: Faulkner and Yoknapatawpha, 1982*, edited by Fowler and Abadie. Historical circumstances regarding race in the period from Reconstruction to the civil rights movement are treated in Neil McMillen, *Dark Journey: Black Mississippians in the Age of Jim Crow*, and James Grossman, *Land of Hope: Chicago, Black Southerners, and the Great Migration*. As noted above, Cheryl Lester comments on the relevance of racial ideology in *The Sound and the Fury* in "Racial Awareness and Arrested Development: *The Sound and the Fury* and the Great Migration."

Audiovisual Resources

In addition to the illustrated books noted above, audiovisual resources can be useful in teaching Faulkner, especially to students outside the South. They vary in quality, however, and an instructor is well-advised to preview material before using it in class.

Documentary Resources

The best overview in a video format of Faulkner's life and works, and of influences on him, is the 1979 PBS–Mississippi Authority for Educational Television production *William Faulkner: A Life on Paper*, screenplay by A. I. "Buzz" Bezzerides. A transcript of the documentary is available, adapted and edited by Ann J. Abadie. The film is constructed through a montage of still photographs, documentary footage, and interviews with members of Faulkner's family (his daughter, Jill Faulkner Summers, and his niece, Dean Faulkner Wells), fellow writers (Robert Penn Warren and Joan Williams), friends (Ben Wasson), Hollywood colleagues and acquaintances (Lauren Bacall and Anita Loos), and scholars (Carvel Collins and Shelby Foote), among many others. If a library has no other Faulkner video, this one is essential. Also available is *Cleanth Brooks: An Introduction to Faulkner's Fiction*, in the Eminent Scholar/Teachers: Modern

American Literature series. While principally a filming of Brooks reading a lecture, this video provides a good summary of Brooks's highly influential approach to Faulkner. These videos are useful both at the college and high school levels.

Documentary films include *William Faulkner of Oxford*, an undated, semidramatized video portrait from the 1950s, which features Faulkner in a mixture of live and awkwardly staged footage on the award of the Nobel Prize, his life on the farm, and his daughter's high school graduation. Other useful resources are *William Faulkner's Mississippi*, narrated by Montgomery Clift and Zachary Scott, and *Faulkner's Mississippi: Land into Legend*, script by Evans Harrington. Especially useful for exploring African American culture and religious traditions is *Two Black Churches*, filmed in Lafayette County, Mississippi, and New Haven, Connecticut. Also on the subject of Faulkner's relation to African American religion is *"Are You Walking with Me?" Sister Thea Bowman, William Faulkner, and African American Culture*. Further information on the availability of these videos can be obtained from the Center for Southern Culture, Univ. of Mississippi, University 38677.

Adaptations

An introduction to Faulkner's work or a change-of-pace assignment can involve one of the better and more reliable film adaptations of his novels and stories. Unfortunately, the 1959 version of *The Sound and the Fury* (starring Yul Brenner as Jason, Jack Warden as Benjy, and Joanne Woodward as Miss Quentin) can hardly qualify in this regard. The film significantly reinterprets the characters and the story line of the novel without providing insight into Faulkner's narrative. The most successful feature-length adaptations of Faulkner's work are *Intruder in the Dust* and *The Reivers*, both filmed on location in Mississippi. Another feature-length work, Horton Foote's adaptation of Faulkner's short story "Tomorrow," is widely regarded as one of the best evocations of Faulkner's themes, although it expands and alters aspects of the narrative. Briefer adaptations of Faulkner's short stories include *William Faulkner's "The Bear,"* in which Faulkner's nephew Jim appears in the role of de Spain; *William Faulkner's "Barn Burning,"* based on a screenplay by Horton Foote (Jim Faulkner again plays de Spain); *Two Soldiers*; and *A Rose for Emily*. (The last is directed and narrated by John Huston and stars Anjelica Huston as Miss Emily. Unfortunately, despite the renown of the principals and the wide distribution of the video, this version renarrates the story in a way that can only loosely be construed as interpretation.) Whatever the quality of the adaptations, they may provide opportunities for instructors to design assignments treating issues of style and point of view. Lively discussions of adaptations of Faulkner's work, his own Hollywood screenwriting, and other more general connections between his writing and cinematic style are available in Bruce F.

Kawin, *Faulkner and Film*; Evans Harrington and Ann J. Abadie, editors, *Faulkner, Modernism, and Film*; and Gene D. Phillips, *Fiction, Film, and Faulkner: The Art of Adaptation*.

Audio Recordings

Important audio resources include Faulkner's reading from portions of his work on a Caedmon recording *William Faulkner Reads*, which is readily available in bookstores and includes Faulkner's reading of his Nobel Prize acceptance speech and various monologues from *As I Lay Dying*. More difficult to find but more pertinent to teachers of *The Sound and the Fury* is *William Faulkner Reads Selections from* Light in August *and* The Sound and the Fury. A very useful documentary in the National Public Radio series *A Question of Place*, with readings by Tennessee Williams and Colleen Dewhurst, is *A Sound Portrait of William Faulkner*, script by Jay Martin.

These resources present teachers and students with many different ways to approach *The Sound and the Fury*. While no class at any level of instruction can bring all of them immediately into play, the production of so many responses to Faulkner's work bespeaks its capacity to stimulate and engage readers on many levels, from many perspectives, and in many forms. *The Sound and the Fury* is eminently teachable in the best sense of the word because it can lead us, and help us as teachers to lead others, to greater literary and human insight.

Part Two

APPROACHES

"Through the Fence, between the Curling Flower Spaces": Teaching the First Section of *The Sound and the Fury*

Robert Dale Parker

Anecdotally, I have heard of many people who were turned away from Faulkner by *The Sound and the Fury*, including bright readers who were led to believe that critical reading in general and especially for Faulkner is little more than an arcane exercise in connecting dots and moving around puzzle pieces. With such readers in mind, I direct the crucial opening class on the novel to the first section's points of greatest resistance: Benjy's eerily simple language and jarring narrative transitions. I try to bring out some linguistic and psychic patterns and then ask about their cultural implications.

Actually, the teaching begins before the opening class. Although I do not like to reveal things about novels ahead of time, for *The Sound and the Fury* that seems excusable and almost necessary. Excusable, because *The Sound and the Fury*, unlike most of Faulkner's novels, proceeds as if readers were already beyond a first reading: it assumes a knowledge of its plot much more than it trades on the suspense that can come from gradually unrolling that plot. And necessary, more or less, to help first-time readers who might be frightened off by the novel's difficulty and by its unfamiliar kind of difficulty. Some teachers go over the plot and form in class before students begin reading. That can help, but it can be hard for students to remember oral explanations, and some students may be absent or late. Therefore, before a class reaches *The Sound and the Fury*, I pass out a genealogy of the Compsons and Gibsons and an introduction that reviews the issues of plot and form that most confuse first-time

ers, while otherwise giving away as little as possible. (The introduction ap-
rs as an appendix to this essay.) I also invite students to consult Edmond L.
Volpe's charts of the scene shifts in the first two sections. While some students
prefer not to look at Volpe's charts until after they read a stretch of text, virtually all of them find the charts immensely helpful.

Then I begin the first class on *The Sound and the Fury* by inviting discussion of an early passage that includes the first two transitions, or scene shifts:

> We went along the fence and came to the garden fence, where our
> shadows were. My shadow was higher than Luster's on the fence. We
> came to the broken place and went through it.
> "Wait a minute." Luster said. "You snagged on that nail again. Cant you
> never crawl through here without snagging on that nail."
> *Caddy uncaught me and we crawled through. Uncle Maury said to not
> let anybody see us, so we better stoop over, Caddy said. Stoop over,
> Benjy. Like this, see. We stooped over and crossed the garden, where the
> flowers rasped and rattled against us. The ground was hard. We climbed
> the fence, where the pigs were grunting and snuffing. . . .*
> *Keep your hands in your pockets, Caddy said. Or they'll get froze. You
> dont want your hands froze on Christmas, do you.*
> "It's too cold out there." Versh said. "You dont want to go out doors."
> (4–5)

Working from this passage, we introduce such concerns as Benjy's minimal differentiation between separate times; his stunning indirectness, as when he lets
us know it is cold but does not register the feeling himself; and his dissociation
of cause from effect. Students often ask why Faulkner does something—for example, why he leaves out question marks—which gives me a chance to suggest
converting questions of why, of intent, to questions of effect. When I then ask
what the effect is of leaving out punctuation marks, they soon convert their
confusions into insights.

Students often refer to Benjy as speaking or telling his story, and I ask what
they mean by those terms or how he can tell his story when he has no language,
which prompts a wider discussion of language in the so-called Benjy section.
This can lead to a formula we later return to and work variations on. In the first
section of *The Sound and the Fury* we get not Benjy's language, although we
might sometimes call it that as a convenient shorthand, but instead we get what
he *would* say, if he *could* say, *which he can't*. That last emphasis on *which he
can't* usually provokes laughter as students recognize the struggle to describe
something outside our epistemological categories. I repeat the formula later
for the Quentin section and then vary it for Jason, illustrating the lack of any
time or place in which Jason actually speaks "his" section by referring to it as
what he would say, if he did say, which he doesn't. In a Faulkner course, we can
return to the same touchstone for *As I Lay Dying*; for unthought thoughts in

the later novels (e.g., Joe Christmas "didn't even think then   *Something is going to happen*" [*Light in August* 118]); for Rosa Coldfield in chapter 5 of *Absalom, Absalom!*; for Ike Snopes in *The Hamlet*, and so on.

When someone remarks the radical simplicity of "Benjy's language," it helps to specify the simplicity: a minimum of subordination, short sentences, little reliance on adverbs and adjectives, heavy reliance on nouns and verbs, and heavy reliance on simple past tense. (A joke about the likeness to Hemingway in these categories can help place Benjy's style in relation to something more familiar.) L. Moffitt Cecil notes that Benjy uses only about five hundred words (38–43). That is the more remarkable given that a fair number of his words— albeit a small proportion—are surprisingly distinct and evocative, as students often note, asking how Benjy can use such words, in this passage, as "rasped and rattled" or "grunting and snuffing." I observe how curious and even comical it is that the novel provokes us to ask such questions when, at the same time, Benjy uses no language at all. In the absence of language, the more unusual words are no more radical a distortion or illusion than the use of any language to render a state of no language—what he *would* say, if he *could* say, *which he can't*. Faulkner has it both ways, forging an impossible compromise that evokes a lack of language and a minimum of intellectual complexity while also maximizing the representation of those incapacities through language.

Indeed, while "Benjy's language" follows a group of radically simple patterns, it also takes up a surprising number of more conceptually demanding variations from those patterns. He says "so," "but," "when," "where," "while," "until," "anymore," "again," "too" (in the sense of also), and even "because," and he uses a number of similes, such as "like trees" (see Cecil 43). The exceptions to these patterns meet the immediate and evolving needs of the narrative as it progresses, much as writers like Mark Twain figured out how to make dialect read more smoothly by using dialect forms or spellings only part of the time. To use them all the time makes the dialect distracting rather than fluent.

Sooner or later, someone mentions the structure of temporal transition or the use of italics. In a remarkable letter, Faulkner argues that what he calls the "thought transference" is "in Ben's mind and not in the reader's eye" (*Selected Letters* 44). Thus the italic and roman typefaces do not represent any given times, but the shift from roman to italics or back from italics to roman usually represents a shift between times, as in our opening example. Benjy snags on a nail, and then the shift in typeface signals that his thoughts transfer to an earlier time when he also snagged on a nail. Students can write papers comparing such bridges, or fulcrums, as I call them, with transitions later in the novel or in novels like *As I Lay Dying*, *Mrs. Dalloway*, *Ulysses*, and many others. Similarly, in a cinematic sound bridge, one scene ends with a sound, such as a train whistle, that then continues into the next scene, so that the sound stays the same while the picture changes. For Benjy, the nail not only bridges the transition and figures it metonymically; the nail also provokes the transition that it bridges.

Throughout, the present retains a privileged position; it interrupts the past without the impetus of any fulcrum. Yet here as in many other works, Faulkner sets up a discernible pattern and then violates it, defying any absolute system. Thus he gives us three time shifts from roman to roman instead of from roman to italics or italics to roman (pp. 38, 43, 53). Sometimes a shift from roman to italics signifies a time shift (e.g., pp. 22, 28, 29), but the following shift back from italics to roman, which usually represents another time shift (thirty-nine out of fifty-two times, by my count, that is, seventy-five percent of the time, by my calculation, not including two uses of incidental italics [pp. 8 and 44]), occurs without a time shift, as if Faulkner decided that once we understand which time we are in, there is no point in holding to italics. I tell students that I write two lines, like an equal sign, where the shift from italics to roman does not mark a time shift, and I write one line, to represent a break, where it does mark a time shift. Then I don't have to rethink each transition from scratch every time I reread a passage. A sharp student might note that, according to Volpe's chart, the second transition in our opening example shifts not between scenes but rather within scenes, as both parts fit in the scene that Volpe dubs "Dec. 23." In that sense this second transition is atypical, but it shows how Benjy's mind does not envision each "scene" as a continuous flow that goes inevitably forward in linear progression. Rather, just as his mind can shift to an earlier scene, so it can shift to an earlier point in the same "scene," thus exposing the artificiality of our (and Volpe's) convenient division of Benjy's memories into distinct scenes.

Still addressing this opening example, I ask whether, if the nail sets off Benjy's shift, something in Benjy determines the thoughts that he shifts to. Or are his responses impersonal and passive? Benjy's seemingly chaotic, rambling memory confines itself to a limited set of scenes. These sixteen or so scenes mirror each other and condense into metaphors and metonymies—the fence, the gate, Caddy's perfume, the slipper, the word "Caddy" or "caddie," the smell of trees, and so on—that the novel contrives to make represent all Benjy's life to that point, as if any thought he might have must come from this narrow repertoire of scenes. Thus André Bleikasten (in what otherwise seems to me the most useful discussion of the novel) finds Benjy impersonal and passive (*Failure* 71–75, *Ink* 58–61). Yet some scenes appear only once, as if they represent selections from a larger repertoire that he doesn't exhaust on any given day or perhaps ever. And if the range of Benjy's scenes feels imposed on him, the selection of any given scene seems less arbitrary, more motivated, and hence more representative of Benjy's mind and memory. The repetition gathers a quality of obsession, of a drive to return over and over to the same scenes and to the same concerns in different scenes. This first scene shift may seem to take Benjy to the least obsessively chosen of his scenes, to the scene least relevant to his pattern of preoccupations. But its turning up here only makes his obsessiveness more striking, especially once we decipher the Uncle Maury–and–Mrs. Patterson plot and see how it presages not so much Caddy's future as, much more narrowly, Benjy's reading of Caddy's future. Caddy crosses the fence-marked boundary of sexual experience, here on Maury's errand and later on her own.

Indeed, in many respects the whole first section of the novel is constructed of fences and openings in fences. Many of the sixteen scenes into which Volpe divides Benjy's section depend on fences: the 23 December delivery of Uncle Maury's message, the end of what Volpe calls the "Uncle Maury–Patterson affair," Benjy's lingering at the gate, Benjy and the Burgess girl. Other scenes depend on fencelike boundaries, as when Caddy climbs the tree to look down through the window after Damuddy's death or when Benjy climbs onto a box to look through the window at Caddy's wedding. Many scenes include fences that echo the more prominent role of fences in other scenes. On the trip to the cemetery, Benjy "thinks," "We went through the gate, where it didn't jolt anymore" (10). In the scene after Quentin's death, he observes, "The calf was in the pig pen. It nuzzled at the wire, bawling" (28). Again, in the scene after Mr. Compson's death, Dilsey builds a fence to contain Benjy: "Dilsey took a long piece of wood and laid it between Luster and me. 'Stay on your side now.' Dilsey said" (32). On the day of Mr. Compson's funeral (listed in Volpe's guide to scene shifts but left out of his chronology, and so a seventeenth scene), when Benjy watches the hearse carry away his father, Benjy and T. P. "ran down to the corner of the fence and watched them pass" (32).

In a way, the novel's first section is about Caddy's crossing to the other side of the fence when Benjy can no longer cross with her. In this opening example, extramarital sexuality—here between Uncle Maury and Mrs. Patterson—is already figured as a crossing of fences, a crossing that Caddy can make with pleasure but that Benjy cannot understand. This passage provides an occasion to ask what it suggests to figure sexual experience as the crossing of a fence and how that figuring looks from the implied perspectives of Caddy, of Benjy, even of Mrs. or Mr. Patterson or Uncle Maury; it also provides an occasion to ask what light Caddy's perspective throws on Benjy's or where either of them gets his or her perspective—an especially tough and perhaps unanswerable question for Benjy.

More answerable, however vaguely, is the question of sources for Faulkner's preoccupation with figuring sexual experience as fence crossing and transgression or as betrayal of the familial bond. We can answer in generalized psychobiographical ways that fit anyone whose experience we describe in oedipal terms. But we can also ask what it tells us culturally that Faulkner figures Benjy's relation to Caddy in terms that condense around her so-called loss of virginity and its metonymies in fence crossing, kissing, wearing perfume, and marrying. What does it mean to "lose" virginity? It is not an object like Luster's quarter or Benjy's testicles. Benjy's preoccupation, and Faulkner's, is culturally produced rather than inevitable, which allows us to read it as a confining and defining cultural fixation rather than a natural or objective marker of Benjy's psyche. The notion that one has or loses something called virginity and the

t the possession or loss of it defines one's essence and the essence of
ion to others represent a deeply implied but largely unspoken cul-
...al assumption that may also burden some of our students. That assumption
can go unrecognized, or unrecognized as culturally received rather than inevitable and natural, but its invisibility helps it settle more stubbornly in the restricted economy of cultural determinants. Thus Benjy is motivated not only by
his own psychology but also by culture, whether directly, unconsciously ab-
sorbing the cultural fixations that motivate those around him (e.g., watching
Dilsey's disdain at Caddy's soiled drawers and bottom), or indirectly, as a site
where Faulkner's conscious and unconscious reproductions of the surrounding
culture congeal and transform.

Benjy's language, then, is only partly his own. What might first appear anar-
chic turns out to have a surplus of system in a context so unfamiliar in some
ways and so excessively familiar in other ways (e.g., in its submission to unconsciously received sexual boundaries) that at first we do not know how to recognize it. On the one hand, Benjy cannot use language directly; he can express
himself only through other characters' registering his nonlinguistic actions and
sounds, even if we discover those through a language that is somehow Benjy's
even as it portrays its own nonexistence. On the other hand, sometimes he does
express himself through language, or at least he tries to. His trying is itself a
kind of expression, as when he is "trying to say" (53) and when he returns so
feelingly to his sister's name:

> "Hush." T. P. said. "They going to hear you. Get down quick." He pulled
> me. Caddy. I clawed my hands against the wall Caddy. T. P. pulled me.
> "Hush." he said. "Hush. Come on here quick." He pulled me on. Caddy
> "Hush up, Benjy. . . ."   (39)

But such cries mark only the more expressive points on a continuum where no
one point is purely expressive or nonexpressive. Even though Benjy's narrative
may seem like arbitrary chaos or neutrally reported dialogue and description,
it is all selected, filtered, and processed in ways that accumulate meaning for
Benjy and his world and for the act of narrating them. If there is no specific
place or time out of which his narrative emerges or is provoked, there is still a
narrative space of characterological, authorial, and cultural motive.

Perhaps the foremost emotion for Benjy is the pain of loss, as so many com-
mentators have observed. Benjy loses so much and fails so dismally to transform his pain over loss into the play and work of culture, in contrast to the little
boy whom Freud watched playing a game of *fort!* and *da!* (gone! and there!) to
sublimate the loss of his mother (see Bleikasten, *Failure* 73–74, *Ink* 60; Freud,
Principle 8–10). It can help students observe and conceptualize Benjy's pain
simply to ask them to brainstorm, to name Benjy's losses while the instructor
records what they name on the board. Usually, their list runs something like
this: Caddy, name, pasture, testicles, fire, flowers, slipper, cushion, Quentin,

Father, Roskus, Versh, T. P., Luster's quarter, language (can he lose what he never had?), and Damuddy. Each loss that students name provides a chance to discuss something that catches someone's interest or leaves someone puzzled. As the losses accumulate in the novel and on the board, it becomes clearer that *The Sound and the Fury* evokes a psychic and narrative development arrested in loss, a fantasy of frustration that almost suggests a degree of narrative or authorial masochism. Yet it also suggests a release from such masochism, for by dwelling on Benjy's frustration it can remind us of our difference from Benjy (or from Quentin or Jason). This is, then, a novel about maturing, about passing from childhood to adulthood, and about resistance to that passing. Students alienated by the novel's form can often snag their interest on its picture of protracted adolescence. *The Sound and the Fury* is also, therefore, a novel of transitions and about transitions and the resistance to transitions. It is about adolescence as a state of transition and also as a state of nontransition at a time when transition is most longed for, a state of forcibly sustained childhood at a time—increasingly prolonged in modern culture—of feeling ready to progress beyond childhood.

Sometimes, when students brainstorm a list of Benjy's losses, they name his mother, perhaps even casting her as the loss that all the other losses displace. Other times I get at the same issue by asking why Benjy loves Caddy. In addition to noting Caddy's love of Benjy, students often point out how differently Caddy and Caroline treat Benjy and how Caddy displaces Caroline in Benjy's erotic economy. Caddy, in turn, is displaced by the transitional objects—slipper, cushion, and the rest—that come to defend against and figure the loss of Caddy and Caroline but that themselves get lost in turn, reproducing the pain they are seized on to resist.

The notion that Benjy's fixation on Caddy displaces the loss of his mother's love is a familiar and useful reading, yet perhaps too useful in its potential to reduce Benjy's emotional economy, in a vulgar Freudianism, to mere finger-pointing at the easy target of his mother. It can suggest Caroline Compson as a transcendent, ultimate source and first cause. We imagine some long-lost imaginary between Benjy and Caroline, or not quite so long-lost imaginary between Benjy and Caddy, lyrically evoked in the smell of trees and the "smooth, bright shapes" (75) and see Benjy as tragically condemned to an endless flip-flop between the imaginary and the symbolic, between the recovered presence and the stubbornly returning absence of his beloved sister or some object or word that evokes her, between the imaginary immediacy of presence and the symbolic distance of mediation and language. It is easy to forget how that imaginary is false and compensatory. Like any imaginary it is constructed retrospectively through a fantasy from within the symbolic. Otherwise it would be real and not imaginary. Thus not only is Caroline not a first cause, but there is no first cause (see Matthews, *Play* 68). Loss is the condition through which we imagine a state before loss that is inconceivable apart from the need to imagine it from the position of loss. That is the exchange of *fort* and *da* through which most of us produce culture, but it is a process that Benjy can only repeat without ever transforming it into a means of production, without ever transforming it, that is, into a means of producing anything except more of itself.

I conclude our discussion of the Benjy section with one long passage where the children play in the branch on the day Damuddy dies, beginning in the present with "He pulled me back. 'Sit down.' I sat down" (17), extending through the scene where Caddy muddies her drawers and then back into the present at "*What is the matter with you, Luster said. Cant you get done with that moaning and play in the branch like folks*" (19). Here I try to bring out the novel's humor and show how the characters' early childhoods already contain their adulthoods, which can help new readers of the novel recognize and learn to work with the distinctive traits and patterns of each character.

Playing in the branch, Quentin and even the more independent Caddy both appeal to Versh's authority, revealing that Versh is a little older and that they all structure authority in terms they will not long sustain. As they grow up, social barriers replace personal connections, leading the white children to assume more authority and lose most of their ability to see authority in blacks. In the meantime, their reliance on personal rather than social distinctions underlines how constructed those social distinctions are. Yet even while they make so few social distinctions, they already diverge sharply in speech dialects. The contrast seems exaggerated, as if even while Faulkner shows the artificiality of those differences he also succumbs to a social pressure to reimpose them.

Quentin, Caddy, and Versh already act in distinguishable patterns. Caddy initiates the action and the others only respond. Her action is corporeal, and Benjy sees or remembers her and her action in terms—"She was wet"—that he cannot recognize as sexual:

> She was wet. We were playing in the branch and Caddy squatted down and got her dress wet and Versh said,
> "Your mommer going to whip you for getting your dress wet."
> "She's not going to do any such thing." Caddy said.
> "How do you know." Quentin said. . . .
> "I'm seven years old." Caddy said. "I guess I know."
> "I'm older than that." Quentin said. "I go to school. Dont I, Versh."
> . . . .
> "You know she whip you when you get your dress wet." Versh said.
> "It's not wet." Caddy said. She stood up in the water and looked at her dress. "I'll take it off." she said. "Then it'll dry."
> "I bet you wont." Quentin said.
> "I bet I will." Caddy said.
> "I bet you better not." Quentin said.   (17–18)

Already, as through the rest of the novel, Caddy plays, improvises, and takes her own self as the authority and as the arbiter of knowledge, whereas

Quentin—and Versh, whom we see less of later—appeal to exterior authority. In a sense the whole novel is about Caddy taking her dress off and about her brothers' reactions to it. Quentin's words are a dare. He desperately wants Caddy to take her dress off, despite his intense resistance to his own desire— and to hers—and so he soon escalates to saying, "You just take your dress off" (18), a plea hardly masked by its feeble sarcasm. In much the same way, the older Quentin will take masochistic delight in his revulsion at Caddy's adventurousness. Here, when she accedes to his command and removes her dress, Quentin slaps her, as he will slap her years later when she kisses a boy and as he will try impossibly to slap Dalton Ames (133, 160).

The scene continues through a series of often comic permutations on the Compsons' lifelong patterns, until finally Caddy, with her bottom "all wet and muddy," says she will run away, and Benjy begins to cry, less a foreshadowing of what happens later than a performance, emotionally and linguistically, of what Benjy—and Caddy, in her brothers' imaginations, at least—already can never do anything but repeat. Then suddenly we learn that "Jason was playing too. He was by himself further down the branch" (19), and it turns out that all through this extended, dramatic, and comic scene, Jason has been there too, on the outside of his siblings' closed drama, without making any difference to them. His sudden visibility hints that he somehow makes a show to remind them that he is there, trying hopelessly to make himself matter to them, much like his efforts through the rest of the novel.

Then Luster, utterly unaware of Benjy's memories, abruptly calls Benjy back to the present, which can always interrupt memory without any narrative fulcrum. In this scene, then, as in the section at large, the novel flaunts its transitions in ways that dramatize the concept of transition itself: narrative transition, emotional transition, transition between memory and present perception, transition from child to adult. At the same time, the same transitions also dramatize the psychological and cultural resistances that clog and thwart transition to lock each Compson in endless repetition. Thus I conclude by asking my students to ponder what it means at the end of the Benjy section when we go to sleep as Benjy, inside Benjy's consciousness as he returns to an imaginary, womblike, lyrical "always," and then turn the page to wake up as Quentin. Does that crossing, that fence gate or transition, release us into a superior or more familiar consciousness, or are we right back in another version of where we began?

APPENDIX
INTRODUCING *THE SOUND AND THE FURY*
(A CLASS HANDOUT)

The Sound and the Fury tells about the Compson family. It is written in four sections (plus an appendix Faulkner added almost two decades later), with each section told from a different perspective. The famous first section comes through the perspective of Benjy Compson, an idiot, not as we use the word colloquially, to mean a fool, but in the sense that denotes someone of extremely low intelligence. Benjy's intelligence is so low that he is not even capable of speech, although Faulkner records his process of mind in a language he might use if he could speak. As a result, Benjy's language is extraordinarily simple, so astonishingly simple that it can be difficult to read. Because Benjy understands so little, he sometimes fails to make connections that we all take for granted, such as between cause and effect; or he makes connections where we would not, such as between a golf caddie and his sister Caddy (Candace). At any moment, particular words or feelings can transport him to some remembered time that he doesn't distinguish from the present, although Faulkner usually gives some clue in language or typography to signal the transition that Benjy himself cannot understand. Gradually, as you read Benjy's section, you will crack the code. You will grow familiar with the different times that occupy Benjy's mind, and grow to recognize them by the people, places, events, and activities of each separate time.

Section 2 comes through the perspective of Benjy's brother Quentin. Quentin is intelligent, anxious, intellectual—in other words, a typical college student. Benjy's and Quentin's sections are the most famous American instances of what has come to be called stream of consciousness; that is, they follow the thoughts of a particular mind in whatever direction those thoughts go, even when those thoughts (like anyone's thoughts, sometimes) refuse to go in directions sensible, convenient, or clear. Benjy's section falls into a pattern, a code that you will eventually crack. You might find Quentin's section more profoundly and permanently difficult.

The third and fourth sections and the appendix offer no special difficulties.

It might help to explain a few details. In three instances, two characters have the same name. Benjy is originally named Maury, after Mrs. Compson's brother. When they realize he is an idiot, they fear that naming him after Maury is in bad taste, so they change his name to Benjamin. Some references to Maury, then, refer to the young Benjy. Jason, the other Compson brother, is named after his father; and Caddy eventually has a daughter, whom she names Quentin after her brother, so that there are two Jasons and two Quentins. The only major confusion might come with the Quentins, but young Quentin has a minor role at first, and the context makes clear which Quentin is which. Also, "Damuddy" is the Compson children's name for their grandmother; "Nancy" is a horse—

presumably part of a matched team with "Fancy"; and when the characters say "branch" they mean a brook or creek. Some readers get confused when Quentin tells his father (or imagines telling his father) that he has committed incest with his sister Caddy. He is lying; he has not committed incest, and his father knows he has not.

You should read *The Sound and the Fury* twice, or at least one and a half times, for you might not get enough from the first two sections until after you finish the whole book. If you read it twice, you might be able to read it in no more time than one careful reading would take. You can first read sections 1 and 2 rather quickly, without worrying about things you don't get. Then after you've finished the whole, you can go back and read it again much more easily. *Start early, so that you can be on your second reading when we get to the novel in class.* At the least, if you only read the novel once, you will probably find it helpful and pleasurable to spend a good deal of time going back over Benjy's and Quentin's sections when you finish.

"Trying to Say": Sound and Silence, Subject and Community in *The Sound and the Fury*

Arnold Weinstein

As a text for teaching in today's critical climate, *The Sound and the Fury* risks appearing decidedly compromised: its modernist, fractured narrative format will alienate many would-be readers, and its representation of particular groups—women and blacks, to name the most obvious—will stick in the craw of those readers intent on mapping the ideological stakes of Faulkner's novel. For this reason I find it crucial in the classroom to focus on what most moved me when I encountered the book some thirty years ago as an undergraduate and what continues to move me today: the sheer emotional power and pathos of the Compson saga and the unprecedented economy with which Faulkner has presented his story of loss. My key terms here—*power, pathos, economy,* and *loss*—are all ways of approaching the core of this novel: the "inside" narrations of the Compson brothers' fates, each dealing with the loss of Caddy and all that that portends; Faulkner's breakthrough in making many of his readers grasp the private landscapes and traumas of these tormented figures, in ways that traditional storytelling cannot manage; the emerging cumulative statement of the novel, generated by its very packaging, about the limits of the first person and the imprisoning nature of self.

The Sound and the Fury possesses, even for the first-time reader, a sensuous immediacy that is rare in fiction, and one wants students to experience as sharply as possible this feature of the novel, to appreciate the novel's revolutionary presentation of feelings and of the wreckages wrought by time—not because this presentation marks a major stage in the development of the modern novel but rather, in more personal terms, because it schools our perceptions, makes us glimpse—and then feel—the awful coherence and pain of twisted lives. Faulkner once said that the writer interested in technique should take up "bricklaying or surgery" (Meriwether and Millgate 244), and I emphasize the affective reaches of this book to rescue it from the web of abstractions that literary criticism frequently treats us to.

The most spectacular exemplar of Faulkner's achievement in this area is, of course, Benjy, and I begin talking about the novel exactly where Faulkner begins, on the first page, with its ominous opening lines, "Through the fence, between the curling flower spaces, I could see them hitting" (3). That innocuous phrase first announces perception as enclosure, with all vision negotiated "through the fence," then announces the violence of the story: "hitting" as the modus operandi of the golf game that Benjy records but does not comprehend. I read much of the page aloud and then ask the students to tell me what is strange here, or, more specifically, what it is that they know but that Benjy apparently doesn't know. They usually explain that Benjy cannot conceptualize golf, that at a certain point he calls the golf course a pasture, that he starts crying for unknown reasons, that he cannot even tell us that he is crying, that the information must come from Luster. We then try to ascertain what is gained by such "naive" narration, in which golf becomes a rather violent affair of hitting and the word *caddie* is mysteriously but crucially overdetermined, since the phrase "Here, caddie" seems to function as a minor explosion in the text, presumably causing the moaning that starts in the next line.

At this point, I usually reverse my question by asking, "What is it that Benjy knows but we don't?" It is rough going for the beginning reader, but there is something irresistible about this line of questioning. We soon begin to gather that Benjy already knows all the things the novel is going to teach us and that Faulkner has put it in plain view for us to make of it what we can. For example, Benjy knows that the golf course was indeed a pasture, the Compson pasture, and at key moments it still is the pasture for him. Those key moments have to do with "Here, caddie"—innocuous words for us, but they have a tragic destiny for Benjy, since the story of his life is that Caddy is not here but that he is here, waiting for her.

"Is you been projecking with his graveyard[?]" Dilsey asks Luster at a later moment in the text (55), and we come to understand that our job is to project with his graveyard, to move inside Benjy so as to know and assess his losses, to see things his way, to know what it means when Caddy smells like trees, to transform his moaning and weeping and even his silence into sounds, our sounds. This is what Faulkner is "trying to say" (53) in *The Sound and the Fury*; and to grasp his affective, sensorial language, we need to shift our customary registers, perhaps to reconceive language as a larger kind of utterance, much the way we know that a moaning, weeping child is trying to say something that needs our attention and that can be comprehended independent of syntax and explanation. Pain speaks its many tongues in this book, and in the Benjy section Faulkner has given us an almost unbearably full picture of Benjy's losses. We see Caddy feeding him, instructing him ("Ice. That means how cold it is" [13]), loving him, mothering him, trying to give up her own wants for him. That is why "Here, caddie" is so devastating.

Much is beautiful in the Benjy section, but I concentrate on the rendition of Benjy's losses, and I look at countless passages—Caddy and Charlie in the swing versus Quentin and the man in the red tie in the swing, Caddy washing her mouth out with soap, Caddy giving perfume to Dilsey ("We dont like perfume ourselves" [43] is among the most poignant lines in fiction)—passages that make visible and palpable the affective economy at work here, the to-the-bone way in which Faulkner tallies Benjy's losses by showing what Benjy had and what it meant.

This sequence of examples is capped by the episode of Benjy's fateful encounter with the schoolgirls who walk by his fence, half fearful and half teasing, until the day he actually breaks out. By this point we know enough to be able to give the episode its fuller assessment, to understand that the girls are a

version of Caddy and that Benjy's entire life consists of waiting for her to return from school to love him, and what must appear to the outside world as
molestation or even attempted rape is—seen from our (now) quasi-inescapable
position as insiders—the desperate attempt to retrieve Caddy, to make good on
love. Faulkner narrates this episode right to its grisly close, where Benjy goes
under the anesthesia for the castration, with the lyric refrain of the scene
(which, again, wants to be read aloud) of "trying to say":

> They came on. I opened the gate and they stopped, turning. I was trying
> to say, and I caught her, trying to say, and she screamed and I was trying
> to say and trying and the bright shapes began to stop and I tried to get
> out. I tried to get it off of my face, but the bright shapes were going
> again. They were going up the hill to where it fell away and I tried to cry.
> But when I breathed in, I couldn't breathe out again to cry, and I tried to
> keep from falling off the hill and I fell off the hill into the bright, whirling
> shapes.   (53)

With this passage we are in a position to leave Benjy's section, but we do so in
full awareness of Faulkner's bold narrative gambit: to fashion a story of brutal
losses (pasture, sister, genitals) in such a way that the reader is virtually trapped
within the character's orbit. We too are now seeing through the fence. And the
world is thereby metamorphosed, personalized into the private calvary of an
idiot for whom every event recasts the presence and loss of his sister. Finding
a language that captures the feeling and pathos of this story is what Faulkner
means by "trying to say."

The Quentin section, larded with speculations about time and shadows, has
a cerebral, indeed literary, coloration and density that can make it even
rougher going for undergraduates than the more limpid and immediate Benjy
material. Again my tactic is to foreground the pathos of this section, to link the
situation of Quentin—freshman at Harvard, far from home, in trouble—with
that of the undergraduates in the course. Sartre once critiqued Faulkner for
failing to verbalize Quentin's reasons for suicide, and I usually start with that
issue: Why does Quentin kill himself? How does Faulkner manage to tell us?
What does it mean to us to "get" it in this way?

Students often want to know if Quentin did or did not commit incest with
Caddy, and this issue leads to the more thorny one of why the incestuous de-
sire/fear is there in the first place and why the claim of incest might substitute
for the deed. At this point the novel is beginning to cohere around one of its
obsessive central issues: the loss of Caddy and the meaning of that loss for
Benjy and Quentin. Benjy's interest in Caddy is all-encompassing and includes
a strong sexual component, but the frame for Quentin's relationship with
Caddy is a kind of sexual crisis, a deep fear of sexuality itself. In that light the
references to Versh's finding a man who mutilated himself, which reflects
Quentin's desire to be free of all sexuality ("O That That's Chinese I dont know

Chinese" [116]), and the references to the stifling smell of honeysuckle, to the fascinating/frightening female body with its mysterious fluids ("Delicate equilibrium of periodical filth between two moons balanced. Moons he said full and yellow as harvest moons her hips thighs" [128]), all speak of Quentin's precariousness, of the libidinal circuitry that governs his life.

Faulkner elects to narrate along just that circuitry. The fateful map of Quentin's tormented sexuality will be drawn. It will interweave the adolescent skirmish with Natalie (*"did you ever dance sitting down?"* [135]) with the nightmarish encounter with the little girl whom Quentin befriends and whom he cannot escape, and we see that this is all Caddy material, this is all about Quentin's suicide. Whereas the Benjy section is a constant to-and-fro between past and present, Quentin's monologue is a shifting, strategic affair, a graphic rendition of the dynamics of repression that have kept him alive up to now and are coming apart. Hence, the story of the past (Caddy's promiscuity, Caddy's pregnancy, Caddy's marriage) trickles, spurts, and surges in Quentin's narrative, flaunting its affective and narrative power, making it evident that this is the true story of Quentin Compson. Nothing better signals the takeover than the moment Quentin greets the little girl with the words, "Hello, sister" (125), announcing the hideous power of the occulted private story, showing us that the ghosts have taken over the script, pointing us to a landscape of fingers like worms, of pink panties, of bread thrusting its nose out of paper, of honeysuckle everywhere. No safe havens are left; the world out there has gone out of business.

Just as "Here, caddie" turns out to be the story of Benjy's life, so too is Quentin's existence musically composed according to that same melody, and Faulkner's writing incessantly returns to the scene of the crime, lays bare the libidinal wiring that will kill this young man. The final, clear sequence of Quentin and Caddy at the branch (149–64)—showing Quentin's powerlessness, Caddy's desire—demonstrates the stranglehold of the past, tells us all we need to know about his death. In looking at how Faulkner has delivered this material, one wants students at the very beginning to grasp Quentin's inside story, in order then to gauge its grisly authority over his everyday life. From here it is but a small step to tackling the real nature of Faulknerian storytelling, which reveals through art the private landscape that otherwise "passeth show," which narrates through the fence. Faulkner's venture consists in showing how imperious (to us) and yet invisible (to others) our private world is, and the truth of this principle is best displayed by asking students what about themselves is visible and narratable. And visible to whom and narratable by whom. Here also is an opportunity to measure the respective "takes" of descriptive mimetic prose versus interior monologue and to pose, finally, the question of whether that darkly coherent inner story (of Benjy and of Quentin) is deciphered, discovered, or invented. Much of the project of twentieth-century modernism comes into focus as the class's investigation reaches its conclusion.

Given my emphasis on assessing the stakes of the interior monologue form in the Benjy and Quentin sections, it would seem appropriate to proceed along the same lines with Jason's. To do so is to acquire a peculiar sympathy with one of Faulkner's most notorious villains, largely because the first person generates, willy-nilly, a readerly bond; it makes us understand that Jason, too, hurts. Yet Jason Compson is also one of the author's supreme comic creations, and Jason's remarks about Jews, blacks, women, and Compsons are hilarious as well as jaundiced and scary. I read some of his passages aloud, partly for comic relief (badly needed at this point), partly to illuminate the amazing spectrum of tonalities that Faulkner achieves. It is also worth asking students which of the Compson brothers most qualifies for the book's title. Although many will make the knee-jerk choice of Benjy, a number will begin to see that Jason Compson—with his raging headaches, repressed desire for his niece, sadism for all around him, control mania of great proportions—is a disturbing contrast to his brothers, since in Faulkner's scheme he seems to represent what happens to those who are lucky enough to grow up.

My parting shot with Jason is that he serves as a foil to the Dilsey chapter, that Faulkner's claim in the appendix that Jason is the "first sane Compson" (*Sound* [Norton] 233) has its grotesque truth. The affective-subjectivist onslaught of the first three chapters whets our appetite for sanity, underscores our readerly need to frame these events and these monologues, to see what the whole venture is leading to. The final section of the novel allows us, more or less, to do just that.

We need to ask first of all whether the chapter deserves to be called Dilsey's chapter, and students will quickly see that she occupies a rather small part of it. Needless to say, this observation leads to very charged issues: What is Dilsey doing in this book? What social order requires black mammies? Why does Dilsey speak so little? Why is Dilsey's consciousness essentially absent from the novel? A discussion of Faulkner's handling of blacks and women will follow, and Caddy belongs in this critical arena as well as Dilsey. For a number of students, the discussion will be the highpoint of reading *The Sound and the Fury*, helping them position Faulkner, gauge his blind spots and liabilities, measure just how much he comes up short in the vexed areas of race and gender.

Yet I submit that the final chapter of Faulkner's book opens up more richly and more rewardingly to a different set of questions, questions that revolve around the Easter sermon. In the Reverend Shegog's performance in the black church, Faulkner takes the measure of his novel and helps us convert our (difficult) reading experience into something we might call knowledge. I say "performance"—and I think it is essential to read aloud, with feeling, chunks of this sermon, as much for the sheer pathos it has as for the light it sheds on all that has preceded—because the text emphasizes the virtuosity and shifting registers of the reverend's sermon, beginning with white-man oratory (compared to acrobatics) and closing with an insistently black and familial rhetoric. As Faulkner moves from "Brethren and sisteren" (294) to "Breddren en sistuhn!" (295), we understand that this story of a broken family, of three brothers and a sister, is coming to a close but is still being told. And the reverend's persistent emphasis on vision—"I sees hit, breddren! I sees hit! Sees the blastin, blindin sight! I sees Calvary" (296)—is cut, over and over, with the collective voice of the congregation, "Mmmmmmmmmmmmmm," calling to mind the book's very first page with its seemingly incoherent moaning.

In a blending of epiphanic vision and collective voice, Faulkner reconceives his entire enterprise of interior monologue and hurting Compsons, and he does so with the severity of a Greek tragedian. The Easter sermon is about re-birth, and it points back to the Crucifixion for its image of a love that gives life rather than takes it, a love that is generosity and grace rather than hurt and anger. It is here that Faulkner is making his largest utterance about the nature of modern life and modern art, because he is indicting consciousness itself (modernism's darling), positing selflessness and love as redemptive values that could illuminate the Compsons' fate. Each of the Compson brothers has tried to hold and possess Caddy, has vampirishly battened on her for the sustenance that makes living possible. That has been precisely the burden of the interior monologues, and we, the readers who have looked through the fence, know how much pathos the brothers' hunger possesses. But the generosity of the Easter sermon helps us to a crucial view of the Compsons themselves as radically selfish and narcissistic, helps us understand that Caddy, and later her daughter Quentin, had to leave in order to live.

These are rich matters, and they transcend issues of narrative technique, perhaps even of ideology. Faulkner's economy consists not only in devising a libidinal, poetic language for the suffering Compsons but also in turning his mosaic of jangled voices ultimately into a picture of what happens when love is reduced to personal need, when generosity of spirit disappears. With its blind Confederate soldier, its watch repairman with a metal tube screwed into his face, its literally imprinted icon that says,

"Keep your 👁 on Mottson" (311),

The Sound and the Fury tells us that genuine vision must be something different from these models, that we are, yes, obliged all our days to see through our own fence, but that we need no less urgently to imagine the vision and needs of others, to see through their eyes. This would be how love is understood in this book.

Life dooms us to the first person. Love moves us beyond it. Reading constitutes our entry into other lives. These issues are at once simple and complex. Faulkner's novel, more than any book I know, gives us a visceral understanding of them. That is what he is trying to say.

Confronting Race in Faulkner:
Strategies for Answering Difficult Questions

Anthony Barthelemy

Professors who decide to include *The Sound and the Fury* or any of several other Faulkner novels in a course syllabus must be prepared to address potentially hostile questions about race and racism in Faulkner's fiction. No one can simply ignore or sidestep these questions by asserting the author's importance to the modernist canon or to American literary history. Failure to acknowledge the significance of the racist past in the construction of Faulkner's fictional world only compromises the critical endeavor. The solution, of course, is more complex than merely deciding that the author or the novel is or is not racist. For me to state that Faulkner is or is not racist—a statement based on years of reading and teaching Faulkner—would be to interfere with any meaningful interrogation by the students of the novel's representation of African Americans. Similarly, such a declaration from me would encourage some readers of this essay to continue reading and others to turn to another essay in the volume. Efforts to provoke inquiry are undermined by an unwillingness to admit that sincere disagreement exists among scholars on this subject. My purpose here, as it is frequently in the classroom, is to guide, not to assert.

In her book *Faulkner's "Negro,"* Thadious Davis addresses the complexity involved in understanding Faulkner's art:

> *The Sound and the Fury* clearly indicates that Faulkner's interest is in the external manifestations of the Negro's inner resources, of which he apparently was firmly convinced. While his literal understanding of blacks is largely shaped by his particular heritage and place in the white world, his artistic development of their presence in plot, structure, themes, and symbols transcends the limitations of his personal perspective.   (70)

Recognition of this intricate weave will stimulate a provocative and useful interrogation of Faulkner's aesthetic and moral ambitions.

To investigate Faulkner's artistic transcendence, the teacher must first frankly discuss the "limitations of his personal perspective." Faulkner's free use of the term *nigger* presents one of the many problems regarding the intersection between that perspective and the work itself. Enough other evidence exists in the novel to justify sincere questions from students about racism. What is one to make, for instance, of Dilsey's self-deprecation (208) or of the parodic portrayal of Luster in broad minstrel terms? How does one interpret the narrator's offensive focus on the shape of Luster's head (285, 289) and the consistent use of animal imagery in referring to the Gibsons in the final section of the book (284, 293, 294)? Are the vignettes of the deacon (96–99) and Uncle

Louis (114–15) irrelevant to the question of the portrayal of African Americans in the novel? The accumulative evidence is troubling and demands answers.

Looking at individual components in isolation does not help the student comprehend the larger picture. Yet the teacher can make great use of the components to develop that picture. The paradox of pedagogy is that we must vivisect the work of art into constituent parts to understand better the meaning of the whole. Thus the method of division and subdivision, the separation of parts from the whole, can determine the meaning we hope to extract from or attribute to the work. Considering the use of the word *nigger* may initially appear to provide too narrow a focus, but the word actually unites the text temporally, geographically, and thematically.

Several possible avenues for discussion open up. The easiest question to present to the class is, Who uses the word and under what circumstances? The teacher might offer several quotations to direct attention to the various characters and the implications of their use of the word. How, for instance, would one compare Dilsey's comment to Luster as recalled in Benjy's section, "Dont you sass me, nigger boy" (55), with Quentin's comment to Caddy, "*Why wont you bring him to the house, Caddy? Why must you do like nigger women do in the pasture the ditches the dark woods hot hidden furious in the dark woods*" (92)? The two statements occur in sections narrated by different people and at different times. In the eighteen years between 2 June 1910, and 7 April 1928 has nothing changed in attitudes toward or treatment of blacks? What do we learn about Quentin and Caddy from Quentin's thought? How does Benjy's mediation affect our attitude toward Dilsey's admonition of her son?

Nigger serves as a remarkable constant in the intervening years. To highlight that constancy, the teacher need only offer a quotation from 6 April 1928, from Jason. Jason seems to use the word *nigger* more than any other character, just as he uses African Americans as a criterion for everything evil, useless, lazy, lucky, and blessed. He tells Dilsey:

> You're a nigger. You're lucky, do you know it? I says I'll swap with you any
> day because it takes a white man not to have anymore sense than to worry
> about what a little slut of a girl does.   (243)

Of course, Jason would not change places with Dilsey or with any other black person, but the irony of the statement reveals much about Jason, his time and place, and the prevailing attitude toward blacks. (The irony further suggests something about the author's perspective.) Thus, by pursuing the problem of *nigger*, we have opened up discussion about character and characterization, self-esteem, racism, and mimesis.

Students can, in fact, gauge how the Compsons feel about themselves by mapping the Compsons' language and expressed attitudes toward black people. Quentin may offer the best advice in devising a hermeneutics for interpreting black people when he reflects on his paradoxical feelings for Dilsey and her family:

> I used to think that a Southerner had to be always conscious of niggers. . . . When I first came East I kept thinking You've got to remember to think of them as colored people not niggers, and if it hadn't happened that I wasn't thrown with many of them, I'd have wasted a lot of time and trouble before I learned that the best way to take all people, black or white, is to take them for what they think they are, then leave them alone. That was when I realised that a nigger is not a person so much as a form of behavior; a sort of obverse reflection of the white people he lives among. But I thought at first that I ought to miss having a lot of them around me . . . , but I didn't know that I really had missed Roskus and Dilsey and them until that morning in Virginia.   (86)

Careful reading of this passage reveals a number of conflicting attitudes, contradictions a teacher should encourage students to pursue. What looks like a genuine epiphany about common humanity, for instance, really denies African American humanity and subject status. Exploring this paradox provides a key to exploring the novel's, and Faulkner's, problem with black people. Black people, to Faulkner, are other; they exist only to help white people understand themselves. Using Quentin's standard, then, we see that while the novel is interested in African Americans as characters, it is fundamentally uninterested in them as people.

Perhaps this lack of interest reflects southern attitudes as well. By constructing a less-than-human identity for blacks, whites celebrate their own supposed superiority. Their humanity finds confirmation in the otherness of the oppressed. Faulkner parodies this feeble logic when Mr. Compson ridicules his brother-in-law Maury: "I admire Maury. He is invaluable to my own sense of racial superiority. I wouldn't swap Maury for a matched team" (43). Because the Bascombs are said to be weak or innately inferior, the comparison renders the Compsons superior to them. Does this comparison reflect an anxiety in the novel about the Gibsons? Dilsey demonstrates fortitude and compassion in the face of adversity. She manages the Compson household with what some might say is too much devotion, while Mrs. Compson (née Bascomb) takes to her bed. Jason's attitude toward Dilsey reflects the degree of her control. Not only does she call him "Jason" even though he is the head of the family; she admonishes and defies him: "You's a cold man, Jason, if man you is. . . . I thank de Lawd I got mo heart dan dat, even ef hit is black" (207–08). Does Dilsey's naming of Jason empower her? How does this naming function in relation to the Compsons' naming of people as "niggers"? In this context, the narrator's decision elsewhere not to use the word becomes relevant; the word's absence in the omniscient narration of the fourth section goes beyond politeness, for it fits in the overall aesthetic composition and moral tenor of the novel.

Dilsey's condemnation of Jason, however, continues to reflect the novel's anxiety about its black characters. Dilsey can only affirm her humanity if she also admits her inferiority. The novel denies her status as subject to highlight Jason's unfeeling selfishness. Jason, however, narrates the section of the novel in which Dilsey condemns him. Thus, even though he possesses none of the love and compassion Dilsey displays, he possesses the authority and power of narrative voice and an unequivocal subject status; he controls a legitimating point of view. Moreover, Dilsey's close identification with the Compsons signals her assent to the Compsons' racist viewpoint. By mastering the role of faithful servant, the character confirms the stereotype and reflects an uneasy acceptance of the economic and political oppression that confines her and her family to the subhuman status demanded and enforced by the South. Dilsey's narrative silence, in fact, implies the author's tacit endorsement of the prevailing southern standard.

Since *The Sound and the Fury*, like many of Faulkner's novels, concerns itself with narration, an obvious question arises: Why do we hear black discourse only indirectly, through the mediation of white voices? Not until the omniscient narration of the events of 8 April 1928 are the Gibsons spared the indignity of a narrator who calls them "niggers," although even this last, omniscient narrator exhibits other forms of racial stereotyping. In a work that authorizes the viewpoint of the retarded Benjy, Dilsey is afforded no opportunity to represent or review her life and the life of the Compsons in a complete narrative unit. She cannot resist in word or deed. Her enforced silence— whether for social, political, or artistic reasons—speaks eloquently about the lack of subject status and the unrelenting alterity of blacks in the white world of Mississippi in 1928 and 1929 and throughout much of American literature and history.

We must not, however, be guilty of the same error; we must not ignore the subject status of the Gibsons. Because the novel suppresses their voices, the teacher in the classroom must attempt to compensate. Obviously, we cannot construct the reality of the African Americans in *The Sound and the Fury*; we cannot give them voice. But we must interrogate the silence, explore its meaning, understand its implications, its ideological and artistic ramifications. Students should also be encouraged to compare the silence of the white women—none of whom narrates a section—with that of African Americans. Such a comparison should help students deduce a theory of alterity to describe the oppression of blacks and women as it occurs in the novel. Dilsey obviously should be the central figure in this discussion, because she suffers from both forms of oppression. Moreover, by focusing on Dilsey, students will be able to discern similarities and differences between racial oppression and sexual oppression.

Any investigation along these lines will inevitably return us to the difficult yet unavoidable question of Faulkner's racism. Since scholars have been unable to agree on an answer, we should not expect our students to agree. But we must help them see the racist past that makes the question necessary; and we must help them see that a great artist remains a fallible human being, capable of remarkable insight but also capable of prejudice.

Toni Morrison suggests in *Playing in the Dark: Whiteness and the Literary Imagination* that in addition to studying the effects of "racial hierarchy" on the lowly, we must study its effects on the masters:

> It seems both poignant and striking how avoided and unanalyzed is the effect of racist inflection on the subject. What I propose . . . is to examine the impact of notions of racial hierarchy, racial exclusion, and racial vulnerability on nonblacks who held, resisted, explored, or altered those notions. The scholarship that looks into the mind, imagination, and behavior of slaves is valuable. But equally valuable is a serious intellectual effort to see what racial ideology does to the mind, imagination, and behavior of masters. (11–12)

By pursuing the problem of the use of the word *nigger*, students can begin to understand how racial attitudes shaped and deformed the oppressor as well as the victim. An investigation of Jason from this perspective may assuage some of the anxieties a few readers feel about Faulkner himself. Regardless of the conclusions reached, an exploration of the use of this word will lead a class through provocative ideas about *The Sound and the Fury*, Faulkner, literary art, race, and American literature.

Using Faulkner's Introduction to Teach *The Sound and the Fury*

Philip Cohen and Doreen Fowler

Unless properly introduced, *The Sound and the Fury* will most likely intimidate students who approach it. Opening the novel and reading "Through the fence, between the curling flower spaces, I could see them hitting" (3), students may turn anxiously to *Monarch Notes on Faulkner's* The Sound and the Fury and substitute an explication of the novel for the experience of reading it. Fortunately, we have available instead Faulkner's own introduction, which is an invaluable aid to teaching the novel. During the summer of 1933, Faulkner wrote draft after draft of this introduction for a limited edition of *The Sound and the Fury* that never materialized. The introduction was thought to be lost until, in 1970, manuscript and typescript fragments and different versions of it were discovered among a cache of Faulkner's papers in the stairwell closet of his home. Soon after, James B. Meriwether published a short version of the introduction in the *Southern Review* and a substantially different and longer version in the *Mississippi Quarterly*. In 1990, Cohen and Fowler published most of the remaining fragments, drafts, and versions of the introduction in *American Literature*. Although we may never know for certain which version Faulkner ultimately sent to his publisher, the evidence points to the long version (Cohen and Fowler 267).

Since their publication, the different versions of the introduction have become the most widely cited of all of Faulkner's prose statements. This attention is well deserved because, despite some contradictions and fabrications, one finds in these materials an openness and sincerity about his life and work that are rare in Faulkner's public statements and that help us understand better various aspects of *The Sound and the Fury*. Instructors may also find that these materials, along with Faulkner's comments on the novel elsewhere, are useful for generating class discussion about some of the basic disputes in literary studies today. Is literary meaning, for example, produced by authors, by texts, by readers, or by a combination of them? How relevant are authorial statements of intention to different methods of interpreting and evaluating literary works? Instructors might also ask students to assess the sincerity of Faulkner's comments in these materials by considering the rhetorical context of their initial appearance.

The drafts for the introduction contain Faulkner's retrospective statements about the genesis and writing of the novel and voice his deeply felt conviction, expressed throughout his career, that it was the book that meant the most to him, his "most splendid failure" (Gwynn and Blotner 77). Thus he writes that "when [he] finished The Sound and the Fury [he] discovered that there is actually something to which the shabby term Art not only can, but must be applied" ("An Introduction" [1st] 708) and that only the writing of this particular novel gave him "that emotion definite and physical and yet nebulous to describe: that ecstasy, that eager and joyous faith and anticipation of surprise which the yet unmarred sheet beneath [his] hand held inviolate and unfailing, waiting for release" (709).

In the introduction, Faulkner describes how he came to write the novel. Before composing *The Sound and the Fury*, he had written, with increasing effort and decreasing remuneration, three good but not great novels. The last, *Flags in the Dust*, was turned down by one publisher after another and accepted and published only in truncated form, as *Sartoris*, in 1929. This experience profoundly influenced the composition of *The Sound and the Fury*. The pain of rejection caused Faulkner to turn deeply inward and led to an artistic breakthrough: "One day I seemed to shut a door between me and all publishers' addresses and book lists. I said to myself, Now I can write" (710). He also recalls that when he wrote the Benjy section, he "was not writing it to be printed" (Cohen and Fowler 277). In other words, unlike its predecessors, *The Sound and the Fury* began as a private novel. It explores an interior landscape, Faulkner's own interior terrain. Students may connect these biographical and psychological circumstances to features of the work. For example, these revelations help explain the intense inwardness of its first three sections, which students can find especially difficult. In these sections Faulkner uses the stream-of-consciousness technique to perform a psychic exploration, to reveal the inner landscape of the person.

Faulkner asserts in this introduction that the novel began with an image, for which, he maintains, the four sections of the novel are less-than-satisfying verbal transactions. In this pivotal mental image, a little girl sits in a pear tree high above her brothers. She is looking through a window at her grandmother's funeral while, beneath her, her brothers are looking up at the muddy seat of her drawers. The image, which Faulkner describes as "perhaps the only thing in literature which would ever move me very much" (710), distills the essence of the novel. Stressing the importance Faulkner attaches to this image, instructors can use it as the centerpiece for class discussion. The following, for example, can be asked: Focus first on the question, Why do you suppose Faulkner found this image so moving? Do you find it moving, and, if so, why? Discuss the significance of the relative positions of Caddy and her brothers: Caddy high above, and her brothers below her. Notice that Caddy is perched in a tree—what associations does a tree have?

Instructors may wish to explore the symbolism of the muddy drawers, asking the students to recall the scene in the novel that led to the soiling. They may direct the students' attention to the important role looking plays in this image; they may suggest that students too are onlookers—like Caddy and her brothers. Eventually, such a line of discussion leads to the conclusion that the novel is a quest for meaning, a quest in which the reader is intimately and intensely involved. Just as Caddy is peering into the house and just as her brothers are peering up at her, so are we, the readers, caught up in the desire to see and know. The object of the quest is implied in Faulkner's image; the fundamental problem of existence, which is nonexistence, death, identified here with women, with Caddy and her grandmother. At this point, the class has fixed on a basic theme of the novel: a male identification of women with death. The little girl in the tree who wears muddy drawers and looks on death represents for her brothers the inevitable flow of time, which irretrievably carries us forward, away from purity and innocence and toward sexuality, decay, and death.

One of the major ways Faulkner's introduction helps us read *The Sound and the Fury* is by focusing on Caddy's symbolic significance. Faulkner suggests that, for her brothers, she embodies the evanescence, the loss, inherent in existence. But Faulkner does not limit himself to this important idea. He goes on to explain, uncharacteristically, what Caddy means to him personally. He created Caddy Compson out of his own sense of loss; he meant for her to fill a lack created by two female vacancies—the absence of a sister and the loss of a daughter. "So I, who never had a sister and was fated to lose my daughter in infancy, set out to make myself a beautiful and tragic little girl" (710).

At this juncture, instructors may wish to introduce some relevant biographical information about Faulkner. Students will most likely already know that Faulkner was the oldest of four brothers. However, they may not know that Faulkner's first child, a daughter, Alabama, was born prematurely on 11 January 1931 and died nine days later of respiratory failure. The infant might possibly have survived had the Oxford hospital owned an incubator. After her death, Faulkner, who at this time was supporting his wife and himself by doing odd jobs, purchased an incubator and donated it to the hospital, apparently in remorse or as penance, as if he felt somehow to blame for the infant's death (Blotner, *Faulkner* [1984] 173–74). This biographical information is relevant to teaching *The Sound and the Fury* since in his introduction Faulkner links Caddy to Alabama as well as to the sister he never had. However, in discussing the relevance of the tragic death of Faulkner's firstborn daughter to Caddy, the instructor should be sure to stress what is easily overlooked—that Faulkner wrote *The Sound and the Fury* in 1928, three years before Alabama's birth and death. Thus in his introduction (written in the summer of 1933) Faulkner is assigning the loss to an earlier time, as if he had always experienced it, as if Alabama's death was one manifestation of a grief he had always lived with. The identification of Caddy with Faulkner's lifelong sense of loss may help to answer another question that students—and scholars—often pose: Why does Caddy Compson not have her own interior monologue in the novel? It may be that we see Caddy only through the eyes of others because Faulkner wants her to remain shadowy, evocative, and evanescent. If he intends Caddy to represent the daughter who will die and the sister he never had or, in other words, to evoke a painful emptiness, the vacancy in his life or in life itself, it would make sense to have Caddy appear throughout the novel as an elusive presence.

Like Faulkner's autobiographical admission of Caddy's origin, some passages that were not included in either of the two published versions of the introduction reveal an extraordinarily probing attempt at self-analysis. Discussing the profoundly intimate nature of the novel, Faulkner seems to be saying that *The Sound and the Fury* is the expression of his unconscious, the articulation of his most deeply repressed fears and desires. Early fragments and drafts, along with some recently discovered letters from him to his friend and agent Ben Wasson, suggest that the author initially conceived of the introduction as a piece of hackwork to be done solely for money (Cohen and Fowler 264, 266). But he soon became inspired, caught up, the authors of this essay believe, in an examination of his career as a writer, of his view of art, and of what the novel, the one he felt "tenderest" toward, meant to him (Meriwether and Millgate 245). Indeed, the sheer amount of surviving manuscript and typescript material suggests that he had written his "guts" into it, as he said he had done—in his 1932 introduction to *Sanctuary*—with *The Sound and the Fury* itself ("Introduction" 338).

The ordering of some of the extant fragments and drafts is problematic. We believe Faulkner cut some of this material because it revealed more about his psychic involvement in his art than he preferred to make known. In one discarded draft, for example, he connects *The Sound and the Fury* to his own unconscious: "I wasn't consciously writing anything to be printed" (Cohen and Fowler 270). This implicit suggestion that in writing the novel Faulkner tapped into his unconscious is supported by his admission that Quentin, Benjy, and Jason are all representations of himself: "I could be in it, the brother and father both. But one brother could not contain all I could feel toward her. I gave her 3." Since Caddy also fills the role of substitute mother for the three brothers, their responses toward her may in fact represent three aspects of Faulkner's complex feelings for the mother or mother figure. In other words, Faulkner's feelings for the mother figure encompass Quentin's, "who loved her . . . as a lover would"; Jason's, "who loved her with the same hatred of [sic] jealous and outraged pride of a father"; and Benjy's, "who loved her with the complete mindlessness of a child" (270). The passage seems an extraordinary confession of the author's obsession with the woman whose body was once connected to his. Even the long version of the introduction contains images that seem to have erupted from Faulkner's unconscious: for example, the image of Caddy as mother, "that fierce, panting, paused and stooping wet figure which smelled like trees." The image of Benjy seems primal in origin: "Without thought or comprehension; shapeless, neuter, like something eyeless and voiceless which might have lived, existed merely because of its ability to suffer, in the beginning of life" ("An Introduction" [2nd] 159, 160).

A man who donned masks all his life as a defense mechanism, Faulkner momentarily dropped his guard in this discarded draft and revealed that he had projected onto the three brothers his most deeply repressed needs and desires, his attachment to the mother, an attachment that he himself described as incestuous, possessively paternal, and regressively childlike. Traces of this self-revelation survive in Faulkner's much more general comments in later drafts on the autobiographical impulse of the southern writer, whose art "is a very personal thing. It is himself that he is writing about. . . . [W]e more than other men unconsciously write ourselves into ever[y] line and phrase" (Cohen and Fowler 279).

The troubles of the Compson brothers, Faulkner implies, are the product of familial conflict. Relating to their surrogate mother, Caddy, as a lover would, or a father or a son, they all obsessively demand from her the gratification and love that their parents, especially the coldly selfish Mrs. Compson, have denied them. Similarly, all three brothers are misogynists, possessing a life-denying view of sexuality, which they inherited from Mr. Compson and the southern Protestant culture that stands behind him. Faulkner's Calvinist linking of sexuality, especially female sexuality, with nature, decay, and death is an authorial signature in much of his fiction, a signature that he sometimes espouses, sometimes dissects, and sometimes both espouses and dissects. The analysis here is predicated primarily on a psychobiographical interpretive framework. In discussion, students might apply other approaches to the same material—reader-response, feminist, sociological—in order to see how critical context shapes textual content.

Criticism of *The Sound and the Fury* often stresses the differences among the three brothers. Thus Cleanth Brooks discusses in his influential *William Faulkner: The Yoknapatawpha Country* the different notions of love and time that each brother embodies (327–31). Michael Millgate, in *The Achievement of William Faulkner*, notes that the novel is concerned with the inevitable subjectivity of truth: "[E]ach man, apprehending some fragment of the truth, seizes upon that fragment as though it were the whole truth and elaborates it into a total vision of the world, rigidly exclusive and hence utterly fallacious" (87). Faulkner's comments, however, suggest that a more recent work such as André Bleikasten's *The Most Splendid Failure: Faulkner's* The Sound and the Fury is closer to the mark when it argues that the three brothers suffer from similar psychological problems but respond to them and to the loss of Caddy in different ways—an argument anticipated in some respects by Carvel Collins's Freudian reading of the novel in his 1952 essay "The Interior Monologues of *The Sound and the Fury.*" The discarded passage from the introduction quoted above (Cohen and Fowler 270) indicates that Faulkner conceived of the three brothers as fundamentally alike despite their surface dissimilarities. And indeed, all three feel abandoned by their parents; all three make impossible demands on Caddy, wanting her to be the mother they never had; all three are obsessed with the loss of Caddy; and all three cannot come to terms with that loss.

As John T. Irwin's *Doubling and Incest / Repetition and Revenge* and Arthur F. Kinney's *Faulkner's Narrative Poetics* have taught us, such a masking of similarity behind difference lies at the heart of Faulkner's narrative technique, not only in *The Sound and the Fury* but throughout his career. Frequently, juxtapositions of disparate blocks of prose—prose different in style, technique, content and in its characters—bewilder readers until they perceive fundamental parallels. As striking incongruities yield to even more striking congruities, we see how characters double and triple one another. Such a strategy reminds us that Faulkner in *The Sound and the Fury* and elsewhere is a novelist less of consciousness than of divided consciousness. As the monologues reveal, the psyches of all three brothers are layered and conflicted in the Freudian sense: the brothers remain mostly unaware of the desires and obsessions that subvert and undermine their intentions. Thus Quentin is *both* the obdurate, idealistic, puritanical protector of lost causes and virginal women *and* the incestuous ravisher, unconsciously, of his sister. Similarly, Jason is only fleetingly aware of the true drives that motivate him. Instead of resorting to an intrusive, omniscient narrator, Faulkner reveals these conflicts by using symbolic imagery, motifs, suggestive parallels, and unusual events like Quentin's adventure with the little Italian immigrant girl. Such parallels and congruities make excellent points in the class discussion of each part of the novel, and locating parallels while evaluating their effects is a good topic for papers and exams.

If Faulkner's introduction, which he eventually sought to suppress, connects the novel to his psychic conflicts, his "Appendix: Compson" seeks to distance *The Sound and the Fury* from him by placing it in a broad social and historical context. In 1945, sixteen years after the publication of *The Sound and the Fury*, Faulkner wrote the appendix for inclusion in Malcolm Cowley's *The Portable Faulkner*. It was subsequently reprinted at either the front or back of numerous editions of the novel. The piece may represent Faulkner's attempt to revive his moribund career and the novel's fortunes by outlining for his readers the novel's plot, characters, and Compson family relationships and genealogy. Arguably, the appendix may also have been an attempt to "rewrite" the novel, without actually rewriting it, to reflect the concerns that dominated Faulkner's work in the late 1930s and the 1940s. Readers who study the novel in the context of the appendix's broad historical framework and in the context of Cowley's influential discussion of Faulkner, in the introduction to *The Portable Faulkner*, as a poetic mythologizer of southern decline often foreground the theme of the fall of the southern aristocracy and downplay the psychological complexity of the Compson family's relationships. This is not to say that readers must approach the novel in terms of Faulkner's conscious and unconscious intentions and desires when he wrote the novel. If one reads and teaches the novel in the context of an authorial orientation as a kind of Freudian family romance as we do, however, the 1933 introduction's biographical revelations and psychological emphases are far more pertinent than either the 1946 appendix or Faulkner's many comments on the novel at the University of Virginia in the late 1950s. To underscore how meanings are produced by the interactions among texts, contexts, and readers, teachers might have their students discuss how reading *The Sound and the Fury* in the light of the introduction and a psychobiographical orientation, on the one hand, and in the light of the appendix and a social-historical orientation, on the other, creates two different novels.

Faulkner's introduction helps us understand the novel in other ways. There is one especially interesting early start at the piece. Presumably, Faulkner's publisher, Bennett Cerf, had provided him with some explicit guidance, because in this early draft Faulkner writes, "Bennett Cerf told me he wants in this introduction, How I came to write The Sound and the Fury, What I think of it after 5 years, and an explanation of the first section; meaning, I think, what Benjy was trying to tell and why I let him tell it" (Cohen and Fowler 266). In another draft, Faulkner tries to answer Cerf's question, writing, "Benjy had to be an idiot: so that he could carry into maturing his feeling for Caddy," and "Ben is the transition: the mausoleum or rather the inviolable alcohol in which the dead sister and brother could be held." The reason he let Benjy "[t]ell this first part, with its concomitant obscuring, is . . . inherent in the inception of Caddy herself: [Faulkner] was not writing it to be printed" (Cohen and Fowler 277–78).

Cerf's desire for an explanation of Benjy's section reminds us that a surprising number of contemporary readers and reviewers of the novel found Benjy's monologue, more so than Quentin's, difficult to the point of obscurity. Since students often have a similar response, it may be helpful to use early reviews to locate and explore some of the interpretive problems the first readers had with the novel. One reviewer, Lyle Saxon, found the writing in Benjy's section "chaotic but pitifully moving" (3), and Basil Davenport noted that Quentin's "thoughts give the tragic occurrences [of the book] more clearly" than does the first section (601). Dudley Fitts observed that "the deliberate obscurity" of Benjy's section "repels rather than invites" and went so far as to recommend that the reader begin the book with Quentin's monologue, saving Benjy's for the last. "In this way [the reader] will not only reassemble the chronology of the narrative, but, thoroughly acquainted with most of the characters, he will better appreciate the significance of Benjy's meditations" (88).

Benjy's section is by no means written in inaccessible prose. This interior monologue of a thirty-three-year-old idiot is characterized throughout by a kind of primitive poetry. Faulkner renders the feebleness of Benjy's mind by employing strikingly literal descriptions that seem like metaphors, concrete and sensuous images rather than abstract and general ones, and a daringly simplified, even monotonous, syntax and punctuation. Benjy cannot use language to discriminate or to create hierarchies or to think conceptually. His passivity and lack of self-consciousness manifest themselves in the way he breathes life into the inanimate world, creating a mysterious and spiritualized natural realm, and in the way the parts of his body operate independently of thought and volition. Benjy's style may be seen in the ruthlessly literal description of a golf game at the novel's opening or in the following passage: "The flower tree by the parlor window wasn't dark, but the thick trees were. The grass was buzzing in the moonlight where my shadow walked on the grass" (46). Frequent time shifts also help make Benjy's monologue confusing, but these transitions, like the language, syntax, and punctuation of the section, operate according to a rigid organizational principle—in this case, the principle of sensuous association.

If the logic dictating the presentation of Benjy's consciousness is initially confusing, it is also an unchanging logic that can be grasped. Quentin's interior monologue, however, strikes many modern readers as more obscure. The narrating mind here is more active, more capable of abstraction, and more self-conscious and sophisticated than Benjy's. Yet it is also a mind in the process of disintegrating. On this day of Quentin's suicide, his mind moves in and out of lucidity. Sometimes, in first-person narration, Quentin may summon memories voluntarily; sometimes, in stream-of-consciousness narration, they may break unbidden into his mind. Unlike Benjy's section with its single style, Quentin's monologue has a variety of linguistic registers, from neutral, detached descriptions to highly stylized, even poetic, meditations that jostle, overlap, and replace each other with astonishing speed. Indeed, some passages are so obscurely personal to Quentin that they remain incomprehensible. And Quentin's monologue, unlike Benjy's, stylizes not only language but also the typography and layout of the printed page. Such stylization reminds us that a characteristic feature of Faulkner's work in particular and of modern fiction in general, a feature especially evident in *The Sound and the Fury*, is the poeticizing of prose. In the novel, Faulkner created the effect of different consciousnesses not only through action, dialogue, and unspoken thought, but also through his wrestling with syntax, punctuation, grammar, typography, and page layout.

Faulkner canceled or discarded some of the introduction's most revelatory passages. Eventually, he disowned the piece completely. When in 1946 Random House was planning to reissue *The Sound and the Fury* and *As I Lay Dying* in one volume, the senior editor Robert Linscott tried to get Faulkner to write an introduction. Faulkner demurred but mentioned the essay he had written earlier. Linscott found the essay in the office files and asked the author to revise it for the forthcoming edition. Faulkner's reply to Linscott, a repudiation of the introduction, was unequivocal:

I had forgotten what smug false sentimental windy shit it was. I will return the money for it, I would be willing to return double the amount for the chance of getting it out of danger and destroyed. . . . I'm certainly glad to have it back. I knew all the time. [sic] I had no business writing an introduction, writing anything just for money. Now I am convinced of it and cured.   (*Selected Letters* 235–36)

The striking vehemence of Faulkner's language here ("out of danger") suggests that the piece still threatened to reveal his psychic involvement with *The Sound and the Fury*—even years after he wrote the piece and even with its most confessional passages excised. Students may propose alternative interpretations of Faulkner's rejection of his introduction, such as genuine disgust with it or a desire for privacy or an emphasis on artistic impersonality. Instructors can use Faulkner's repudiation of the introduction to return to the vexing relationship between authorial statements of purpose and the text. Because it sheds so much light on *The Sound and the Fury*, however, the authors of this essay along with many readers of the novel consider it fortunate that Faulkner's wishes concerning the introduction were not respected.

Private Writing and the Published Novel: Letters and Gifts

James G. Watson

Writing to his Aunt Alabama McLean in 1928, Faulkner called *The Sound and the Fury* "the damndest book I ever read" (*Selected Letters* 41). Many students would agree. But if their first question is likely to be, What does it all mean? it may be followed by that sense of aesthetic wonder that urges our reading and rereading of the novel and finds expression in the question, How did he do it? One approach that I find especially rewarding, once students are familiar enough with the book to phrase the second question, is through a small, readily available body of private writing, peripheral to the novel proper and autobiographical but revealing much about both the matter and the making of the novel. This material consists of, first, an introduction to *The Sound and the Fury* that Faulkner drafted in 1933 but never published ("An Introduction" [2nd]), and, second, a collection of private writing that includes letters to his parents in 1918 (*Thinking of Home*); an illustrated fairy tale (*Mayday*) and a book of sonnets (*Helen: A Courtship*), both privately made for a young woman in 1926; and a short correspondence with his publisher in 1927–28 about the novel that preceded *The Sound and the Fury*. The introduction is retrospective, and I ask that students read it toward the end of our discussion, as an authorial self-appraisal of a favorite work. I do the same with Henry James's preface to *The Portrait of a Lady*, which I like to teach with *The Sound and the Fury* in a course on the American novel. Faulkner's introduction, they find, is more impressionistic and far more personal than James's preface. Faulkner recalls "that emotion definite and physical and yet nebulous to describe which the writing of Benjy's section of *The Sound and the Fury* gave [him]." Comparing himself to the Roman of an old story, he says, "I had made myself a vase, but I suppose I knew all the time that I could not live forever inside of it" ("An Introduction" [2nd] 160, 161). The introduction, as much a representation of himself as an account of the novel, is thereby connected to other self-representations in his letters and gift books. Whether assigned singly or together, these materials provide background for the substantive discussion of authorial intention and of the relation and adaptation of the author's life to his art.

  The Sound and the Fury was accomplished in part by Faulkner's sense that he was writing not for a publisher but for himself. In his introduction, he describes the writing as a release; he recalls, "[O]ne day it suddenly seemed as if a door had clapped silently and forever to between me and all publishers' addresses and booklists and I said to myself, Now I can write. Now I can just write" (158–59). His sense of personal release, in turn, released to his use his private writing of the previous decade, writing in which he had depicted both real and imagined experience and that now provided him with people, situations, and events he could draw on as he worked. "[I]t is himself that the Southerner is writing about," he says in the introduction, "not about his environment," explaining that the southern writer "unconsciously writes into every line and phrase his violent despairs and rages and frustrations or his violent prophecies of still more violent hopes" (158). I suggest to my students at the outset that self-representation of the kind Faulkner describes is in fact self-fictionalization and that it is a feature of all writing where a first-person narrator represents himself or herself to readers. We begin to see that as Faulkner is reflected in the gathering pool of his private writing, so he is present, more obliquely though no less certainly, in the novel into which he incorporated that writing,

Developing biographical connections in criticism is always problematic, especially when the novel is as challenging as *The Sound and the Fury* and the writer a man at once as private and as protean as William Faulkner. Most instructors would agree, moreover, that Faulkner's life is simply too large and too complex a subject to assign to any but the most advanced students. Selections from his letters and gift books are more accessible, and, read together with the novel, they uncover connections between the public book and its private antecedents, between his art and his life. I find it enough to say that Faulkner, like Quentin, left Mississippi at the age of twenty and went to live for a time on the East Coast at a New England Ivy League college. Quentin's Harvard roommate is a Canadian student, and Faulkner knew Canadian RAF officers at Yale and was housed with them as an RAF cadet at the University of Toronto. As Quentin loses Caddy in April 1910 to Sydney Herbert Head, so Faulkner lost Estelle Oldham when she married Cornell Sidney Franklin in April 1918. Ten years later, Estelle's divorce made that old attachment immediately present to him as he was working to revise Quentin's section of *The Sound and the Fury* in the spring of 1928.

Given these parallels, it is not hard for students to find echoes from the novel in letters Faulkner wrote his family from Yale. The surnames of the Harvard womanizers who torment Quentin are borrowed from a shell-shocked British officer named Bland and a Yale poet named Arthur Head. Both would have been the objects of mixed admiration and envy to the would-be soldier and poet from Oxford, Mississippi, in 1918. In a letter of 2 June 1918, Faulkner wrote about the Harvard-Yale boat races that Quentin alludes to on 2 June 1910 and, in a passage recalling Quentin's return to Cambridge from his fight with Gerald Bland, described the train ride home as "the most uncomfortable trip of my life." The same letter contains an account of the New Haven Decoration Day parade of Civil War veterans, transcribed into the novel in 1928 almost word for word, and concludes with a suggestive passage about drowning: "I went out to double beach [*sic*] this afternoon and had my first swim in the ocean. I dont see how any one ever drowns in the sea. You can float like a cigar box" (*Thinking* 61, 62). Whether or not it is possible to trace Quentin's comings and goings on a 1918 map of New Haven, as Joyceans do for the comings and goings of Stephen Dedalus and Leopold Bloom in Dublin, it is clear from the dates of these letters and those of 1921, when Faulkner was again in New

Haven and New York, that he would not have had time to visit Cambridge, Massachusetts. Quentin's Harvard, the letters strongly suggest, was Faulkner's Yale.

At this point, students can agree that the factual parallels between events in Faulkner's novels and his life cannot be accidental. The question remains whether the factual material adapted from the letters was generative as well as descriptive. In this regard, I ask students to list differences between Faulkner's experience, as he reported it to his parents, and his representation of Quentin's fictional experience. One important difference is in the letters themselves, and in their lack. Faulkner came to love New Haven, but his 1918 correspondence shows that at first he was intensely lonely there and wrote every day to his parents, urging them to write him. Often he addressed his mother "Darling Momsey," saying in one letter, "Momsey: I couldn't live here at all but for your letters. I love you, darling" (*Thinking* 53). Conversely, Quentin, who shares significant details of Faulkner's experience, fears and refuses to read the wedding invitation from "Mr and Mrs Jason Richmond Compson" (*Sound* [Vintage] 93) and a letter from Mrs. Bland, whom he and Shreve call Semiramis (101). He blames his dissociation from his family on his mother, lamenting at the end of the day, "*[I]f I'd just had a mother so I could say Mother Mother*" (172). I explain to students that this difference between Faulkner and his character Quentin has to do with the special nature of letters as a genre of writing, and this observation also provides an opportunity to introduce students to the epistolary conventions that laid the foundation for the novel in English. Faulkner discovered those conventions in his early reading of novelists such as Samuel Richardson, mastered them in his own correspondence from 1918 to 1925, and appropriated them for his novel.

To begin with, all letters are generated by absence. They attempt to span separation by figuratively putting the writer's hand—handwriting—into the hand of his or her correspondent. By denying Quentin access to letters from home, Faulkner effectively—and I believe intentionally—intensified in his character the loneliness and isolation that Faulkner felt in New Haven and that generated not only his letters but also his parents' comforting replies. Among the fictional letters I ask students to consider is the ironically unwritten one in which Quentin sends his father a blank sheet in an envelope containing the key to his trunk of clothes and books. In April 1918, Faulkner asked his father for advice about locating a lost trunk and wrote, "Dad, I got your letter today. Thank you, sir, and I love you" (*Thinking* 53). If his epistolary image of the reportedly dour and unresponsive Murry Falkner was a conscious invention, that device is echoed in the novel when Quentin ironically thinks of himself as "*my fathers Progenitive I invented him created I him*" (122). In such convergences, students can see that Faulkner used his state of mind in 1918 as one basis for the unrelieved despair that drives Quentin to drown himself—weighted down, it should be noted, by two six-pound flatirons, the need for which Faulkner discovered when he first swam in the sea at Double Beach, floating, as he reported in his letter, "like a cigar box."

If "all writing that aspires to be literature is autobiography and nothing else," as James Olney has argued (4), letters—and by extension the letterlike gift books Faulkner made and addressed to Helen Baird—may be read as fragments of autobiographical fiction (see Watson). Self-consciously literary in their portrayal of sender and receiver, letters hold the writer also separate from his or her written image. It is the written, invented self that letters transmit into the hands of the receiver and that answering letters confirm. In his letters from New Haven, Faulkner was writing himself into being as a dutiful son, needful and deserving of parental support, which that spring was forthcoming in surprising profusion. He was doing the same, in another guise, when he portrayed himself to Helen Baird in *Mayday* (1926). Again, students are quick to see parallels between the privately written gift of love and the published novel. Faulkner's allegorical Sir Galwyn of Arthgyl is a romantic idealist who drowns himself for love in the arms of "Little sister Death" (87). The language and situation of the gift book are carried into the novel, as are the knight's—and presumably Faulkner's—character traits. Another example of letterlike self-representation may be found at the end of the sonnet sequence *Helen: A Courtship* (1926): the poet named Bill forfeits life and love for his art, forsaking the Pascagoula beach, where he once courted Helen, for the page of his book, that "stubborn leaf" (126) on which the man is the writing. Here and in *Mayday*, as in Faulkner's conventional letters, the writer is both the maker of the text and a part of it. As Faulkner named himself in *Helen*, so he illustrated the *Mayday* endpapers with a pen-and-ink drawing of a faun that has his face and pipes the self-reflecting music of seduction. In the letters and in the gift books, the writing is the surrogate for the writer; the self and the word are one.

The self and the word are also one, though less directly, in *The Sound and the Fury*, where Faulkner's written image is in the novel, in Quentin, by way of his private writing. The private writing helps make this subtle issue sensible for students. The point is not that Quentin Compson is William Faulkner but that Faulkner found in intimate aspects of his own life and art a conception of Quentin and the means to portray him (Watson 55). As his letters show, he is in the book in other characters as well, sometimes surprisingly so. Working on *Flags in the Dust*, in 1927, Faulkner carried on a lighthearted and self-assured correspondence with his New York publisher that took an abrupt and bitter turn when Horace Liveright rejected the novel that November (see *Selected Letters* 33–40). Thereafter, and for a period that extended into his early work on *The Sound and the Fury*, Faulkner depicted himself in letters to Liveright as a victim. Like Faulkner in that correspondence, Jason Compson is betrayed in the novel by "one of the biggest manipulators in New York" (192), loses the same amount of money (two hundred dollars) in the cotton market that Faulkner claimed to have lost gambling, and blames his lack of ready cash on the same 1927 flood. In life as in the novel, identity is crucially at issue—Faulkner's as a novelist, Jason's as a man.

The letters in the novel itself suggest that Faulkner's private writing was a resource for the form as well as the matter of his first masterwork. The letters and letterlike materials that generated the book also in part compose it. There are twenty-one letters and telegrams in *The Sound and the Fury*, and by cataloging them students can discover their many forms and uses. They are transcribed (Lorraine to Jason, 193) and untranscribed (Uncle Maury to Mrs. Patterson, 13–14); fragmented (the wedding invitation, 77) and whole (Uncle Maury to Jason, 223–24); read (Caddy to Miss Quentin, 213) and unread (Mrs. Bland to Quentin, 101, 107); written (Quentin to Shreve, 99), unwritten (Quentin to Mr. Compson, 81), and imagined (Quentin to Mrs. Bland, 107). It is another aspect of the striking form of the book that the characters write and read parts of it through these letters, which, again, are governed by and employ the same epistolary conventions Faulkner used in his own. Like his and all letters, fictional letters depict sender and receiver, establish relationships, and span distances between correspondents. In *The Sound and the Fury*, their "delays, misdirections, and interceptions move the plots of the novel and convey the themes of failed communication and broken identity proposed by the sound and the fury of the title" (Watson 78). Thus Uncle Maury's untranscribed love letters to Mrs. Patterson may be read as elements in the recurrent pattern of "trying to say," wherein communication is forestalled, desire frustrated, and private writing punished. The blank page Quentin sends to his father amounts to a self-erasure analogous to suicide. The suicide itself is enacted only in unwritten writing—in Quentin's pointedly untranscribed letter to Shreve, the suicide note Mrs. Compson refers to on April 8 (283)—but the suicide is postponed in enactment by his carrying the letter with him all day on June 2, and the section ends with his preparing to mail it. The power of private writing to define the correspondents is suggested by Jason's burning of Lorraine's balefully misaddressed note to "Dear daddy" and by his insistence that he makes it a rule "never to keep a scrap of paper bearing a woman's hand" and that he "never writes them at all" (193). The vulnerability of letters and letter writers is dramatized by the ease with which Jason robs Caddy's letters of the money she sends for Quentin and by the care he takes not to sign his lying telegram, "All well. Q writing today" (193). For such reasons, Caddy's letter to Jason lacks both salutation and signature. It is the only instance in the novel when she speaks in her own voice. Anonymously pleading for a responding letter that never comes, asking only to be recognized, Caddy is only a voice, an *idea*, as she is to her brothers; in her letter she is as disembodied as the ideal woman in Sir Galwyn's vision in *Mayday* or as the unattainable Helen in *Helen: A Courtship*.

By itself, the perspective of Faulkner's personal accounts of himself in private writing will hardly explain *The Sound and the Fury*. The autobiographical dimension it adds, however, underscores, as it adds to our understanding of, the reflexive form of the book. Faulkner's insistent subject was not only his "little postage stamp of native soil," as he called it, but the "cosmos of [his] own"

(Meriwether and Millgate 255) that he created from it in his writing. In his novels as in his letters, he was self-consciously writing about writing. He was a written presence in his writing, however directly or obliquely represented and in whatever guise, trying the versatility of writing, testing its limits, tapping its potential. In being a written presence, he was no less a *writer* writing letters than he was a writer writing poems and stories and novels, and it is little wonder that letters—his own letters especially—found their way into his fiction from the start. It is no small irony that his private writing, the publication of which would have appalled him, is so deeply and expressively embedded in the writing he chose to have published.

The Compson Appendix as an Aid to Teaching *The Sound and the Fury*

Walter Taylor

For some years, Faulkner's "Appendix: Compson: 1699–1945," published in 1946, has been considered a standard device for introducing students to *The Sound and the Fury*, published in 1929. Faulkner himself fostered this notion. The appendix was "the key to the whole book," he wrote to Random House editor Robert Linscott in 1946; he wanted it printed at the beginning of subsequent editions because after one read it, the novel's four sections "[fell] into clarity and place" (*Selected Letters* 220). For first-time readers, however, the appendix may create as many problems as it solves. In the assessment of its value as a teaching tool, the following questions should be addressed.

How was the appendix conceived?

By 1944 Faulkner's work was falling into neglect and nearly all his books were out of print. Malcolm Cowley conceived *The Portable Faulkner*, a collection of stories and selections from the novels, as a device for reviving Faulkner's career; in particular, he wanted to show the thematic unity of Faulkner's canon, which, taken as a whole, provides a fictional history of his mythical Yoknapatawpha County. When Cowley inquired about what to include from *The Sound and the Fury*, Faulkner suggested "the last section, the Dilsey one" and offered to write "a page or two of synopsis to preface it, a condensation of the first 3 sections." When the new material arrived, Cowley found "something vastly different" from what he had expected: "a manuscript of twenty or thirty pages, a genealogy, rich in newly imagined episodes, of the Compson family over a period of almost exactly two centuries, beginning with the battle of Culloden in 1745" (Cowley, *File* 31, 36).

How does reading the appendix before reading the novel help the reader to understand the novel?

The appendix provides brief sketches of all the novel's major characters and some minor ones. Often these sketches contain short, pithy statements that identify core aspects of personality. Quentin "loved not the idea of the incest which he would not commit, but some presbyterian concept of its eternal punishment" ("Appendix" 743). Caddy was "doomed and knew it" (744). Jason was "the first sane Compson since before Culloden" (750). These sketches can be helpful in understanding difficult passages in the novel, as can some of the information in the new episodes.

What new information is supplied by the appendix?

New narratives extend the history of Yoknapatawpha County back to the time of the first settlements and the history of the Compson family back to the birth of Quentin MacLachan Compson in 1699. The Yoknapatawpha material includes narratives about the Chickasaw chieftain Ikkemotubbe ("Doom"), who granted the first Yoknapatawpha soil to the Compson family, and about President Andrew Jackson, "who patented, sealed and countersigned the grant" (738). The Compson family material provides characterizations of the male Compsons from the time of Quentin MacLachan, "son of a Glasgow printer," who "fled to Carolina from Culloden Moor" (738), then fled to Kentucky to avoid the American Revolution. Quentin MacLachan's gambler son, Charles Stuart, survived the revolutionary war and followed his father to Kentucky, but he was forced to leave after a failed "plot to secede the whole Mississippi Valley from the United States and join it to Spain" (739). Charles Stuart's son, Jason Lycurgus, came to Mississippi, where he swapped Ikkemotubbe a mare for the first square mile of Compson land. The Jason Lycurgus narrative also tells of two of his descendants: Quentin MacLachan II, who became governor, and Jason Lycurgus II, who became a Confederate general.

The appendix supplies new information about most of the novel's major characters and some minor ones, updating to 1945 the stories of those who were alive on 8 April 1928, the last day dramatized in the novel. This material has Caddy marrying and divorcing a "minor movingpicture magnate" (745) before disappearing in Paris in 1940 and includes a tale suggesting her possible liaison with a German general. It has Jason sending Benjy to the state asylum in Jackson after the death of Caroline Compson. And it shows Dilsey moving to Memphis to live in a black middle-class neighborhood with Frony, who has married a Pullman porter.

All this material is related by a historian narrator whose commentary on the characters is often ironic: a perspective that the novel's impressionistic technique does not supply.

How reliable is the appendix as a guide to understanding the novel?

Some information in the appendix conflicts with that supplied in the 1929 text. The characterizations of Luster and Jason illustrate this discrepancy. The appendix describes Luster, with no apparent irony, as a "man, aged 14. Who was not only capable of the complete care and security of an idiot twice his age and three times his size, but could keep him entertained" (756). The Luster of 1929 is no such paragon. On Easter morning he forgets his obligation to bring firewood for the household while he experiments with making music from a handsaw. Sometimes, rather than keep Benjy quiet, he deliberately upsets him by whispering Caddy's name. He starts Benjy bellowing in the final scene when he takes their surrey for an unauthorized turn around the square. Such behavior may well be a passive protest against the social role fourteen-year-old Luster knows he must face in a segregated society. In any case, it suggests a complexity not visible in the Luster of the appendix. (In *Faulkner's Search for a South*, I argue that Faulkner never truly resolved his ambivalence toward race. The Faulkner of 1945 and the Faulkner of 1928–29, however, had very different notions about race; particularly different was the theory of "endurance" he created through Isaac McCaslin in *Go Down, Moses* in 1942.)

The Jason narrative reveals other difficulties. Readers familiar with the novel may be jarred when the narrator of the appendix calls Jason "the first sane Compson since before Culloden" and asserts that he is "logical" and "rational" (750). Such descriptions can only be read for irony when applied to a character who is a basket case of misogyny, xenophobia, and racism, a man whose deepest fear is that he will be thought as insane as his siblings. But the rest of the Jason material in the appendix gives another image: a survivor "who not only fended off and held his own with Compsons, but competed and held his own with the Snopeses" (750). We are told that Jason "used his own niggard savings out of his meager wages as a storeclerk to send himself to a Memphis school, where he learned to class and grade cotton." In this way, he "established his own business" and was able, after his father died, to assume "the entire burden of the . . . family" and to save a sum of $2,840.50 in addition to what he had stolen from the money Caddy sent to support her daughter, Quentin IV (751). Jason's familiar anger and paranoia are clearly represented in the appendix; still, the new information has a cosmetic effect on one of the most negative characters in Faulkner's canon.

The conflicting characterizations of Luster and Jason reveal the basic problem of the appendix as a supplement to the novel: although much of the material in the appendix is helpful in understanding the novel, all its information must ultimately be validated by comparison with the 1929 text.

What was Faulkner's idea of the relation between the appendix and the novel?

A note to Cowley accompanying the appendix manuscript indicates that Faulkner saw it as a new section of the novel: "I should have done this when I wrote the book," he told Cowley. "Then the whole thing would have fallen into pattern like a jigsaw puzzle when the magician's wand touched it" (Cowley, *File* 36). As a result, the appendix has been included in some subsequent editions of the book. Still, Faulkner was aware of what he called "inconsistencies in the appendix" with the 1929 text, and he admitted that when he wrote the appendix, he did not have access to a copy of the novel (*File* 36). His justification of the discrepancies is suggestive not only of his notions about the appendix but also of his attitude toward his canon. He told Cowley that as a younger man he "did not know these people" as he did at forty-five; thus he "was even wrong now and then [in the 1929 text] in the very conclusions [he] drew from watching them, and the information [he] once believed." Since "the appendix was done at the same heat [of inspiration] as the book, even though 15 years later," he concluded, "it is the book itself which is inconsistent: not the appendix." What that meant was that "the inconsistencies in the appendix" proved to him that the novel was "still alive after 15 years, and being still alive [was] growing, changing" (*File* 90).

The statement reveals Faulkner's idea of the relation of the appendix to the original: Faulkner was not simply bent on explaining his novel, he was rewriting it. The statement also implies that he considered an understanding of the contours of his career more important than an understanding of an individual novel. It thus suggests a question fundamental to the study of Faulkner's canon: To what degree is each work to be read as a separate artistic entity, and to what degree must each also be read for its role in the canon?

In what ways does a prior reading of the appendix detract from the appreciation of the novel as a separate work of art?

That some of the information in the appendix conflicts with information in the novel is confusing. Moreover, since the appendix supplies not only new characters but also information on old characters that is not in the novel, readers who go to the appendix first will have an experience of the novel different from that of those who do not. The novel's impressionistic techniques are designed to force the reader to discover the characters; to be told in advance, for example, that Caddy was "doomed and knew it" undermines the process of discovery. The historical narratives of the appendix create a similar problem. A central irony of the novel is that although all the Compsons are aware of a family genealogy that includes a governor and a general, only the alcoholic Mr. Compson remembers that family history in any significant fashion. Thus each of the Compson children searches for a modern identity in a historical vacuum; the family identity, which the children believe was clear and coherent to their ancestors, remains a mystery to the children. Although Faulkner's fleshing out of that identity may add to the irony, it undermines the mystery.

What are the advantages of reading the appendix after reading the novel?

The advantages consist almost entirely in whatever is to be gained from visualizing the novel from the standpoint of the Faulkner of 1945. The appendix adds to the reader's perspective by placing the novel in the context of Yoknapatawpha history. Moreover, since Faulkner's own statements favor an understanding of that history over an understanding of individual works, the appendix emerges as an important feature of his canon, a link in a chain that includes all the Yoknapatawpha fiction, the historical chapters of *Requiem for a Nun* (1951), and the fictionalized essay "Mississippi" (1954).

Order and Flight: Teaching
The Sound and the Fury Using the Appendix

Charles Peek

Using Faulkner's 1946 appendix to teach *The Sound and the Fury* has many advantages. My students always ask, "Why did Faulkner write the story this way?" Their question raises issues of authorial intention that Faulkner's insistence to Robert Linscott, in a letter of February 1946, to "be sure and print the appendix *first*" (*Selected Letters* 221) opens for classroom discussion. The appendix is written in a more accessible style than the novel; it gives more explicit order to the chronology of events and provides a discursive frame of reference for the world explored in the novel. Further, the appendix makes connections between Faulkner's fiction and historical events, such as the Battle of Culloden and Scots-Irish emigration to the American South, as well as between the novel and biblical stories, such as the story of Benjamin. Finally, approaching the novel through the appendix, readers can engage issues of race and gender without being so influenced by Dilsey's indomitability or distracted by the Compson brothers' obsessions with their sister, Caddy. While these two features dominate the experience of many first-time readers of the novel, reading the appendix first takes readers away from these intensities and allows them to perceive more readily other organizing motifs of the novel. Thus, instead of encountering characters whose stories unfold in a stream-of-consciousness narrative that confuses the temporal sequence of events, students can come to appreciate how Faulkner ordered his fictional world and to what effect.

One effect of approaching the novel through the appendix is to focus on the motif through which Quentin IV's flight brings the Compson saga full circle to the stories of flight at the beginning of its chronology. To introduce students to Faulkner's use of motifs as a structural device, I ask them to keep journals in which they complete several assignments leading to a short essay on the novel. (See Arrington on the use of motifs as organizing tropes.) I ask them in their first reading of the appendix—in the Norton edition of *The Sound and the Fury*—to note the number of times the narrator uses the word *fled* or some literal or metaphorical variation of it. Then, following the theory of the reading process articulated by Louise Rosenblatt in *Literature as Exploration*, I ask them to write short narratives about significant moments of flight in their own lives or in the lives of people they know. I work from the assumption that readers come to appreciate the formal and aesthetic dimensions of a text by reflecting first on its expressive significance and that they can be led to do this by comparing literary narratives with their own experiences.

These journal assignments remain ungraded, although the journal (like attendance) is required for credit. Students share their accounts in small group discussions in class. We discuss how the structure and significance of their personal stories compare with the structure and significance of stories told in the appendix.

I ask, What motivates our flights? Is it fear? or escape? or shame? Does Jason's supposed sanity ("a sane man always" ["Appendix" 212, Norton ed. of *Sound*]) form a confining environment from which Quentin IV flees, as English repression of Scots culture (e.g., proscription of the clan tartan) formed a confining environment that prompted Quentin I's flight? Discussion brings the personal thoughts and feelings of students into relation with events in the novel, leading to an examination of how one might approach a literary text so as to interact with it.

Having connected motifs to the ascription of motives through the use of the students' own writings, I then ask students to summarize the story of one character's flight in the appendix. A student might focus on Quentin IV's flight, as suggested above, observing that she takes off with Jason's secret "hoard" ("Appendix" 212), which consists largely of her own money; that she runs off to the more exciting life of carnivals that travel across America; that the pitchman she runs off with is a bigamist; and that she, seventeen years old, repeats a pattern set by her mother. Since I frequently respond to journal entries, I might ask the student if Quentin IV's future looks like her mother's with its chromium Mercedes and German staff officers or if the student personally knows any "Quentins" and how they compare with the characters in the book.

Once our observations on the patterns of flight have enabled us to explore the relation between motif and motive and to expose relations between order and flight, I ask students to note how the motif of flight causes readers to focus on those sites that are either barriers or thresholds. I provide students with examples of these images from the appendix, we discuss them in class, and then we turn to the text of the novel itself. As the students begin to read the novel, I ask them again to note and discuss the significance of passages with key words relating to barriers that hinder flight or openings that serve as thresholds to flight. Students may note that several sections of the novel begin or end at such places. The first section, for instance, begins at a fence through which, as Luster says, Benjy can't "never crawl . . . without snagging" (4), a fence whose gate is the site of important interactions. Students expand on the assignment, providing their own examples, such as Quentin's hearing Shreve "[t]hrough the wall" (77) and waking to watch him, through the window, "running for chapel" (77–78); Dilsey's emerging from and returning to her door (265); Jason's threatening to kill Luster if he ever crosses "that gate . . . again" (320); and of course the central window through which Quentin IV escapes with her money, circumventing the locked door of Jason's room.

Here I point out one of the intertextual connections Faulkner's "little sister" motif establishes with metaphors of promiscuity and chastity, citing Song of Solomon:

> We have a little sister, and she hath no breasts: what shall we do for our sister in the day when she shall be spoken for?
> If she be a wall, we will build upon her a palace of silver; and if she be a door, we will inclose her with boards of cedar.

> I am a wall, and my breasts like towers; then was I in his eyes as one
> that found favour. (King James Version 8.8–10)

We discuss how stories can establish motifs by drawing on culturally encoded metaphors that are at once the vehicles for public, shared meaning and private thought and feeling. I also introduce a passage from Eliot's notes to *The Waste Land*, undoubtedly known to Faulkner, in which Eliot quotes from F. H. Bradley:

> My external sensations are no less private to myself than are my thoughts
> and feelings. In either case my experience falls within my own circle, a
> circle closed on the outside; and, with all its elements alike, every sphere
> is opaque to the others which surround it. . . . In brief, regarded as an ex-
> istence which appears in a soul, the whole world for each is peculiar and
> private to that soul. (92)

Considering passages in the novel in the light of these passages, we discuss further the issues of point-of-view implied by the difference in narrative strategy between the novel and the appendix.

We have now gathered enough information to assess whatever order comes from within as a result of our own perception, reflection, and exertion of will and whatever order comes from the external world, an order that is already in place and that both enables and constrains our exertion of will. We return to the opening of the appendix and its curious nominative phrase, "A dispossessed American king" (203), describing Ikkemotubbe, where "dispossessed" means a displacement from subjective ordering, as one political or cultural order displaces another. I ask my students to consider how the flights we have observed are related to the theme of dispossession, literal and metaphoric, and to the idea of an "ordered place," the phrase with which the novel ends. Are there assertions of order that do not imply a related dispossession? Do the dispossessed go on to set up the next "ordered place" from which someone else must flee in the long succession of flight described in the appendix? Do the dispossessed have any alternative?

Using especially the long account of Jason Lycurgus in the appendix, I ask my students to trace the course by which the "solid square mile of virgin North Mississippi dirt as truly angled as the four corners of a cardtable top" ("Appendix" 203), later "still the square intact mile" (206), becomes the "cornice and façade [that] flowed smoothly . . . from left to right" (*Sound* 321). The Lycurgus narrative provides an account of the cultural geography informing the novel, from the first Compson flight and those following ("[f]led to Carolina from the Culloden Moor"; "fled again one night in 1779" ["Appendix" 204]) to the present. As each flight is placed in context, students see how the motif of flight is connected to the theme of honor, as the first Compsons defend themselves from dispossession by "an English king," only to participate in the later dispossession of Ikkemotubbe, until Quentin III becomes an "inflexible . . .

judge of what he consider[s] the family's honor" (204, 208). Students collaborate to make a master list of references to characters who are trying to hang on
to or defend something they see endangered, and that list provides the basis
for a writing assignment in which students discuss the conjunction of motifs
and themes of honor and possession.

The writing assignment leads us to a discussion of the kinds of ordering in
which cultural constructions of honor, chastity, gender, and race have come together by way of the protection of bloodlines, family names, and inheritances—a discussion that enables us to put the story of the present-day
Compsons in a broader historical context. Caroline Bascomb Compson's repeated references to "[her] flesh and blood" (104) establish a focus on family
that inevitably leads us to Caddy's naming of her daughter after her brother
and the renaming of Benjy. Because I do not assume that my students bring to
their reading a knowledge of Bible stories, I trace for them the narrative of the
biblical Benjamin (Gen. 42–47) and explain how it is related to the motif of
flight we have been exploring; and I explain how the flight of Jacob's family to
Egypt to escape famine comes full circle with the story of the flight led by
Moses out of Egypt (Exod. 3–15), which is referred to twice in the novel (174,
295). Finally I point out how the New Testament writers, especially Matthew,
cast the Passover and the flight from Egypt as prefigurations of the Crucifixion
and Resurrection (Matt. 26–28); with this I establish the significance of the
dating of events in the novel, specifically the escape of Quentin IV, "[w]ho at
seventeen, on the one thousand eight hundred ninetyfifth anniversary of the
day before the resurrection of Our Lord, swung herself by a rainpipe from the
window . . . and climbed down the same rainpipe in the dusk and ran away"
("Appendix" 214).

While students may not be rhetorically sophisticated enough to perceive connections between Faulkner's use of devices such as anaphora in his appendix genealogy and similar devices in the Bible, they are impressed by the specificity
with which Faulkner establishes the date of Quentin IV's escape, subtracting the
presumed age of Jesus at the time of the Crucifixion from the calendar date to
arrive at the commemorative dating of the event. What is the significance of this
specificity? Here we are led again to note the number of times that the crossing
of a threshold is metaphorically related to the pattern of defeat and victory established through biblical allusions, as in Reverend Shegog's sermon: "'Dey kilt
me dat ye shall live again; I died dat dem whut sees en believes shall never die'"
(297). The paradox that death produces life and dispossession freedom brings
us to the heart of the peculiar paradoxes of Faulkner's themes of endurance.
Against the background of our delineation of motifs involving various geographical and physical barriers and the emotional longings they signify, we are
able to explore what might be called the spiritual resonances of the novel and
the appendix. What are we to make of the quasi-biblical narrative repetitions
and reversals that structure this text and establish the triadic pattern of order,
dispossession, and flight toward (perhaps) an as yet unknown future order?

Our final exploration of the relevance of the appendix to an understanding of the novel begins at the end of the appendix with our examination of the famous phrase "They endured," which occurs under the heading "Dilsey." Working back, we note that this terse expression and the preceding portraits of Luster, Frony, and T. P. occur under the rubric "These others were not Compsons. They were black" ("Appendix" 215). Reading down the column of biographies, we observe that each begins with the pronoun *who* until we reach Dilsey, where *who* changes to *they*. Conventionally, this *they* is taken to refer back to the statement "these others were not Compsons" and by extension perhaps to blacks in general, but the grammar is ambiguous. Who is it that has endured and what is the meaning of enduring? Is the action of enduring specifically that of not fleeing? Yet Dilsey, Frony, and T. P. apparently escape from the Compson mile to cities like Memphis and Saint Louis.

Here we return to the issue of the relation of the appendix to the novel and Faulkner's insistence on the integral quality of that relation. Much as the critical tradition wants to see texts as self-enclosed entities and as much as Faulkner at some points in his career gave homage to the symbolist aesthetic, which is the source of that tradition, the open-endedness of these narratives—Faulkner's gestures suggesting that no story is ever finished—frustrates such an approach. The ambiguity of the final phrase of the appendix, its reference back to an uncertain collective, keeps us from closing off interpretation. The succession of order and dispossession we trace in the appendix leads us to consider these patterns as typical of the history in which we participate with Faulkner and his characters. Entering the novel through the appendix highlights the patterns and motifs of the novel sufficiently for students to relate to "that long line . . . who had had something in them of decency and pride even after they had begun to fail at the integrity and the pride had become mostly vanity and self-pity" ("Appendix" 210). Just as Quentin IV's escape holds out the possibility of another chronicle, comparable to that of Quentin MacLachan, so *The Sound and the Fury* and its appendix, read together, hold out the possibility that no story is ever finished because it is never discrete, never without relation to some other story. The stories that my students begin by telling about themselves and their acquaintances become points of reference for their understanding of how Faulkner establishes narrative patterns more characteristic than eccentric when viewed in the context of American life. These stories enable my students to consider the relevance of the novel and the appendix to their own lives and to consider the narratives of their own lives as constructions of meaning in which they exert an authorial hand.

Teaching *The Sound and the Fury* with Freud

Judith Bryant Wittenberg

On at least two public occasions, Faulkner disavowed any direct knowledge of Freud's work. In 1955, he said to an interviewer, "Everybody talked about Freud when I lived in New Orleans, but I have never read him" (Meriwether and Millgate 251). Three years later, he told a group of psychiatrists, "What little of psychology I know the characters I have invented and playing poker have taught me. Freud I'm not familiar with" (Gwynn and Blotner 268). Yet John T. Irwin suggests that it may have been Faulkner's awareness of similarities between his own work and Freud's that elicited such denials (*Doubling* 5). In any case, Faulkner's fiction manifests—sometimes, in the early work, by explicit reference to psychoanalytic principles—a knowledge of Freudian theory, and virtually all his fiction yields effectively to psychoanalytic interpretation.

The Sound and the Fury, perhaps more than any other novel by Faulkner, invites a Freudian approach. Its claustrophobic portrait of a dysfunctional family in which the children have been crippled by the failures of their parents, its thorough depiction of a series of "normal" yet psychically traumatic events involving sexuality and death, and its stream-of-consciousness method—all these qualities make the text an ideal candidate for psychoanalytically informed exploration. Indeed, for novice readers its daunting complexities can come to appear not only explicable but appropriate when viewed through a Freudian lens.

There are several things to keep in mind when approaching this or any work of fiction by way of Freudian concepts. First, Freud wrote and published an enormous body of work over several decades, and because of his extraordinary capacity for intellectual reflection, he tended to qualify and sometimes revise his principles over time. Thus it is necessary both to be selective with regard to the concepts emphasized and to acknowledge that what the public regards as

Freud's theory may constitute an oversimplification of a Freudian text and may represent Freud's early ruminations rather than his revisionary work of subsequent years. Another problem is that some Freudian criticism of literary texts, whether by students or psychoanalysts or literary critics, has been embarrassingly reductive and thus has given the entire enterprise a poor reputation in some quarters. Some Freudian critics have even gone so far as to refute the method publicly. In addition, in the 1990s, a purely Freudian approach seems outmoded. Critics interested in psychoanalytic approaches are increasingly turning to Lacanian theory, in part because of its relative newness (although Lacan's work dates to the 1930s, almost none of it was published in English until the 1970s) but also because, as James Mellard points out, it has a greater capacity to deal with the "normal" subject and its focus on language and figures of speech is more literary (56–57).

Still, there are a number of reasons to use Freudian ideas to approach *The Sound and the Fury* in the classroom, beyond the novel's interiorized technique and its concern with family dynamics, developmental traumas, and pathological behavior—beyond, that is, its status as a compelling "case history" that also attempts to capture the mental processes of disturbed individuals. One reason is that Faulkner's own description of the novel's creation reveals that it was a less than purely rational exercise in artistry and thus called for psychological assessment. He said that the title "came out of [his] unconscious" (Coindreau 109); that he wrote the book "five separate times trying to tell the story, to rid [himself] of the dream which would continue to anguish [him] until [he] did" (Meriwether and Millgate 244); and that he experienced a sort of catharsis in writing it, an "ecstacy" that was "waiting for release" in the process of creation (*Sound* [Norton] 219).

More important, perhaps, is the cultural context from which the book emerged. Some of Freud's work was translated into English just before the First World War, and in the postwar years, as Frederick Hoffman points out (*Freudianism* 55–75), the intelligentsia—particularly those in urban areas such as New Orleans and New York, where Faulkner spent time during the years *The Sound and the Fury* was taking shape in his mind—became fascinated with Freud's ideas. In interviews, members of a group with which Faulkner associated in the 1920s told Carvel Collins that their talk "was full of" Freudian theory (Collins 226). And the writer who was Faulkner's mentor at the time, Sherwood Anderson, was hailed by critics as "the American Freudian" (Hoffman, *Freudianism* 229). Faulkner also later spoke publicly of the way in which ideas are often widely disseminated at a particular historical moment and can become the seed from which fictional and other texts emerge. As he said, "[T]he writer don't have to know Freud to have written things which anyone who does know Freud can divine and reduce into symbols" (Gwynn and Blotner 147). Moreover, as Hoffman notes, *The Sound and the Fury*, along with *As I Lay Dying*, is one of the best American examples of a writer's trying to capture those psychic sources usually kept below the level of consciousness (*Freudianism* 127–30).

While a Freudian approach to *The Sound and the Fury* may seem almost a requirement given the novel's background, content, and method, its application will vary according to the context in which it is taught. In an introductory course on theoretical approaches to the novel, one might begin with an essay like Ross Murfin's "What Is Psychoanalytic Criticism?" to gain an overview of key psychoanalytic concepts. One might also provide a list of study questions that the psychoanalytically oriented reader can ask of any fictional text, along the lines of the questions appended to this essay. If the approach is to be strictly Freudian, one might assign a paperback "primer" of Freudian concepts or an actual essay of Freud's, such as *The Ego and the Id* (1923), which is especially appropriate for *The Sound and the Fury*. If, however, only a class or two can be devoted to a psychological approach, it is often sufficient to begin with a basic review of Freudian terms, since so many of Freud's ideas have entered into common parlance and are taught in general courses on psychology and human behavior.

If the course is more specialized or advanced—for example, Psychoanalysis and the American Novel or Psychological Approaches to Faulkner—relevant critical essays could be assigned. An early one is Collins's study "The Interior Monologues of *The Sound and the Fury*," which asserts that Faulkner consciously drew from Freudian theory and modeled Benjy's monologue on the concept of the id, Quentin's on the ego, and Jason's on the superego. This thesis can be supplemented with commentary that qualifies or questions it, that questions particularly the Jason-superego equivalency. Brief and helpful also are Freudian summaries of the novel such as that in Victor Strandberg's *A Faulkner Overview* (63–70). More complex and provocative is Irwin's intertextual reading of Faulkner and Freud, lengthy portions of which analyze Quentin's psychological plight. Also useful for analyses of the interrelation between Faulkner's psyche and the psychodynamics of the novel are the relevant chapters in Judith Bryant Wittenberg's *Faulkner: The Transfiguration of Biography* (72–88) and David Minter's *William Faulkner: His Life and Work* (93–107).

The problematic conjunction of Freudian theory and feminist awareness in a psychoanalytic interpretation of *The Sound and the Fury* also warrants discussion; it certainly has been an issue in my all-female classes. Just as Freud was assailed for his phallocentric emphasis on oedipal structure, so Faulkner has been criticized by my students. They have noted his privileging of the male point of view in this novel, observing, for example, that Caddy, despite being an emotionally crucial figure, has no interior monologue of her own. They are bothered by the extreme negativity of the portrait of Mrs. Compson and by the biological and racial marginalization of the surrogate mother Dilsey. Juliet Mitchell's *Psychoanalysis and Feminism* attempts to retrieve Freud from the feminists' repudiation, and an essay of mine, "William Faulkner: A Feminist Consideration," argues that certain psychoanalytic principles are relevant to a feminist reassessment of Faulkner's work, although I make only limited reference to *The Sound and the Fury*. Faulkner, asked why he portrayed Caddy only indirectly, answered that she was nevertheless at the center of the book, "the beautiful one, . . . my heart's darling," and that his methods seemed like "the proper tools" to tell her story (Gwynn and Blotner 6). Joan Williams's essay on Mrs. Compson attempts to put that character's flaws in the context of the era. And the marginal status of Dilsey is explicable from a number of vantage points. For advanced students, a long essay in Minrose Gwin's *The Feminine and Faulkner* addresses the "silencing" of Caddy Compson—and is indebted as much to contemporary neo-Freudians as to Freud himself. Gwin asserts that Caddy and other Faulkner females occupy a textual space that "speaks of women's libidinal energies" and that the works in which they appear are characterized by powerful "bisexual tensions" (37).

One may, however, decide to eschew such aids as psychoanalytically oriented study questions, Freudian primers, and psychoanalytic evaluations and instead to have students plunge unassisted into the novel. I have done this, influenced by my own first reading, which occurred outside course work and with limited knowledge of Faulkner or his texts. I was mystified but compelled by the novel's fluid prose and the strange and terrible beauty of what I could discern. "Understanding" seemed somehow irrelevant then. I sometimes ask my students to begin their reading the same way; I know that class discussion will clear up much of their confusion. At other times, I provide a rudimentary section-by-section guide to events. This guide includes brief comments or questions about the brothers' mental states, the parents' attitudes, the family's dynamics, and Faulkner's stream-of-consciousness technique. I point out Faulkner's use of italics to indicate (although only partially) the shifts between past and present in Benjy's and Quentin's sections and Faulkner's original desire to have the different passages printed in different colors of ink to assist his readers in intuiting the shifts.

Assuming students have read at least the first two sections of the novel for the initial class discussion (although an introductory course may proceed at a slower pace), I often begin by reviewing the events accorded significance in the brothers' minds, attempting to explore the reasons the brothers have been so traumatized by seemingly typical occurrences—the death of a grandmother, the wedding of a sister. It is useful to consider Benjy and Quentin as psychologically arrested in developmental stages—Benjy in early childhood, Quentin in early adolescence; this observation raises intriguing questions for a later discussion of Jason's "adulthood." Attention to the nature of memory and the associational process by which interior monologues develop is also helpful in clarifying these two sections, so difficult for first-time readers. One assignment is a brief in-class freewriting that focuses on a single passage and discusses the psychic problems and processes evident there. An ongoing reading journal allows students to reflect informally on their responses and to analyze the text in a preliminary way.

To continue a psychoanalytic exploration of the novel, while Freud's theory of the oedipal stage is so familiar that it hardly needs discussion, the first two

Compson brothers' neurotic obsession with their sister as representing a displacement of attachment to the mother merits review, as do the various quasi-oedipal triangles in which they find themselves and the sense in which they have been literally or psychically emasculated by familial deficiencies. In the early pages of Benjy's section, the appearance of a series of parental figures, most of them profoundly flawed, is revealing, linked as they are to his tremendous grief at the loss of his maternalistic sister and to memories of earlier portents of that loss. Although intellectually limited and unable to make judgments, Benjy—in his fixations, in the associational trajectory of his thoughts, and in his despair—is psychically a mirror image of his more cerebral brother Quentin, who is for most readers the central figure of the novel. Discussions about Quentin focus on the reasons for his suicide—the terrible emotional wound inflicted by his sister's marriage, his problems with his sexuality, the eruption of troubling memories. The way the events of the present and Quentin's itinerary around Boston echo or invert situations of the past is also relevant, as is his inexorable movement toward death by water and all that that signifies psychoanalytically.

The portrait of Jason poses fascinating problems; while his paranoia, cruelty, greed, misogyny, and xenophobia all make him a villain par excellence, a psychoanalytically informed analysis results in a more sympathetic appraisal. His misogyny is a consequence of his crippling ties to his mother, who did nothing to foster his psychic independence, and of his anger at the loss of the bank job. Likewise his theft of money earmarked for other family members represents a displacement of what could be seen as an understandable resentment of parental failures. To be sure, Jason, unlike his brothers, seems to have become a functional adult, acting as a sort of father-provider. Faulkner, with considerable irony, described Jason as "logical rational contained" in his 1946 appendix to the novel (*Sound* [Norton] 233). Nevertheless, Jason's isolation and emotional sadism suggest that he too has been victimized by the familial inadequacies.

In this sort of reading of *The Sound and the Fury*, Benjy, Quentin, and Jason are all seen as psychologically stunted—one of them fatally so—by the dynamics of their early upbringing, and Caddy's sexual promiscuity and eventual estrangement become more explicable, perhaps, than her constant compassion for family members. The parents' deficiencies as individuals and as nurturers may be responsible for their children's difficulties, but they too represent instances of arrested development and might be viewed as having been victimized by the failure of previous generations or by the failure of the values of their culture. Indeed, the novel is not only a portrait of psycho-familial breakdown but also a fictional casebook of individual psychological disorders—including fetishism, narcissism, hypochondria, paranoia, and suicidal despair. Extreme in its bleakness and emotional intensity, *The Sound and the Fury* is a brilliant, compelling example of psychoanalytically informed fiction.

APPENDIX
QUESTIONS FOR A FREUDIAN APPROACH TO
THE SOUND AND THE FURY

1. What parts of the text seem to be dreamlike disguises for repressed wishes (in dreamwork, a repressed wish can be expressed as a fear)?
2. What set of repressed wishes or dream fantasies does the text seem to revolve around?
3. How are the different psychic registers (id, ego, superego) represented in the text?
4. What sort of neuroses or psychoses are evident in the characters?
5. What images of events have taken on deep symbolic significance for the characters (or the author)? What do they appear to symbolize?
6. What evidence is there of condensation or displacement—of doubles, surrogates, composite characters or locales, loaded verbal ambiguities, obvious disguises?
7. Are any of your own repressed wishes or fears brought to the surface or exposed by the text? Do you find yourself censoring your reading to keep under control the thoughts and feelings evoked by the text?
8. Does the text imply a possible cure or only offer a diagnostic narrative of a subject or subjects in a psychological bind?

Giving Jung a Crack at the Compsons

Terrell L. Tebbetts

Jung's theory of individuation gives students a useful tool for probing *The Sound and the Fury*. The theory's focus on wholeness helps students grasp the novel's fragmentations; the roles it ascribes to parents deepen students' understanding of the novel's inadequate family; its analysis of the source of human idealism helps them see the relation between characters as diverse as the Compson brothers and Dilsey; and its analysis of the source of human love brings some coherence to their experience of the alienation of all the characters except Dilsey.

Perhaps better known in English departments for his writings on the collective unconscious and its archetypes, Jung devoted one of his last major works to individuation, the process of realizing full human wholeness. M. L. von Franz, a colleague of Jung and coeditor with him of *Man and His Symbols*, describes individuation as a "slow, powerful, involuntary" process of "psychic growth" and "maturation" that is "possible with every individual" but is not always achieved (161). The idea of individuation rests on the theory that human beings are first conscious of only a part of the Self, which Jungians understand as both "the organizing center" of the psyche and, at the same time, "the totality of the whole psyche" (161). At first conscious of only the Self's first part, the ego, human beings mature when they become conscious of the other two parts of the Self. These other two parts are the shadow (the dark, rejected part of the Self) and the anima in men or animus in women (the female side of the male self and the male side of the female self), and they make their presence known whether or not the ego consents, often through dreams.

Jung held that the ego is immensely stronger when it submits to the whole Self. Of course, the ego can so fear other parts of the Self that it refuses to recognize and accept them, thus preventing the emergence of the larger Self. If we thus buy safety for our egos, we remain petty, partial human beings. But if we have egos strong enough to accept the shadow and the anima or animus as working partners, the Self will emerge and we will become mature, flexible, and complete human beings.

Students always need help in grasping the process of individuation. Although they might be familiar with Jungian constructs like shadow and anima or animus, they usually associate them solely with Jungian projection and related Jungian concepts like scapegoat and femme fatale. Illustrations from literature can help students grasp individuation. Goethe's *Faust* works especially well, for students can quickly see that Mephistopheles (shadow), although a devil and thus fearful, has God's sanction and is an agent of Faust's maturation and ultimate salvation. Blake's *The Marriage of Heaven and Hell*, *The Book of Thel*, and *Songs of Innocence and Experience* also provide portraits of friendly menace sometimes rejected, to the individual's loss (Thel), but sometimes embraced, to the individual's immense gain (the angel of *Marriage*). In addition, students must be acquainted with the Jungian view of the roles of parents in preparing individuals to negotiate the ego's fear of shadow and anima or animus, especially as *The Sound and the Fury* connects the younger Compsons' dysfunctions to their experiences as children.

The work of the Jungian psychologist Edward Edinger helps students grasp one parental role. Edinger shows that children project the Self on their parents and that the later, adult "ego-Self relationship" grows out of "the relationship between parents and child" (39). This point made, students are ready to deal with Jason and Caroline Compson's inadequacies as parents, to discuss the effects of Jason's nihilism and alcoholism and of Caroline's self-centered hypochondria on their children. Students come to see the alienation that grows between ego and Self when problems distance parents from children. They see how Jason III's nihilism increases his children's fear of Self since in him Self represents not completion but annihilation of the ego. When students see the Compson children cut off from Self and trapped in a frightened and limited ego, the work of E. A. Bennett helps them understand also that the child's ego learns about itself from the child's same-sex parent (115–16). At this point students ask what the male ego learns from the father and the female ego from the mother.

Jung himself will answer this question and in doing so provoke further discussion. He teaches that fathers model the masculine principles associated with logos, giving sons a sense of the positive function of idealism in focusing and perhaps even in shaping the experiential world (175). (Some students will question Jung's gender distinctions, but generally students accept them as representative of the period of the novel.) The father's function in modeling idealism gives students a useful entry to discussing the nihilism of Jason III, which absolutely denies the idealism his sons' egos need. Comprehending the organizing power of logos, the word, the ideal, students are ready to confront Benjy, who is as incapable of forming ideals as he is of forming words. Yet the need remains whether or not logos is available. When asked how Benjy's depiction in the opening section expresses this need, students begin to see that his fixation on particular memories, his fascination with fire, and his resistance to change can be his substitutions for the ordering power of the ideal. And students relate the chaos of his memories and the directionlessness of his life to the inadequacy of those substitutions. Benjy becomes the perfect introduction to his brothers, to Quentin's despair and to Jason's hypocritical materialism.

Leaving Benjy, students are ready to discuss Quentin's fixation on Caddy's affair, his fantasy of incest, his furious attack on Gerald Bland, his concern with time, his fastidiousness, and of course his suicide. They explore these matters in relation to the masculine ego's rage for order—order normally supplied by ideals that Quentin sorely lacks. Quentin's storybook dungeon (173) can provoke strong discussion at this point, for it suggests the ego's alienation from both the light of ideals and the fullness of Self. Students now consider Jason's fixation on wealth from this perspective: Money is the vain substitution of abstract wealth for the larger abstractions of ideals, and its worship is more the misrule of Mammon than the rule of logos. In this light they understand his hypocrisy: he talks about the value of work and of female respectability and says he admires the Christian forbearance shown by his mother—while he evades work, keeps a whore, and regularly robs his mother. Gerald Bland offers an effective way of focusing on missing ideals and of linking Quentin and Jason. Quentin attacks Bland because Bland is a hypocrite, apparently embodying southern ideals but actually betraying them; Jason half becomes Bland, mouthing the southern gentleman's ideals occasionally but no more allowing those ideals to direct his behavior than Bland does. Jason lives in his father's nihilism as surely as Quentin dies in it.

To comprehend the absent Caddy's feminine ego, and also her brothers' anima, students need to know Jung's analysis of the feminine ego. According to Jung, it thrives on "love alone" (185). In the first and second sections of the novel, students can now interpret Caddy's care for Benjy and concern for Quentin as signs of a nature with a propensity to love. Discussion may move to the depiction of Caroline Compson as a mother as empty of love as her husband is of ideals. Her self-pity, accusations, ineffectuality with Benjy, and infatuation with the younger Jason and with S. H. Head suggest an absence of love and her varying substitutions for it. Discussion might end with Caddy's promiscuity and abandonment of her daughter, the teacher inviting students to compare the Caddy they glimpse as an adult with her adult brothers. Given that she has no apparent family or home of her own, whatever love she has attained, it is a poor substitution for the love she was born capable of, just as Benjy's cries for continuity, Quentin's fastidious suicide, and Jason's fixation on money are poor substitutions for the ordering power of ideals, of the word, of logos.

To complete their understanding of parents' roles in individuation, students need to know about the influence of parents on opposite-sex children. Jungian psychology is clear about the father's responsibility for the daughter's animus. Although students will not see a healthy animus in Caddy, they need to know that Jungians believe a healthy animus strengthens a woman by giving her special qualities associated with logos—"spiritual firmness, an invisible inner support" and "meaning" (von Franz 189, 194). (They will want to discuss these qualities in relation to Dilsey when they reach the fourth section.) With the same father her brother has, Caddy has little access to logos, to guiding ideals and meaning. Students can now understand Caddy's (and her daughter's) promiscuity, her ineffectuality in dealing with Jason, and even her subsequent association (for those who teach the appendix to the novel) with Nazis. The discussion may also take up her rootlessness, relating it to the purposeless movements of Benjy, the wandering of Quentin through Massachusetts byways, the erratic and vain pursuits of Jason—each brother having a destination set by others or no destination at all.

Jungians are equally clear about the mother's responsibility for the son's anima. Von Franz writes that the "negative mother-*anima* figure" gives life "a sad and oppressive aspect" that "can even lure a man to suicide" (178). The application to Quentin is obvious, as it is to Caddy's dual role for him as mother-substitute and "Little Sister Death" (*Sound* 76). The application to Jason stimulates discussion as well; he lives with an imaginary invalid who has death constantly on her lips and lies all day in her room as in a mausoleum. Von Franz writes that the negative anima shows up in a man's "waspish, poisonous, effeminate remarks by which he devalues everything" (179). Students armed with this knowledge can understand the bigotry that characterizes Jason's monologue, his "bitch" (180), "old woman" (184), "jellybeans" (184), "dam little slut" (185), "old half dead nigger" (185), "dam squirts" (188), "nigger wench" (189), "no-count nigger" (189), "dam eastern jews" (191), "dam redneck" (194), and "Great American Gelding" (263). Finally, von Franz's assertion that a man's "capacity for personal love" depends on a positive anima (177) opens up a discussion of all three brothers' capacity to love women, with Benjy's castration given fresh meaning as the outward and visible absence suggesting the inner absence in his brothers.

Before leaving Quentin and Jason, students inevitably want to discuss the state of their shadows. Although shadow has no direct relation to parents' influence, it is essential in assessing the brothers' failed individuation. Students note Quentin's fascination with hell and his attention to his physical shadow during his day in the country. Students can discuss the degree to which he has finally denied ego and identified with shadow in his longing to find ultimate meanings normally supplied by logos, as if choosing hell in the absence of heaven. Students sometimes feel that Quentin's unindividuated shadow has come to dominate him directly. They also note Jason's scapegoating: his projection of his shiftlessness onto blacks, of his thievery onto "eastern jews," and of his pimping (living off his mother and niece) onto women ("bitch" and "slut"). They can see these projections as another sign of an unindividuated shadow, but Jason's shadow dominates him indirectly. The brothers thus exemplify two extremes of the unindividuated shadow, which, when denied, dominates ego either directly or indirectly.

A Jungian analysis of the Compson children leads to a positive understanding of Dilsey. Students usually see her as the one character in the novel who reaches full individuation, her ego in harmony with animus and shadow alike. When asked to apply Jung's assertion that the feminine ego must love, students offer numerous examples of Dilsey's love. Dilsey's acceptance of shadow, though more difficult for students to see, becomes apparent through discussion of the Easter sermon on the Christian doctrine of atonement, with the blood of the Lamb cleansing "de thief en de murderer" with whom Dilsey and other Christians identify themselves (296). Jesus becomes a peculiar scapegoat on whom Dilsey, as a Christian, casts the consequences of her sins but not the sins themselves. Her ability to see herself as both sinner and saved suggests the harmony of shadow and ego. The doctrine of atonement thus established, students often want to discuss Dilsey's comments on Luster's "devilment" (276, 317) and on "Compson devilment" (276) in relation to shadow.

Students' understanding of Dilsey's animus grows from earlier discussions of its weakness in Caddy. Alert to the spiritual firmness, inner support, and meaning in Dilsey, students find abundant signs of a healthy animus, from small matters (she knows what time it is no matter what someone else's clock says) to large (she takes Benjy to church no matter what Frony or the neighbors say) to grand (when she says she sees the beginning and the ending, she implies she sees not only the events of life but the meaning that runs through them, giving them the very linearity that beginning and ending require [297]). Students will want to relate these signs of Dilsey's individuation to her status in her largely unindividuated society. As a black woman, she is the object of frightened projections of racists' shadow and sexists' anima—Jason, of course, embodying both. Students find their understanding of her response to those projections enriched by intertextual studies of such Faulkner characters as Joe Christmas (*Light in August*), Charles and Etienne Bon (*Absalom, Absalom!*), and Lucas Beauchamp (*Go Down, Moses*). They also benefit from reading studies of Faulkner's black characters by critics like Thadious Davis and Lee Jenkins. Jenkins's psychoanalytic approach in *Faulkner and Black-White Relations* dovetails well with a Jungian approach.

Finally, students might take a look at Dilsey's singing. Before church "she sang, to herself at first . . . and presently she was singing louder" (270). After church "she sang" again, a hymn this time (301). Dilsey alone among the characters sings. Her singing joins the bellowing of Benjy, the whining of Caroline Compson, the confessions of Quentin, and the cursing of Jason as a characteristic and characterizing expression in *The Sound and the Fury*. Asking students to identify and contrast such expressions of the major characters makes a compelling conclusion to a Jungian study of the novel.

Teaching Religion and Philosophy
in *The Sound and the Fury*

John F. Desmond

Understanding Faulkner's presentation of religious values in *The Sound and the Fury* is a formidable task, one complicated by the technical complexities of the novel. To shape class discussion, I focus on the meaning of Quentin Compson's suicide in the second section, with a twofold purpose: to illuminate the problem of religious values in the novel and to relate it more generally to spiritual themes in twentieth-century southern literature. I begin by pointing out how prevalent the theme of suicide is in the works of modern southern writers—Allen Tate, Robert Penn Warren, Eudora Welty, Flannery O'Connor, William Styron, Walker Percy—and then suggest how suicide serves as a metaphor for a pervasive spiritual malaise. To explain this metaphoric notion of suicide, I introduce Kierkegaard's concept of "spiritual suicide" or despair. I have students read portions of *The Sickness unto Death* (133–214) to familiarize them with Kierkegaard's concepts. For Kierkegaard, despair involves a refusal to be a self "transparently under God"; it is a denial of spirit. To be in despair is "not to be able to die"; it is to suffer a "sickness unto death" (147–62). Conversely, to be able to die, in the sense of relinquishing an inauthentic selfhood in order to become an authentic self "transparently under God," is to escape spiritual suicide or despair.

Further elaborating Kierkegaard's ideas, I explain how language is central to the act of authentic self-affirmation. Naming is a way to overcome the despair of silence before reality, what Kierkegaard describes as a condition of "introversion" (196–200). Naming is also a way to avoid the inauthenticity that occurs when one simply defers to the language and vision of another; Kierkegaard calls such deferring being "defrauded by 'the others'" (166). Finally we discuss Kierkegaard's idea of another type of despair, one in which the self affirms itself defiantly as independent of any divine power, with the human being alone the measure of reality, a stance Kierkegaard calls stoicism. The aim of this preliminary discussion is to prepare students to consider Quentin's losing struggle against his father's language and stoical value system in the second section of the novel.

Having established the philosophical context, we relate Kierkegaard's idea of stoicism to the cultural code of stoicism that dominated genteel society in the ante- and postbellum South. I have students read two short essays on this subject—Allen Tate's "Religion and the Old South" and Walker Percy's "Stoicism in the South"—both of which reveal the stoical ethos that underlies the trappings of Christianity in the South. I ask the class to consider how the stoical code of gentlemanly honor and noblesse oblige is viewed in the Compson family, especially by Quentin's father. Students now see how this decadent stoicism, this nihilism, can be linked to Kierkegaard's idea of defiant despair. I emphasize how the stoical code of values is antithetical to genuine Christian beliefs (particularly regarding the meaning of time and human redemption), and I note how Faulkner establishes stoicism and Christianity as opposing visions of experience throughout the novel.

Before going to the second section, I ask the class to describe the difficulties they faced in reading the novel because of Faulkner's technical innovations. They discuss how Faulkner frequently abandons the conventional distinctions between objective and subjective reality, fusing past and present and real and imagined events in a continuous flow of language, often without regular punctuation. To clarify Faulkner's strategy, I distribute copies of Edmond L. Volpe's short summary of the major actions in the second section (373–77). I also ask members of the class to read aloud brief portions of Quentin's debates with himself, with his sister, Caddy, and with his father to help capture the flow of Quentin's inner struggle.

After clarifying the basic action and the strategies of this section, I relate Faulkner's unconventional narrative technique to the larger theme of the collapse of values in Quentin's world. The class looks at the nihilistic view of time expressed by Mr. Compson on the opening page of the section and discusses Quentin's own obsession with time. I emphasize how Faulkner's disruption of the chronology of the narrative reinforces the theme of despair and how this despair is the result of the loss of a transcendent religious perspective through which mundane time and action within time receive ultimate significance. We discuss how the Christian view of time and history is informed by a belief in the possibility of spiritual redemption, a belief that the Compsons have lost. I ask the class to compare Faulkner's treatment of time in this section of the novel with his treatment of time in the other sections, especially Benjy's and Jason's. Students are quick to see how Quentin's anguish over the meaning of time is mirrored in these two sections. The class considers how time is presented in the fourth section, both thematically and technically; they focus especially on Dilsey's understanding of human time, in the light of her Christian belief in the resurrection and eternal salvation, which is best seen in the Easter service scene.

We now discuss in detail Quentin's struggle with suicidal despair, to see how he is a victim of the South's stoicism and his father's stoicism. His relationship with his father is crucial, both psychologically and spiritually. Quentin looks to him as a moral authority, whereas his father rejects all religious values, especially logocentric Christianity, the Word made flesh. We examine Quentin's failed attempt to convince his father that he committed incest with Caddy, since this claim goes to the heart of his despair. Students realize that the defense of a woman's virtue and good name was central to the southern stoic code of honor. But, as Mr. Compson informs Quentin, terms like "honor" and "virtue" no longer signify:

> Women are never virgins. Purity is a negative state and therefore contrary to nature. It's nature is hurting you not Caddy and I said That's just

words and he said So is virginity and I said you dont know. You cant know and he said Yes. On the instant when we come to realise that tragedy is second-hand. (116)

In this view, Caddy's loss of virginity is morally meaningless because biological drives are the only forces governing her behavior.

Quentin attempts to break free of his father's influence but cannot overcome or escape his father's nihilism. Consequently, he cannot affirm himself as a moral being either in terms of the bankrupt stoic code of honor or in terms of a Christian vision of lost innocence and possible redemption. I have the class discuss Faulkner's ironic allusions to those authentic Christian heroes—Jesus and Saint Francis of Assisi—who haunt Quentin's consciousness as examples of meaningful action he cannot emulate, since his father has taught him that "all men are just accumulations dolls stuffed with sawdust swept up from the trash heaps where all previous dolls had been thrown away the sawdust flowing from what wound in what side that not for me died not" (175–76). In this ironic allusion to Christ's crucifixion, Mr. Compson nullifies any hope of redemption. Likewise, Quentin observes despondently that Jesus "had no sister" (77). I point out to the class that whereas Saint Francis in faith joyfully embraced death as his "Little Sister," Quentin is doom-haunted by the memory of his promiscuous sister, Caddy. His one attempt to act heroically by helping the lost little Italian girl, whom he calls sister, ends ignominiously in his arrest as a child abductor. Quentin is again completely ineffectual as savior—a primary role in the stoic code of the gentleman. I also discuss how this stoic role of savior-gentleman involves a tacit displacement of the Christian savior in favor of the man of honor and how the collapse of Quentin's attempts to fulfill this role will lead directly to his acceptance of suicide.

Our discussion of Quentin's failure as self-appointed savior and guardian of female virtue leads to a closer look at the psychological and spiritual roots of his condition. We examine the crucial scene of Quentin's sexual initiation with Natalie (133–39). As André Bleikasten has demonstrated, Quentin's struggle with Caddy during this scene with Natalie reveals his fear of sexual maturation (*Failure* 97–106). The acceptance of maturation means the acknowledgment of sexual differentiation and therefore separation from Caddy, that is, the destruction of the bond with his sister he longs to preserve. Quentin's concern to protect Caddy's virtue is really a masked attempt to preserve his own innocence. Thus Caddy functions as a projection of Quentin's narcissism (since he wants to be the sole object of her desire), a projection of his refusal to "fall" into adult sexuality.

As the class discusses the dynamics of the Natalie episode, I extend Bleikasten's psychological reading by linking Quentin's rejection of mature sexuality to the larger religious context, particularly the meaning of sexuality in history. I ask the class to consider two views of human sexuality. The first, expressed in religion and myth, sees sexuality as divine in origin, a manifestation of humankind's participation in transcendent power and mystery. The second regards sexuality solely as a cultural or biological phenomenon, bound within history. I relate these two views to the opposing Christian and stoic perspectives in the novel.

From the religious perspective, Quentin's attempt to reject adult sexuality involves a refusal to fall into history and time. He desires to remain inviolate, innocent, and morally self-sufficient. Students recognize how this attempt underlies Quentin's motive in claiming to have committed incest with Caddy: his wish to preserve them together from the world and the inescapable contaminations of evil, time, and change. Conversely, for Quentin to accept a fallen world would mean accepting fallibility, mortality, and the need for a transcendent savior. But, following his father, he rejects this Christian vision of history and possible redemption: "Christ was not crucified: he was worn away by a minute clicking of little wheels. That had no sister" (77).

Once the class has understood the spiritual implications of Quentin's rejection of sexuality, we discuss how this rejection drives him to invent for himself an idealized identity as savior figure. In short, we see how he tries to become his own self-appointed, pure redeemer. But since he is not the God-man and since he is locked in history, his attempt is doomed to failure. Like his father he thus assumes the stoic's response to the fall into history—a passive forbearance rooted in despair over the possibility of redemption. He is trapped in a world where all humans are "dolls stuffed with sawdust" (175).

To anchor these large thematic considerations in the text, I relate them to major image patterns in the second section of the novel. I stress Faulkner's practice of building meaning through a repetition-with-variation strategy. My aim is twofold: to demonstrate how Quentin's spiritual predicament is embodied in specific repeated images and, particularly important, in the language itself; and to link this section imagistically to the rest of the novel. First I concentrate on images of time (the watch, clocks, flowing water, tolling bells, moving shadows). I ask students to cite similar images of time in other places in the novel. They point to Benjy's synchronous experience of time, Jason's desperate obsession with time, and Dilsey's sacralizing of mundane time through a belief in eternal salvation.

Similarly I have the class discuss images of the body (sexuality, shadows, physical dirtiness, corruption, blood, bodily mutilation); images of nature (the branch, rivers, the tree, rain, flowers); and images of death and resurrection (suicide, drowning, Easter and the resurrection of Jesus). For example, we look at Quentin's association of honeysuckle and roses with Caddy's sexuality and Benjy's association of flowers (narcissus and his poisonous "jimson weed" [14]) with his love for and loss of Caddy. We compare Benjy's mutilation, his castration by the family, with Quentin's unsuccessful attempt to "mutilate" himself and Caddy in a suicide pact, and I emphasize how the image of castration serves in both cases as a metaphor for spiritual impotence. Finally, we link Quentin's concern with death's finality (weighting his body for the drowning) to the motif of Christian resurrection developed during the Easter service attended by Dilsey and Benjy, a scene that underscores Christian redemptive love in contrast to the destructive self-love of the Compsons. Throughout our discussion I show how Faulkner's nuanced, often ambiguous, evocation of religious themes through these images resonates dynamically against opposing ideas and values—with no definitive resolution by the author. I stress that Faulkner is presenting an anatomy of the modern spiritual condition, not prescribing simplistic solutions.

After examining important image patterns, we analyze the major actions (actual, remembered, and imagined) of Quentin's final day, observing again how Faulkner's strategy of repetition with variation dramatizes Quentin's entrapment in despair. Of particular importance here, in addition to his conversations with Caddy and his father, are his encounters with Caddy's various lovers and their contemporary counterpart, Gerald Bland. I ask the class to discuss how each of these encounters ends in Quentin's defeat and to consider the cumulative effect of the defeats. Students note how Quentin faints during his confrontation with Dalton Ames and fails to drive him away; how he fails to stop Caddy's marriage to "that blackguard" Herbert Head (111); and how he loses a fight to Bland, a casual seducer who is the antithesis of Quentin's code of virtue. Having discussed this pattern of defeats, we put them into the larger perspective of Quentin's stoicism and eventual suicide. Aware that his stoic code of virtue is ineffective in the world and that there is no way to redeem it, Quentin concludes that the only recourse for a man of honor is to refuse participation in such a world. His suicide is the culmination of the spiritual suicide he has been committing (with his father's help) throughout the novel; therefore I link his suicide to the Kierkegaardian concept of suicide with which our discussion began. I reiterate how Quentin's despair constitutes the essence of spiritual suicide, how he tries desperately to wrest moral meaning from his experience but is defeated by his father's stoicism. Finally, the class looks closely at Quentin's last debate with his father's voice (172–79) to see how Quentin is absorbed and defrauded by Mr. Compson's viewpoint and rhetoric. This absorption drowns Quentin so that he cannot achieve any independent spiritual identity, drowns him just as fatally as his plunge into the Charles River.

Nihilists and Their Relations: A Nietzschean Approach to Teaching *The Sound and the Fury*

Jun Liu

Many college instructors agree that teaching an undergraduate class in modernist literature sometimes requires the careful introduction of ideas of such significant modern thinkers as Freud, Bergson, and Nietzsche, especially when the class is taught in the context of a humanities course that treats literary and philosophical themes comparatively. If the teacher knows how to begin and, perhaps, when to stop, such ideas can facilitate the students' comprehension of rather difficult texts. In teaching *The Sound and the Fury*, I find that Nietzsche lends theoretical insights. Without them, students may not be able to see the various types of nihilism represented in the relations of the Compsons, and they may fail to note that the novel as a whole shows a tragic strength tested at the edge of nothingness. In offering students this aid, however, I limit my introduction of Nietzsche to his typology of nihilisms, illustrated by fragments from *The Will to Power*. (See the appendix to this essay. For a more detailed explanation of the typology, see chapter 5 of Gilles Deleuze's *Nietzsche and Philosophy*.) These few fragments provide an orientation for our exploration of nihilism in the novel.

I sometimes declare to my class, at the outset, that *The Sound and the Fury* "signifies nothing." This does not mean, I add quickly, that the novel is meaningless. It means that the novel signifies the tragic will in struggle with nothingness. The form of the novel—tortured, some say—in fact highlights the complexity of nihilism as a modern reality. But what is modern nihilism? What do I mean by the tragic will? I tell my class that answers to these questions will be deferred, and I hand out Macbeth's soliloquy from which the novel's published title is drawn:

> To-morrow, and to-morrow, and to-morrow,
> Creeps in this petty pace from day to day,
> To the last syllable of recorded time;
> And all our yesterdays have lighted fools
> The way to dusty death. Out, out, brief candle!
> Life's but a walking shadow, a poor player
> That struts and frets his hour upon the stage,
> And then is heard no more. It is a tale
> Told by an idiot, full of sound and fury,
> Signifying nothing.   (5.5.19–28)

Since my students have already been instructed to read the entire novel once, it does not take them long to discover that Faulkner has borrowed from this passage more than the words "sound and fury." The class then explores the extent of that borrowing. Shakespeare's metaphorical variations on the theme of nothingness are translated by Faulkner into fictive details: a "walking shadow" follows Quentin while he is deciding whether to be or not to be; Benjy, "an idiot," moans and howls, figuring a tale of sound and fury. Sooner or later in our discussion, students point out that there is also a "candle" for Benjy's birthday and that Jason is not unlike a "poor player" who "struts and frets" but soon is "heard no more." They may also suggest that the rhythm of "to-morrow, and to-morrow, and to-morrow" is reproduced by Faulkner. This observation results in a brief discussion of the sections of the novel as reiterations or repetitions of these themes.

I emphasize that the novel and the soliloquy are linked, first and foremost, in vision. Macbeth utters the terrible truth of nothingness. However, that truth is also defied by a spirit of affirmation—expressed by Shakespeare's voice—that stubbornly follows tomorrow "to the last syllable of recorded time" and that dances in the rhythm and in the poetic play of words. Such affirmation is, according to Nietzsche, a strength beyond the normal human limits; it characterizes tragic art, which we need in order not to perish of the truth. By both admitting the value of nothingness and implying the need to overcome it, Shakespeare teaches the paradox of nihilism that is at the heart of tragedy. This point can be reinforced by the instructor's reading the last paragraph of Faulkner's Nobel Prize acceptance speech regarding the "poet's voice" that asserts the tragic will in the struggle with nothingness. The same paradox is also illustrated by Wallace Stevens's "The Snow Man," which the instructor could use.

The class is now ready for Nietzsche. I pass around a sheet containing six fragments from *The Will to Power*, renumbered in my order (see appendix). I ask the students to look at fragments 1–4 while I define, initially, two types of nihilism. In its basic sense, nihilism, a form of pessimism, applies the value of nil (nothing) to life. Life is thus depreciated, denied; it becomes unreal. According to Nietzsche, the higher values in Western civilization—the idea of another world or a suprasensible world in all its manifestations (including a God of a moral world order and the separation of body and soul), exemplified especially by Christian moral interpretations—are ironically created on a nihilistic ground. These values are products of the will to nothingness because they rely on a grand fiction whose purpose is to annihilate this life. This kind of nihilism, since its distinctive quality is negation of this life, is negative nihilism. More than a trace of it is detectable, for instance, in Mrs. Compson.

In nihilism in the modern context, higher values now experience a deep crisis and they are reacted against. The "father" in God is dead. So modern nihilism, says Deleuze, is "no longer the devaluation of life in the name of higher values but rather the devaluation of higher values themselves" (148). Modern nihilism may lead to the further decline of the human spirit. When the possibilities to create values are denied, the human will yields silently to the nonhuman; there is then only nothingness of the will (a Schopenhauerian concept, which Nietzsche also critiques). Tragedy cannot be reborn under such conditions. This second type of nihilism, insofar as it is characterized by merely reactive forces, is reactive nihilism. Both negative nihilism and reactive nihilism are harmful to life (fragment 4).

Nietzsche and Faulkner seem to share the view that both types of nihilism are unfinished and are the opposite of tragic strength. If experiencing nihilism makes one wise about truths and nonetheless steels one's will, it can increase strength (fragments 5 and 6). In that sense, the tragic can be defined as accomplished nihilism. Accomplished nihilism is paradoxical. To explain this with Wallace Stevens's "The Snow Man," precisely because of one's recognition of "the nothing that is," one gains the wisdom that human creativity is everything and one sees, with the will strengthened, "[n]othing that is not there" (10). What is crucial to tragedy, then, is will: the tragic response to nihilism must be completed by converting the will to nothingness (which says that there is nothing) to the will of affirmation (which says that there is nothing except the will to power). Nothingness is thus overcome.

An outline of the three types of nihilism is all the theory I need from Nietzsche to highlight two points. First, *The Sound and the Fury* represents Faulkner's struggle with nihilism as a historical phenomenon. "Signifying nothing" is a serious mission to redeem humanity from nothingness. (On many occasions, Faulkner insisted on the need to overcome nothingness. For instance, in a letter to Marjorie Lyons, he concluded by quoting from his novel *The Wild Palms*: "Between grief and nothing, I will take grief" [*Faulkner on Love*].) Second, as suggested by the form of the novel, Faulkner also understood the need to provide a typology of nihilisms for the purpose of distinguishing the tragic from the nontragic.

In class, I elaborate on the second point in order to move to another stage of exploration, another question: How are the various types of nihilism embodied in the novel? They are embodied in relations. Faulkner uses troubled kinships as the foundation for plot situations and the novel's structure. The African American characters and their culture, in a subplot, represent accomplished nihilism. This strategy associates Faulkner with a long tradition of tragedy: intrafamilial problems of extremity—the murder of parents or children, incest, suicide, betrayal—are brought to the fore in classical tragedies. Allegorically, the famous houses in tragedies are prototypical, signifying problems that concern social values, the foundation of civilization, and humanity's uncertain status in the universe. In *The Sound and the Fury*, Faulkner adopts traditional motifs to convey a profound sense of loss. At the most immediate level, loss is felt by the Compson children as the lack of parental love. Mr. and Mrs. Compson not only stop functioning as adequate parents but have split the family into two camps: the Compsons (Father, Quentin, Caddy, and Benjy) and the Bascombs (Mother, Uncle Maury, and Jason). As in Macbeth's soliloquy, these intrafamilial problems signify nothing metaphorically; they signify the deeper ambiguity and larger sense of loss that is modern nihilism.

Because of my emphasis on nihilism, I give the Quentin section more weight and teach it before the others. Quentin's internalized dialogue with his father focuses mostly on Caddy. He wills a Caddy in the roles of sister, mother, girlfriend, and bride. Worth noting is that he insists to Mr. Compson: "*I have committed incest I said Father it was I it was not Dalton Ames*" (79). When I ask the class to explain why Quentin makes this claim, I usually get the following answers, which I push to their limits. Quentin's yearning for maternal love is perhaps confused in his mind as well as in his loins, some students suggest. This, they say, is a morbid passion. I ask them why Quentin, who did not commit incest as a deed, should insist to his father that he did. Isn't he playing a game with his father? Isn't Faulkner replacing the "Father in Heaven" with a nihilist Father (always capitalized in the text), making an appropriate comment on the modern era? If so, I suggest, a moral judgment is an inadequate explanation of Quentin's motives. Students sometimes make an apt observation: Since there is an overwhelming sense of loss—signified by the ineptitude of the parents, the division of the family into Compsons and Bascombs, the selling of forty acres to send Quentin to Harvard for a "fine dead sound" (174), the loss of a sister (with her loss of virginity as a central metaphor)—Quentin turns to the father, perhaps hoping to hear something he can still believe in. If the father would say something like "Son, incest is wrong," he would be admitting the validity of some values, and that might console his son. But the father never wavers in his view that all human experience is "reducto absurdum" [sic] (76), that no battle is ever won or even fought, that time (symbolized by the watch) is the "mausoleum of all hope and desire" (76). Mr. Compson does not believe that Quentin is capable of incest either. In effect, he removes all the illusions Quentin needs to live.

Students readily grasp the point that Quentin, an artist of sorts, struggles with this Father who represents nothingness of the will, that is, reactive nihilism. The Father's denial of the human will is so thorough that it also seems as if he were the nonhuman given a human voice, uttering the truth that Silenus was forced to utter (Nietzsche, *Birth* 42). He is of course human, especially when one considers how frail and weak he is. Life may have taught him how to reflect, but reflection has not taught him how to live. Yet his perspective that reduces humans to nothing is one beyond tragedy, which freezes Quentin. Quentin, however, becomes the tragic artist when he both recognizes the value of seeing humans as nothing and resists it. This ambiguity characterizes his internal world until the end and is best reflected in the long, unpunctuated passages (176–78) in which the father's and son's words merge.

Invariably, students ask if the value of nil is any value at all and what its effect is on Quentin. A short answer is that Quentin has learned from his nihilist father that human reality is a translation of desires into words. In the scene of the three boys with fishing rods, when Quentin hears the boys talking about what they will do with the hypothetical twenty-five-dollar reward for a trout that has not been caught for twenty-five years, he thinks that they are making "of unreality a possibility, then a probability, then an incontrovertible fact, as people will when their desires become words" (117). He realizes that this is how humans cope with nothingness. At the same time he understands that the boy who does not boast enjoys a "silent superiority" and that "people, using themselves and each other so much by words, are at least consistent in attributing wisdom to a still tongue" (118). The "silent superiority" implies the superiority of the nonhuman perspective.

The effect of this value of nil on Quentin is obvious. He realizes, for instance, that he has invented Father (122). In imagining an incestuous relationship with Caddy, he is not unlike the boys imagining what they could do with a fish not yet caught. He thus plays with "all forms, moods, and shows of grief" (*Hamlet* 1.2.82) in order to translate his desires into reality. Quentin's final choice—turning his wake into a wedding with Caddy—is based on pure fiction. While this choice may be called, romantically, the overflowing desire of life expressed in the form of death, it is also, from the perspective of the nonhuman, "a piece of natural human folly" (177). Who wins in the game? At the moment of Quentin's death, it seems that the nonhuman perspective (which laughs at the apotheosis of human folly) prevails. It is ironic that Quentin, challenging Mr. Compson's nothingness of will, should himself choose the will to nothingness. Trying to overcome nihilism in one mode, he succumbs to it in another. But the courage in his folly is precisely tragedy.

Mrs. Compson, however, exemplifies the Christian moral belief that this life is too sinful to be meaningful and is thus only transition. This negative nihilism is responsible for her insistence on "virtues" that are harmful not only to herself but also to her children. When I ask my class if they can identify what she cares about above all else, the word "name" or "reputation" usually comes first or is high on their list. She cares only for the nominal, neglecting the real substance of life. She changes Benjy's name from Maury to avoid embarrassment; she wants Benjy's pasture sold in order to send Quentin to Harvard; she wants Caddy married in order to give the unborn child a proper name; and she forbids Quentin IV from knowing her mother's name. Jason both collaborates with and defies his mother's value system. Consistent in his cynicism (another form of reactive nihilism), Jason does not believe in sin. One should, however, refrain from reading him too moralistically. The teacher may want to draw the students' attention to what Faulkner wrote about Jason in the appendix, namely, that he is "[l]ogical and rational contained and even a philosopher in the stoic tradition: thinking nothing whatever of God one way or another and simply considering the police and fearing and respecting only the Negro woman" ("Appendix" 212). Pretending to burn the checks Caddy sends is a game he plays. Perhaps there is even love in this game. After all, Uncle Maury wants Jason to consider it their "duty to shield [Mrs. Compson] from the crass material world as much as possible" (*Sound* 224), and Jason may be acting accordingly.

The overture and coda of the novel are Faulkner's poetic play on the theme of nihilism. Faulkner seems to have found in Benjy the most apt vehicle for expressing the tragic paradox. The Benjy section is a poetic simulation of what Benjy might have thought and said but cannot, since he is speechless. So Benjy's narrative space is also Faulkner's (play)ground on which he allows his pessimism to rollick, roam, and sometimes roar in the figure of a perpetual idiot. A golfer shouting "Here, caddie" (3) initiates Benjy's mental search. Some students quickly see this scene as embodying the double loss of the pasture and Caddy. Yet, I suggest to them, idiocy may also be figured as the idiot's blessing, since the association of caddie with Caddy erases the double loss. Benjy begins to search but cannot name his loss. With Benjy, the reader enters a world tenuously suspended between despair and consolation, meaninglessness and meaning.

The novel also seems to suggest that Benjy has to be left in someone's proper care for there to be redemption. But whose? This question warrants a discussion of mothering presence repeated with variations that agree with the novel's typology of nihilisms. For visual illustration and analogy, I show my students a reproduction of Picasso's *La vie* (1903), a painting in which the gesture of embrace is repeated in every detail, introducing into an otherwise cold priming a sense of human warmth. In Benjy's section, the memory of a lost sister intimates a sensuality that a child would associate with its mother, and the section ends with Benjy's inchoate memory of Caddy's embrace; Caddy thus substitutes for Mrs. Compson. Caddy plays the role of mother also in Quentin's peregrinations. And Mrs. Compson, of course, is mother for Jason. In the fourth section Dilsey emerges as mother, taking the idiot child to the Easter service. Dilsey is highly significant since she is part of the African American culture, which the novel offers as an alternative to the general decline symbolized by the Compsons. The Easter ritual in an African American church of this kind also represents a Christianity that contrasts with Mrs. Compson's impoverished version. The African American form of Christianity, whose history can be traced back to the struggle against slavery, emphasizes the renewal of strength in the face of nothingness and thus represents the paradox of accomplished nihilism, as in this passage:

> And the congregation seemed to watch with its own eyes while the voice consumed [Reverend Shegog], until he was nothing and they were nothing and there was not even a voice but instead their hearts were speaking to one another in chanting measures beyond the need for words. . . .
> (294)

After the Easter service, Dilsey visits Mrs. Compson, who has been sleeping and who does not even have the strength—or the will—to pick up the Bible left by Dilsey on the edge of the bed. Dilsey, handing her the Bible, says, "You cant see to read, noways. . . . You want me to raise de shade a little?" (300). The scene has a distinctly Joycean, epiphanic quality; Dilsey is contesting Mrs. Compson for the role of real mother (and real Christian, in Faulkner's scheme). Her words are both diagnosis and prescription: Mrs. Compson needs more light. In daylight, Dilsey has "seed de first en de last" (297). Although she won't say exactly what she has seen, it can be inferred that it is the history of the Compsons that has run its course; moreover, she is aware that there is something beyond that history. Meanwhile Benjy roars, reminding us once again of the sound and the fury. When he is not roaring, he is as mute as the ultimate silence. Could this roar be the sound of the nonhuman translated into a human sound? While it takes a leap of imagination to grasp the idea, it is a possibility worth entertaining, and I ask my students to think about it. After all, what would the sound that signifies nothing sound like?

APPENDIX
EXCERPTS FROM NIETZSCHE'S
THE WILL TO POWER

1. What does nihilism mean? *That the highest values devalue themselves*. The aim is lacking; "why?" finds no answer. (9)
2. The end of the moral interpretation of the world, which no longer has any sanction after it has tried to escape into some beyond, leads to nihilism. (7)
3. Since Copernicus man has been rolling from the center toward X. (8)
4. Against "meaninglessness" on the one hand, against moral value judgments on the other . . . A *critique of Christian morality* is still lacking. (7)
5. A philosopher recuperates differently and with different means: he recuperates, e.g., with nihilism. Belief that there is no truth at all, the nihilistic belief, is a great relaxation for one who, as a warrior of knowledge, is ceaselessly fighting ugly truths. For truth is ugly. (325)
6. Nihilism as a normal phenomenon can be a symptom of increasing *strength* or of increasing *weakness*. (319)

CONTEXTUAL AND COMPARATIVE APPROACHES

History on the Margins and in the Mainstream: Teaching *The Sound and the Fury* in Its Southern Historical Context

Daniel J. Holtz

The Sound and the Fury, like any of William Faulkner's novels, is not a historical novel. It does not set out primarily to reconstruct a historical era or to recreate the lives and times of historically important people. However, students who understand important facets of the southern legacy can more readily grasp some of the novel's implications, because the novel resonates with history and with Faulkner's ever-apparent sense of the past in the present. My job in teaching *The Sound and the Fury* has been to identify aspects of southern history that best illustrate the novel's themes and best fill the gaps in my students' knowledge. I synthesize this approach with an analysis of the novel's structure and narrative technique. I have found the following areas of information most useful.

First of all, I want my students to understand that southern history in general and Mississippi history in particular are not typical of the American experience in the early twentieth century. They include large measures of frustration and defeat: economical, social, and political—a point best brought out in C. Vann Woodward's *The Burden of Southern History*. While America was moving quickly to become the dominant power in the world, the South was emerging from what some historians call the colonial occupation of the Reconstruction period. Therefore, unlike most other Americans, southerners had little reason to believe that they could accomplish almost anything.

One need only look at economic contrasts in the South and in Mississippi before and after the Civil War. In Mississippi from 1860 to 1900, the average size of farms decreased from 370 acres to 83. And in 1860, as the historian James Oakes notes in *The Ruling Race: A History of American Slaveholders*, the twelve wealthiest counties in America lay below the Mason-Dixon line. Adams County, Mississippi, in the southwest corner of the state, had the highest wealth per capita of any county in the country. And many of the wealthiest people in the United States were scattered throughout the state. That glittering legacy contrasts markedly with the poverty and deprivation of the early twentieth century.

Second, I want my students to understand how the legacy of plantation life as an ideal still held sway in Mississippi in the early twentieth century, though it was changing and had to change. The plantation ideal, as Joel Williamson notes in *William Faulkner and Southern History*, prescribed how men and women, and blacks and whites, ought to live with each other and treat each other in almost any situation. Extended patriarchy was the cornerstone; the white father headed the household, both black and white, and made the important decisions. He was provider, protector. Another cornerstone was the concept of the southern belle—beautiful, chaste, pious, domestic, submissive, gracious—who married and grew to be a woman protected, placed on a pedestal, and isolated as much as possible from the cares of everyday life. Although the roots of the plantation legacy lay in the antebellum South, its mindset continued into the twentieth century in a somewhat altered state that Williamson calls "placeness" (403)—the need for every person to occupy a specified place in society. Indeed, Williamson calls placeness the essence of southern society because of the white South's exaggerated need to keep blacks in their place, a need exacerbated by the abolition of slavery.

Consequently, different social arrangements had to evolve after the Civil War, although the plantation society still remained a desirable and comfortable vision for the vast majority of whites. In fact, Williamson says the South probably was never so united as it was in the 1920s and 1930s, when it envisioned a return to "moonlight and magnolias" (401). However, the press of economic necessity had created new roles and attitudes for both blacks and whites, even though whites wanted to keep the former slaves in their previous economic and social positions. They almost completely succeeded in this, through terror, control of land ownership, and, later, Jim Crow laws. The former slaves, however, resisted any return to plantation life. As Michael Wayne notes in *The Reshaping of Plantation Society: The Natchez District, 1860–1880*, black men removed their wives from the fields, tried to get their own land, and pushed for education and a secure family life. What these efforts, in part, led to, though, was a gradual decline in noblesse oblige support from whites. The slaves, although they might be harshly punished, had belonged to an extended family and been under the paternalistic care and concern of the master. Free blacks were more nearly part of a business equation, and when times were tough and the agricultural economy depressed, as in the late 1880s and on into the 1890s, they had to fend for themselves.

Because of this situation, many black males moved to the cities. The exodus, according to Williamson in *A Rage for Order: Black-White Relations in the American South since Emancipation*, created two new roles for southern blacks: the "nigger loose" and "black matriarchy" (58–59). "Nigger loose" refers to black males in southern cities who often could not find jobs and thus operated on the margins of society, posing a threat in the minds of whites because such blacks owed loyalty to no one. "Black matriarchy" refers to the women who, working as domestic servants for upper-class whites, became the providers and supporters for those black men who were unemployed.

Finally, I want my students to be more aware of other patterns of race relations in turn-of-the-century Mississippi. In *Dark Journey: Black Mississippians in the Age of Jim Crow*, the historian Neil McMillen says that Mississippi was the most notorious state in the Union for racial violence. It had the most lynchings, 486 from 1889 to 1945 (4 of those occurred in Lafayette County), and it had the highest rate of lynchings per capita. In fact, from 1904 through 1908, Mississippi averaged one lynching every twenty-five days. By 1928, however, the number of lynchings had fallen considerably (there was an average of fewer than ten a year in the 1920s), as it had in other southern states, although fear of the "white death," as Richard Wright called lynching, was ever-present. The decline reflected not a greater benevolence of whites but, rather, an increased confidence about their control over the lives of blacks. After the long reign of terror, most whites felt that lynchings were necessary primarily as an occasional object lesson for the black population. Unfortunately, as lynchings became less frequent, McMillen notes, they became more brutal and sadistic. Burning, mutilation, and other forms of torture grew more common.

I give my students this historical background, but, more important, I ask them to use it as a basis to raise questions about *The Sound and the Fury*. I model questions to begin but later allow and expect students to formulate their own. I expect the questions to be open-ended and to require analysis or synthesis of passages from the book, along with information, when necessary, outside the novel. Examples of questions arising from the first section of historical information I discuss are the following: Does the South's legacy of frustration and defeat manifest itself in *The Sound and the Fury*? If so, which characters seem most affected? Why? Questions from the background on racial roles may include these: Dilsey is a fictional example of a historical type, the black matriarch. Through her character, what does Faulkner suggest about the power and potential of black women? Why can she wield the kinds of authority, with both whites and blacks, that she does?

To assist students further with this question-raising process, I put them in groups of three or four and assign each group a topic. Some of the topics are the American dream in the South before and after the war; the plantation legacy and postwar carryovers in male and female roles; and race relations, including black-white rearrangements in the New South. Before students begin their inquiry, I encourage them to think of the journalists' list of six questions: Who, what, when, where, why, and how.

Through their questions, our discussions, and my prodding, students often discover a number of correlations between Faulkner's novel and history. They discuss transitions between the old and the new South, which various members of the Compson family illustrate. Jason and Quentin, for example, have grown up in the same environment, but they are separated by a chasm in attitudes. I ask my students: What does this separation indicate? Is it some sort of biological predetermination, the Bascomb blood, as Mrs. Compson believes? Or does it represent a broader change that was going on in much of the South? And how do these questions correlate with Faulkner's comment that Jason was the only Compson who held his own with the Snopeses? By responding to historically based questions like these, my students can begin to see other reasons behind the attitudes of Quentin, who remains troublingly tied to the past, and of Jason, who in his savagely practical way is breaking from it.

Because of Williamson's concept of placeness, they can also see the broader context for the objections of the poor whites ("[t]rash white folks," as Dilsey calls them [290]) to Dilsey's taking Benjy to her church. When I ask why these whites object, my students quickly respond, Because of the color line, and wonder why I have asked a question to which the answer seems so obvious. But then I ask, Why do these whites object; why not upper-class whites? Then they have to think more fully about the concept of place and why poor whites and not the upper-class whites felt their positions threatened. These questions dovetail well with a discussion of the fact that mob violence against blacks was usually carried out by poor whites, although it could not have continued without the consent and support of the upper class.

As we continue to discuss how history illuminates themes in the novel, I also want my students to understand that *The Sound and the Fury* makes commentary on history in addition to reflecting it. Typically, Faulkner tries more to re-form history than to reflect it. For instance, when students view Caddy in the context of the plantation legacy, they find that she represents not only a source of vexation to her mother but also a sharp break with her mother's tradition. Caddy follows the norms prescribed for her only when they coincide with her nature. She is not pious, chaste, or domestic in any socially acceptable sense; however, she loves her offspring (the cornerstone of a woman's role in the Victorian-based plantation tradition) more fully and honestly than her mother ever loved hers. In other words, as Williamson observes (in *Faulkner*), Faulkner challenges and exposes the artificiality of female roles in the South, just as he challenges other social relations (365–66).

Faulkner's "That Evening Sun," a story I like to teach before we begin studying the novel, offers additional insights into black-white relations and into the Compson family. It demonstrates the Compsons' detachment from their black servants, and it shows—in Nancy's man Jesus—a troubling example of a black person operating on the margins of society. With this additional context, my students can better understand the social criticism Faulkner makes in *The Sound and the Fury* and better respond to such questions as, What is the nature of the

Compsons' relationship to their servants? What factors for both blacks and whites hold this relationship together: loyalty, mutual care and concern, economic necessity, or other kinds of interdependence? What do the answers to these questions say about this kind of society? I try to get my students to understand that although the historical context illuminates themes and incidents in the novel, the novel continually criticizes the keystone of southern history, its social fabric, and therefore it illuminates that history. The principal characters, almost without exception, strain society's limits; they push normal sensibilities to the extremes. The Compsons, most certainly, are the early twentieth-century paradigm of the dysfunctional family. Yet their story is remarkable, as is its ability to reflect mainstream historical trends while simultaneously revealing the hollowness and inhumanity of some of those trends.

Finally, looking at the novel from a historical standpoint helps students handle its narrative structure as well. As my students and I discuss the novel's historical background, we also briefly discuss methods of historical research, how historians must sift through a variety of artifacts and data to reach conclusions. Because parts of those data may be contradictory and reflect the prejudices and misinformation of their presenters, historians must evaluate their data with a good dose of skepticism and detachment. Paradoxically, they must also try to identify and empathize with their sources, the people behind the data, in order to understand their motivations. Reading *The Sound and the Fury* involves much the same process. Faulkner presents history through a number of different perspectives, some of them reliable, some not so reliable; some straightforward, some enigmatic and convoluted. Furthermore, the story occurs over a number of years, but it is not told in a linear fashion. We must reconstruct it as a historian reconstructs, and we can do that fully only after we have listened to and evaluated all the sources, seeing how they confirm or contradict one another. This process takes patience and understanding. It also takes the ability to examine our own prejudices to see why we empathize more with one character than with another.

Contextualizing *The Sound and the Fury*: Sex, Gender, and Community in Modern American Fiction

John N. Duvall

A modernist theme that deserves careful scrutiny when one teaches *The Sound and the Fury* is the relationship between women and men, particularly the confusion, nervousness, and anger men express about women. To a significant degree, men's anger may be linked to women's demands in the first third of the twentieth century for greater political power and sexual autonomy, demands that began to reshape the boundaries of previously accepted gender roles. On this general topic, Carroll Smith-Rosenberg's *Disorderly Conduct* provides useful background, particularly its concluding chapter, "The New Woman as Androgyne: Social Order and Gender Crises, 1870–1936," which recounts the hostility toward women entering the university and the attempt of medical and sexological discourse to categorize women's desires for economic and intellectual development as signs of lesbianism. Also useful is volume 1 of Sandra M. Gilbert and Susan Gubar's revisionist history, *No Man's Land: The Place of the Woman Writer in the Twentieth Century*. According to Gilbert and Gubar, "male thinkers were daunted by women's new-found libidinous energy, and literary men tended to re-envision the battle of the sexes as an erotically charged sexual struggle" (35). It is hardly an exaggeration to say that there developed during the transition from the Victorian to the modern period an epistemic crisis regarding the sexual behavior of women and men. What does it mean if the sexual woman is no longer exactly a fallen woman? This crisis can be seen as the beginning of an unhinging of biological sex from culturally constructed gender roles.

As portrayed in canonical modernist literature, this unhinging of gender from biology often is experienced as a threat, so that the American family and community frequently are represented more by their rupture than by any sense of wholeness. In *Gender Trouble*, Judith Butler more radically argues that the sex-gender distinction collapses at the point where one realizes that "this construct called 'sex' is as culturally constructed as gender" (7). While Butler's deconstruction of the sex-gender opposition is interesting, more useful for developing undergraduates' understanding is Myra Jehlen's short essay "Gender," which makes clear the notion of gender as an enactment.

This essay considers how an instructor can group *The Sound and the Fury* with other texts in a modern American literature survey course to emphasize the significance of gender issues for notions of American community. I do not wish to suggest that sexual politics alone charts the coordinates of identity or that any discussion of Faulkner's novel would be complete without a consideration of race. A study unit on gender matters, though, can help place *The Sound and the Fury* within a specifically modernist context: the parallel historical development of psychoanalysis and the discourse of literary modernism. In the teaching of modernism, some background lectures on Freud's concepts of the unconscious and the dreamwork are indispensable for students' understanding of both the form and content of the stream-of-consciousness technique that plays along the associative chain of language. Chapters 1 and 2 of Elizabeth Wright's *Psychoanalytic Criticism* provide useful background on key psychoanalytic concepts. An introduction to psychoanalysis shows students that the foregrounding of the sexual nature of identity was not isolated to literature but indeed was crucial to a whole new science of humankind. And if Freud's notions of female sexuality seem trapped in the sexism of his age, other concepts, such as that of the polymorphously perverse infant, show the debt that later gender theory owes to psychoanalysis.

Although male characters in canonical modernist texts experience confusion and hostility toward women, such feelings are at least as much an expression of anxiety about themselves and the status of their masculinity. The ur-texts in this regard are T. S. Eliot's "The Love Song of J. Alfred Prufrock" and *The Waste Land*. The psychologically impotent Prufrock, as well as the more elusive yet equally wounded Fisher King narrator of *The Waste Land*, serves as a basis for understanding a variety of Faulkner's male characters, particularly Quentin Compson. The effeminate, middle-aged Prufrock's inability to act on his desire—he is unable even to summon the courage to speak to a woman at a tea party—prefigures virginal Quentin's inability to enter the world of adult sexuality. More telling, perhaps, is the narrator in *The Waste Land*. For this narrator, the wholesale reshaping of the geopolitical world in the aftermath of World War I points to the failure of cultural institutions (i.e., the church, the monarchical state, the university, the family) that previously had sustained values. But almost as much to blame for the wasteland of modernity, from his perspective, is the behavior of women, who now seem to attach no importance to the sex act. Sexual union, as represented in Western culture, from Greek myth to English history to German literature, is spiritual and transcendent and should give us access to the timeless essences of our masculinity and femininity—or so Eliot suggests by the range of his allusions. But what Eliot finds in his contemporary moment rocks the history of Western representation; there is nothing but failed relations between women and men, regardless of social class, as "A Game of Chess" makes clear. It is in "The Fire Sermon," particularly the clerk's seduction of the typist, narrated by Tiresias, that Eliot's disgust with sexuality in the modern world is clearest. What horrifies him is that this woman is not horrified by what has happened to her. Cut off from prior representations of the spirituality of sexuality, women and men in the modern world are reduced to mere animal ruttings that are devoid of intimacy and produce no significant communion. It is as if Western culture is ruined when women no longer know that they are ruined.

Eliot's assessment of the degradation of human sexuality (for which women, again, are primarily to blame) leads almost directly to an understanding both of the central "crime" of *The Sound and the Fury*—Caddy Compson's becoming pregnant out of wedlock and giving birth to a child with no father name—and of Quentin's tortured response to this situation. Caddy's sexuality is related to the unmanning of all the Compson brothers. Benjy's castration, resulting from his displaced attempt to have Caddy sexually, surely figures the symbolic castration of the other two Compson brothers. The communal judgment against Caddy's pregnancy reminds us of how traditional the southern community was and in some ways still is. The elaborate fictions of noblesse oblige and of the southern lady and gentleman mask the underlying reason why the transition from virginity to marriage is the only socially sanctioned course for a young woman. For a culture so invested in blood and lineage, the uncertainty of fatherhood can never be acknowledged. Thus transgressions such as Caddy's threaten to disrupt the communal order. But it is an order already waning, and there is a moment in Benjy's narration that signals that waning. Almost every time I teach *The Sound and the Fury*, someone asks what the reference to Agnes Mabel Becky means (50). It is what Quentin's latest lover, the man with the red tie from the traveling show, reads off the small metal disk that Luster thought was a quarter. The showman takes the disk as evidence of her previous sexual activity. Calvin S. Brown points out that these names are part of the logo of a brand of condoms popular in the 1920s (19). But it is not sufficient for teachers merely to pass on this bit of information, lest we reproduce the sexism of the showman's comment to Luster as the showman returns the metal case to Benjy. More than an index of Quentin's sexuality, the condom case needs to be seen in its broader social context, namely, that "the dissemination of birth-control information and equipment in the 1910s and 1920s disengaged reproduction sexuality, removing one major impediment to female erotic freedom" (Gilbert and Gubar 35). (But Smith-Rosenberg argues that sexual freedom at times could be a divisive issue among women. To the extent that men were successful in portraying as repressed the new woman who desired political and economic opportunity, they succeeded in making "her the enemy of the 'liberated' woman of the 1920s—the flapper" [282].) It is not flippant to conclude, as one of my students did, that had this birth-control technology been available to Caddy eighteen years earlier, the multiple tragedies of *The Sound , and the Fury* might never have occurred.

Although Benjy's "narration" poses an undeniable challenge to students, I find that Quentin's section presents more problems. I have turned increasingly toward assigning short papers to give students focus in their reading and to serve as the basis for longer papers. The topics that follow can help students see how masculinity is an enactment, in the context of Quentin's failure to enact successfully his culture's code of masculinity. These short essays (600–900 words) are due the second or third day of our study of the novel, when we begin discussion of Quentin's narration. Since students write without the benefit of class discussion, I hold these papers to a lower standard of scrutiny than I do longer essays. Using this format also improves class discussion, since students already have thought through a particular problem.

1. Compare Julio's protection of his younger sister with Quentin's failure to protect Caddy from Dalton Ames. What is the implied norm of masculine behavior behind these two moments? How might Quentin's failure to live up to the code of masculinity in his confrontation with Ames affect his sense of self?

2. Given Quentin's incestuous thoughts about Caddy, might Quentin's relation to the little Italian girl (whom he calls sister) be less innocent than he believes it to be?

3. Why does Quentin strike Gerald Bland? Look closely at what precedes Quentin's action, particularly his line "Did you ever have a sister? did you?" What relation, if any, do you see between this scene and Quentin's confrontation with Dalton Ames?

Having worked through these topics, students can begin to contextualize their observations about Quentin. Quentin Compson well understands what is expected of him as a brother whose sister has been wronged. Yet the Quentin who faces Dalton Ames on the bridge is a young Prufrock, feminized in a Freudian sense (castrated, made impotent) by the fact of his sister's sexuality. What Quentin really desires is more than castration, as indicated by the moment when he recalls the story of a man who mutilated himself: "But that's not it. It's not not having them [testicles]. It's never to have had them then I could say O That That's Chinese I dont know Chinese" (116). Quentin's desire for childhood innocence before the knowledge of sexual difference registers his unconscious awareness of the codes that map gender on the body and provides a significant clue to the nature of a particular gender reversal: Quentin is what the culture demands Caddy should be, a virgin, while Caddy's sexual experience is precisely what the culture tells Quentin he should have. He is disturbed by something similar to what Joe Christmas experiences in *Light in August* when he decides that his lover, Joanna Burden, is a better man than he is. If the woman has a firmer grasp on masculinity than the man does, then the man is emasculated—cut off from his masculinity because something has intervened to demonstrate that masculinity is an enactment, not an essence.

When Quentin attempts to insert himself self-consciously into the role of protector, his efforts are ineffectual. Standing on the bridge, he tells Ames to leave town by sundown, but he slaps at rather than hits Ames, only to have Ames hold both his wrists in one hand. Ames pulls out a pistol and demonstrates his marksmanship by hitting pieces of bark in the water. When Ames offers the gun to Quentin, however, Quentin refuses it, and his refusal can be seen as the inability to seize phallic authority. Instead, he "passe[s] out like a girl" (162). The whole scene so profoundly marks Quentin's psychosexual landscape that he will turn to another bridge to commit suicide. Quentin is at least as obsessed with Dalton Ames as Caddy ever was. Near the beginning of his narration, Quentin thinks, "When he put the pistol in my hand I didn't" (79). Didn't what? Didn't shoot him. That's because Quentin can never conceive of himself as the one who penetrates, and indeed just a few lines later Quentin imaginatively transforms his refusal of Ames's gun, the symbolic phallus, into a way to defeat Ames by a refusal of the literal phallus—that is, Quentin imagines preventing the conception of Ames through coitus interruptus: "If I could have been his mother lying with open body lifted laughing, holding his father with my hand refraining, seeing, watching him die before he lived" (80).

Quentin also fails to wield the symbolic phallus effectively when he puts his pocketknife to Caddy's throat and suggests a murder-suicide. This scene, real or imagined, is rife with sexual imagery, as are so many moments in *The Sound and the Fury*, conflating sex and death. The sexually experienced Caddy, who has "died" for Ames, tries to guide Quentin: "no like this youll have to push it harder," while Quentin can only ask for assistance—"touch your hand to it" (152). But though Caddy says she wants him to penetrate her, Quentin loses his knife and his opportunity to consummate the incestuous union he desires.

After teaching *The Sound and the Fury*, I try to build on what students have learned from reading Eliot and Faulkner so that these ambiguities and tensions of gender will not be seen as isolated within discrete works. Quentin's and Jason's psychological impotence, for example, can serve as a touchstone when one turns to Hemingway's *The Sun Also Rises*. Jake Barnes, whose unmanning is as much the effect of Brett Ashley's sexual freedom as of his war wound, can serve as the basis for another short paper:

1. On their fishing trip, Bill Gorton banters with Jake Barnes about "irony and pity" (113, 114), and Jake seems to alternate between self-pity and self-irony. Compare Jake's self-presentation with that of Jason Compson. How do their less admirable traits—Jake's homophobia, Jason's racism, and their shared anti-Semitism—get played out with pity and irony? How do their other prejudices reflect on their attitudes toward women?

2. Compare Jake's sense of Brett in his discussion of "the presentation of the bill" and "exchange of values" (*Sun* 148) with Jason's sense of Lorraine, the Memphis prostitute he regularly visits, expressed after he gives her money: "After all, like I say money has no value; it's just the way you spend it" (194). For Jason and Jake, what do men owe women? What do women give that merits payment?

Hemingway's figurative use of the opposition between bulls and steers to comment on the relations among Jake and his friends in Pamplona provides a good way to keep the issue of gender ambiguity in the forefront, especially when students realize that Brett has more bull-like qualities than any other member of their band of expatriates.

Tennessee Williams's *A Streetcar Named Desire* provides an apt end point in this approach, a place to consider the male judgment of female sexuality.

Blanche Dubois's arrival by streetcars named Desire and Cemeteries once again reminds us of modernism's almost pathological conflation of sex and death. The punishment of Blanche at the conclusion of *Streetcar*—sexual violence against the sexual woman—participates in an intertextual logic that reflects on Caddy and Brett as well. At this point, I find it useful to have students write a longer paper (6–8 pages) that draws on their shorter papers. Here are some possible topics:

1. Explore the ways in which T. S. Eliot's *Waste Land* speaks through *The Sound and the Fury, The Sun Also Rises,* and *A Streetcar Named Desire.* Pay particular attention to the treatment of male-female relations. Do the other texts simply reflect the dynamics of *The Waste Land* or do they modify them in some way?
2. Blanche Dubois tells us that "a woman's charm is fifty percent illusion" (41), which reminds us of Jehlen's point about gender as an enactment. Discuss specific scenes in *Streetcar, The Sun Also Rises,* and *The Sound and the Fury* in which masculinity is at least fifty-percent illusion.

Against these canonical male texts, I usually turn to women's fiction as a way to reconstellate the issue of gender and its relation to community. Two novels that work well are Willa Cather's *O Pioneers!* and Zora Neale Hurston's *Their Eyes Were Watching God*. In Cather's novel, the fertility of the Nebraska farmland presents an immediate contrast to the wasteland visions the students have read. At the same time, the triangular desire that ends in Frank Shabata's killing his wife, Marie, and Emil Bergson lets the reader touch base once again with the Dalton Ames–Caddy–Quentin triangle in *The Sound and the Fury*. The difference here is that Cather does not allow the violence of romantic love to stand uncontested. The proposed marriage at the conclusion of the novel between the ambiguously gendered Alexandra Bergson, who embodies traits of the cultural masculine, and Carl Linstrum, who is aligned with the cultural feminine, serves to devalue heterosexual battling.

Hurston's exploration of African American community offers a different kind of counterbalance to male modernist literature. The frame for Janie's telling her life's history, the fulfillment "of that oldest human longing—self-revelation" (6), emphasizes the importance of women's friendship. The intimacy between Janie and Pheoby can be played off against Hemingway's celebration of male bonding between Bill and Jake and Faulkner's "marriage" of Quentin and Shreve. Logan Killicks and Joe Starks, Janie's two husbands, embody a number of the same traditional male conceptions of a woman's role that students encountered in previous texts, but the difference is that these male attitudes are now filtered through a female point of view. Janie's relationship with the younger Tea Cake, a man who allows her to be a subject rather than an object, holds out hope for intimacy and love between women and men.

To end on a cautionary note: Perhaps because I teach in the Bible Belt, I find that a number of students are uncomfortable both with the emphasis psychoanalysis places on the sexual nature of identity and with the anti-essentialist implications of gender theory. The assignments I suggest do create a kind of coherence, but I also give options for papers (omitted here for reasons of focus and concision) that do not involve issues of sex and gender. Whatever vision of a more just future one may have becomes unjust if it means forcing students to confront matters that they find too alienating.

Teaching *The Sound and the Fury*
in the Context of European Modernism

Philip M. Weinstein

Teaching a course on Proust, Joyce, and Faulkner every other year, I know I will be greeted by students frightened by the notorious "difficulty" of these three literary masters. So I begin by rehearsing the traditions of the nineteenth-century novel that modernism will so powerfully revise. Most of my students have read at least one of these earlier canonical texts (*Pride and Prejudice, Great Expectations, The Mill on the Floss, Madame Bovary, Anna Karenina, The Portrait of a Lady*, to name six), even though few have speculated on the formal and ideological tenets such texts share. Before we move on to the ferocious experimentation that fuels *Ulysses* and *The Sound and the Fury*, it makes sense to map the more familiar field of realism. (Good background reading to help students construct this map may be found in Elizabeth Ermath's *Realism and Consensus in the English Novel*. Ermath analyzes sympathetically the shared values required for the realist text to speak with its characteristic authority.)

We examine four key components of realism: coherent characterization, developmental plots, a central narrative intelligence, and general readability. Characters in realist novels come to the reader properly introduced, carefully located in social space and genealogical time, and assembled by a cluster of summarized, compatible traits. Their minds are accessible in traditional language. The coherence of Elizabeth, Pip, Maggie, Emma, Anna, and Isabel is textually produced through a detailed repertory that orients the reader both to their internal resources and to their external conditions. The subsequent interplay between the characters' resources and their social conditions unfolds as the realist plot. Although the verbs that pass this plot on are in the past tense, the reader's overwhelming temporal experience is of a future being generated. Realist plots span many years, typically concluding with the maturation (or destruction) of the protagonist.

Because the realist writer charges a central narrative voice with the responsibility of organizing the novel's materials, nuances of character and plot are faithfully communicated to the reader. The narrator of the realist text sifts, selects, makes transitions that—however confusing at first—promise to be richly intelligible. From start to finish we as readers are in the narrator's hands, and the narrator's combination of reliability and omniscience encourages us to align ourselves with the ongoing assessments. Like God in a religious scenario, like perspective in Western painting from the Renaissance through impressionism, the narrator is the principle that guarantees that we as readers are granted a privileged, noncontradictory relation to what we encounter. The realist text seems written for us. The linguistic procedures of the narrator are recognizable and trustworthy—a vocabulary we have learned and a syntax we have read before, in the service of a plot we are familiar with.

We spend several weeks rehearsing these realist procedures as background for the unconventionality of modernist procedures, confirming for the students that the reading habits they bring to the course are relevant, precisely, as learned orientations that will be deliberately attacked by modernist practice. In this way the students realize that their trouble with the texts is not personal but cultural. Their way of reading earlier texts has been taught within one cultural paradigm, and it will not work adequately for texts written within another cultural paradigm.

The critic whose work most dazzlingly opens up the concealed constructedness of realism—its status as a cultural paradigm rather than "the way things are"—is probably Roland Barthes. Both his *S/Z* and *The Pleasure of the Text* dissect the status quo inertia of the reader-friendly text (what Barthes calls the "readerly text"). Students may also consult Catherine Belsey's *Critical Practice* for a straightforward (if at times simplistic) poststructuralist analysis of realism's assumptions.

But the two thinkers most helpful in illuminating the cultural transition from realism to modernism are Nietzsche and Freud. Nietzsche's insistence that all seeing and knowing is perspectival reminds students that even a voice as generally authoritative as a typical nineteenth-century narrator's actually embodies a limited point of view. Instructors might ask their students to consider, for example, this passage from Nietzsche's *On the Genealogy of Morals*:

> Henceforth, my dear philosophers, let us be on guard against the dangerous old conceptual fiction that posited a "pure, will-less, painless, timeless knowing subject"; let us guard against the snares of such concepts as "pure reason," "absolute spirituality," "knowledge in itself": these always demand that we should think of an eye that is completely unthinkable, an eye turned in no particular direction, in which the active and interpreting forces, through which alone seeing becomes seeing something, are supposed to be lacking; these always demand of the eye an absurdity and a nonsense. There is only a perspective seeing, only a perspective "knowing"; and the more affects we allow to speak about one thing, the more eyes, different eyes, we can use to observe one thing, the more complete will our "concept" of this thing, our "objectivity," be.
>
> (119)

It would be hard to find a more pertinent philosophical rationale for Faulkner's reliance on such aggressively perspectival narrators as Benjy and Quentin and Jason. More, when Nietzsche claims "I'm afraid we are not rid of God because we still have faith in grammar" (*Twilight of the Idols* 483), he draws an explicit analogy between the orderliness of a grammatically coherent narrative and the legitimacy of a divinely sanctioned cosmos.

Along the same lines, Freud's model of consciousness as a battleground for conflicting impulses prepares students for the jaggedness of Faulknerian stream of consciousness in the first two sections of *The Sound and the Fury*. The Freudian model's refusal of future-oriented time, its insistence on returning to the still-entrapping entanglements of the past, serves as a paradigm for the modernist text's refusal of the developmental plot of realism. "There was no hope for him this time," the first story of Joyce's *Dubliners* begins (9). That text joins Faulkner's texts in proposing a modernist interrogation of the labyrinths of the past rather than a realist exploration of the projects of the future.

My students enter *The Sound and the Fury* by way of Proust's "Combray" and Joyce's *Dubliners*. The Proustian text features a narrator (Marcel) lacking both plans for a future and a grasp on the past. The stories of *Dubliners*, even more tellingly, go nowhere, and my students gradually understand that its embattled protagonists are as much imprisoned by their clichéd dreams of escape as they are by their daily routines. Rather than rehearse his culture's feasible projects, Joyce dissects his culture's paralysis—its ways of unintentionally training its adherents to fail through what they aspire to as much as through what they submit to. In this he perfectly prepares a reading of *The Sound and the Fury*. There, too, the stories that the Old South licenses are already foredoomed. Different though the brothers may be, Benjy, Quentin, and Jason share an incapacity either to activate the South's older convictions or to make good on its shabby substitutions for them. No one in that text manages to fulfill a culturally approved project. Failure, Faulkner never tires of repeating, is the ground note of *The Sound and the Fury*. (An exploration of the cunning uses to which he puts failure in the novel may be found in my *Faulkner's Subject* 156–62.)

In Benjy and Quentin character emerges as a mosaic made up of echoes and insistences. Rather than use the lucid coherence of realistic characterization, Faulkner chooses to represent Quentin's consciousness as follows:

> Because it means less to women, Father said. He said it was men invented virginity not women. Father said it's like death: only a state in which the others are left and I said, But to believe it doesn't matter and he said, That's what's so sad about anything: not only virginity and I said, Why couldn't it have been me and not her who is unvirgin and he said, That's why that's sad too; nothing is even worth the changing of it, and Shreve said if he's got better sense than to chase after the little dirty sluts and I said Did you ever have a sister? Did you? Did you?   (78)

Quentin's head is filled to bursting with such contradictory utterances, here of his father and his roommate, elsewhere of his mother, his sister, Dalton Ames, Herbert Head, and others. Instead of being a coherent self-with-purposes summarized by a trustworthy narrator, the character of Quentin is produced as the repository of cryptic thoughts that moment by moment assault his mind. His life endures a day, not a lifetime. Of course, Faulkner did not invent Quentin out of whole cloth. Joyce's Stephen Dedalus, alien in his own culture, too self-conscious to adopt its licensed roles, is already there, waiting for Faulkner to rewrite him. Even more, in *Ulysses* Faulkner found to hand not only the character of Stephen but also the most powerful mode of producing him: stream of consciousness. Stephen in Joyce's *Portrait of the Artist as a Young Man*, still invested in the developmental plot (becoming an artist), appears to the reader as a figure of increasingly coherent views and desires, whereas Stephen in *Ulysses*—no longer going anywhere, explored by the text during a single day (6 June 1904)—is an inexhaustible field of competing thoughts, feelings, sensations. The reader witnesses here, as with Faulkner's Quentin, not the strategic behavior of an individual pursuing his goals against the stable backdrop of a larger culture but the dizzying encounter of cultural assertions pulsating microcosmically within a single mind.

Joyce's *Ulysses* served *The Sound and the Fury* in other ways as well, and my students discover these connections during their reading of both texts. Refusing to make peace with its reader, to settle into a sustained contract about how it should be read, *Ulysses* revises its procedures with each new section. Its "verbal, situational, and narrative texture is too polytropic [full of turns] for our customary inertia," as Fritz Senn puts it (41). Likewise, Faulkner changes the readerly contract of *The Sound and the Fury* with each new chapter, reminding the reader that all seeing and knowing is perspectival and refusing to offer any narrator's overview that might reconcile, godlike, the competing biases. As with Braque's or Picasso's cubism, in which a reassuringly unified perspective on the object disappears (leaving the disconcerted viewer with simultaneous and incompatible facets of the "same" object), so Caddy appears as Benjy's mother, Quentin's sister-lover, Jason's sworn enemy—each time shaped to the insistent optic of the male viewing her. There are only Caddys in *The Sound and the Fury*, no Caddy.

Technically, Joyce more than any other modernist writer made possible Faulkner's breakthrough in *The Sound and the Fury*, Faulkner's fourth novel and first thoroughly modernist one. Faulkner can emerge as Faulkner only through the detour of Joyce. Before (as in *Flags in the Dust*), he is still—on balance—a restless regionalist, inserted by his procedures even more than by his themes into the character and plot conventions of twentieth-century American realism and naturalism. (For a range of accounts of Faulkner's development into his modernist phase, students might consult Stonum; Kreiswirth; Bleikasten, *Failure* 1–37; and Matthews, *Play* 3–33.) Joyce enables not only *The Sound and the Fury* but also Faulkner's modernist masterpieces that follow: *As I Lay Dying* (1930), *Light in August* (1932), and *Absalom, Absalom!* (1936). Joyce enables these achievements, but this is only to say that through them Faulkner becomes Faulkner. Their urgency, obsession with race, and Gothic intensity keep these texts from ever being mistaken for Joyce's.

The light Proust sheds on *The Sound and the Fury* is metaphysical, not technical. *Remembrance of Things Past* (1913–27) is modernism's supreme interrogation of time, revealing patiently time's cunning, its ways of fracturing identity into time-entrapped, contingent selves. Proust's novel keeps proposing that over the years we enact different selves, each cued to a forgotten time and place. Marcel's goal is to redeem this unacknowledged multiplicity of selves by unearthing, through involuntary memory and relentless self-analysis, the ignored continuities of subjective desire. Such a multiplicity of selves is what the developmental novel of realism systematically obscures in its insistence on social surfaces: on a common vocabulary, a cultural space shared with others, an accumulating selfhood that adopts social goals as it matures over time. Faulknerian time, in contrast, is very close to Proustian lost time, without Proust's visionary goal of recovering it. Quentin's horrified "temporary" (177)—his anguish that time crushes all values, eats away all commitments—echoes Marcel's thoroughly modernist recognition that time shatters human identity into uncohering fragments.

Indeed, Quentin's suicide receives its fullest gloss in Proust's analysis of the inhuman dynamic of time. Uncannily resembling Quentin in his anguish at the emotional infidelities enforced by time, Marcel speculates on the strangeness with which we outlive ourselves as we abandon earlier relationships and take on new ones:

> And our dread of a future in which we must forgo the sight of faces and the sound of voices which we love and from which today we derive our dearest joy, this dread, far from being dissipated, is intensified, if to the pain of such a privation we feel that there will be added what seems to us now in anticipation more painful still: not to feel it as a pain at all—to remain indifferent; for then our old self would have changed . . . so that it would be in a real sense the death of the self, a death followed, it is true, by resurrection, but in a different self, to the love of which the elements of the old self that are condemned to die cannot bring themselves to aspire. (1: 721–22)

That inhuman dynamic certainly governs the wasteland of Faulkner's text, but it would be an error to see such cultural futility as metaphysically sanctioned (despite Mr. Compson's claim that "no battle is ever won" and that "victory is an illusion of philosophers and fools" [76]). Rather, the resources of a specific culture at a specific moment (the American South of the early twentieth century) have given out, and *The Sound and the Fury* articulates this exhaustion with stunning intelligence: Benjy's idiocy, Quentin's suicide, Jason's self-destroying meanness, both parents' parental incapacity, the daughter and granddaughter's flight from the South. Like Joyce's Ireland and Proust's France, Faulkner's South is incapable of enculturating its young. It will take a later generation of writers and readers (the postmodernists) to discern in what ways this supposedly objective revelation—the modernist attempt at Olympian detachment—is itself steeped in cultural assumptions. (For a shrewdly postmodernist critique of Faulknerian modernism, see Moreland.)

Yet I try to keep the current critical distance from modernism from blinding my students to modernism's remarkable vitality as a set of ideological convictions and aesthetic practices. By refusing the narrative premise of linear time (a liberal commitment to the protagonist's unfolding projects), Faulkner achieves cultural diagnoses of rare power. The two swing scenes, one involving Caddy and Dalton Ames and the other Miss Quentin and the man with the red tie (simultaneous in Benjy's mind but twenty years apart in clock time), are unimaginable in realism, yet they reveal—in small—the cheapening and toughening of an entire culture's sexual attitudes. Likewise, through Benjy's conjoined flashbacks, Faulkner telescopes Damuddy's funeral (1898) with Caddy's wedding (1910), fusing into one imagistic cluster the discovery of death, the advent of sexuality (Caddy's muddy drawers), the defection of the mother (one dead, the other fleeing in marriage), and the larger sense that, for this would-be incestuous family, marriage and funeral are interchangeable rituals of depletion and betrayal.

Realism—faithful to the discrete unfoldings of time—is incapable of such poetic condensation. More, realism refuses to entrust to the relation between reader and text its most precious transactions. Still committed to articulating its insights through the vehicle of plot, realism generates its essential meanings through characters and events. What is achieved in that way is what counts. Modernism, by contrast, visits an often unredeemable social scene yet reserves its finest utopian energies for rewriting the contract between reader and text, permitting (as in the Faulknerian sequences mentioned above) extraordinary recognitions to which the characters themselves remain blind. We as readers must labor hard to put such modernist texts together. In doing so we achieve the coherent vision of social interconnectedness—what in *Absalom, Absalom!* Faulkner calls the "might-have-been" (115)—so painfully lacking at the level of plot and characterization.

Moreover, this vision—precisely because it is forged through the writer's reconfigured relation with the reader, a relation partially freed from complicity with cultural norms as these are embodied in conventional practice—invites my students to do what realism rarely solicits: to glimpse their own insertion within their culture's most intricate arrangements. Relying less on the verisimilitude (the givenness) of the stories that fiction relates, modernism inquires into the array of reasons why a culture tells the stories it tells. *The Sound and the Fury* doesn't just tell the story of Caddy. It shows what is at stake when the Caddy stories of the Compson brothers reveal not Caddy's recognizable picture in the mirror but the constructedness of the mirror itself—indeed, of the overarching patriarchal culture—that keeps insisting on such pictures. By the end of the course, most of my students realize that, for writers to diagnose critically the obviousness of their culture's representations, an unobvious (and at first incoherent) formal procedure may be most effective. They recognize that the difficulty of *The Sound and the Fury* is inseparable from its achievement.

Teaching *The Sound and the Fury* as a Postimpressionist Novel

Panthea Reid

When I teach *The Sound and the Fury*, I offer the students some basic information about Faulkner's life, especially his voracious reading, his 1918 disappointments in love and war, and the static poetry of longing that he wrote between 1917 and 1925. I suggest that his 1925 sojourns in New Orleans and Paris were liberating exposures to new movements in the arts that inspired and invigorated his sudden shift from poet to fiction writer. I distribute a handout (see appendix) and explain the key memories in the Benjy and Quentin sections. We go over these sections almost page by page. Jason's section we consider more quickly, focusing on his finances and on the weave of past and present in his narration. This inductive method enables students to understand the text at its most basic level and offers me the chance to illustrate the interplay of motifs within the fragmented structure. Then I reintroduce biography and introduce art history. I explain that Faulkner's mother, Maud Butler Falkner, was a painter and once admitted that she had "tried too hard to steer [William] into being a sketcher and painter" ("*McCall's* Visits Miss Maud"). Apparently she had good reasons. As a child, Faulkner drew what he could not describe verbally (see Reid 84). As a young man, he drew a number of highly stylized drawings for Ole Miss publications. He also hand-lettered and illustrated an early verse drama and several collections of his poems. But despite his mother's prodding and his considerable artistic gifts, Faulkner felt himself a failure as a painter. His New Orleans friend in 1925, the artist and architect William Spratling, thought Faulkner's drawing "lousy" (Reid 88). And by this time Faulkner conceded, describing Spratling as a man "whose hand has been shaped to brush as mine has (alas!) not" (*William Faulkner: New Orleans* 46). That "alas!" echoes the tone of longing for a lost woman typical of his early poetry.

Shaped for pen rather than for brush, Faulkner's hand nevertheless learned in New Orleans and then in Paris that it could borrow from the brush. In New Orleans, Faulkner often spent afternoons "at the Museum looking at the pictures, and the evenings talking with painters and writers and musicians" (*Thinking* 181). In recurring discussions with his new Bohemian friends, he argued that plot was now passé (Reid 89–90). He objected to linear plot, which moves from problem to complication, along a neat line of rising action to a climactic scene, then to a falling action, and then to a conclusive resolution. Along with other modernists such as Marcel Proust, James Joyce, and Virginia Woolf, Faulkner thought that a design so neat could not embody the fragmentation and uncertainty of a world in which, to quote his Quentin Compson, "all stable things had become shadowy paradoxical" (170).

If linear plotting was no longer expressive of a modernist sensibility, Faulkner recognized that some other organizing principle must shape the novel. When he arrived in Paris in August 1925, he saw at first hand experiments in the visual arts that he had only read or heard about. He lived near the Luxembourg Museum, where he saw the "more or less moderns, like Degas and Manet and Chavannes" (*Selected Letters* 13). At that time the Parisian art world was furious because the Luxembourg and the Louvre Museums had hung so few avantgarde paintings. The newest, most exciting paintings could be seen only in private galleries. Faulkner, whose acquaintances seem to have been mostly visual artists, was aware of and possibly embroiled in this controversy. He went to "a very very modernist exhibition the other day—futurist and vorticist" (*Selected Letters* 13). He was also able to view private collections of Matisse and Picasso (Blotner, *Faulkner* [1984] 160). Unlike the "more or less moderns," these revolutionary artists shattered preconceived notions of representation.

Faulkner's Parisian experience culminated the personal and aesthetic growth he had begun in New Orleans. His writing process changed in ways that are closely associated with the lessons he learned from postimpressionist art. If linear plots were outdated, these paintings showed him that a work of art might be organized by repeating patterns, that wholes might be fragmented or faceted to achieve a new sort of order. They inspired him to structure his great experiments with narrative form, to use pattern rather than plot (Broughton, "Cubist Novel" 58, "Faulkner's Cubist Novels" 82). They also showed him that art might be autonomous, independent of the world as people know it. This exposure in New Orleans and in Paris strongly affected the three novels he wrote between 1925 and 1927. Only with *The Sound and the Fury* (written in 1928, published in 1929), however, did Faulkner create something radically new.

After covering the first three sections of the novel, I summarize for the students this biographical information. Then we view slides of postimpressionist paintings, especially works by Cézanne, Manet, Chavannes, Duchamp, Matisse, Picasso, and Braque. We observe how Cézanne's still lifes allow one to see both the inside and outside of a basket; how his landscapes bring the sky or background into prominence so that background and foreground have equal emphasis; how his late paintings reduce their subject matter to elemental geometric shapes such as triangles and cylinders; and how the technique known as *petites sensations*, whereby small details of, say, leaves or clouds receive as much attention from the artist's brush as do large ones, flattens the canvas and deprivileges conventionally important material.

I use Matisse's still lifes to show how various inside scenes incorporate outside subjects so that neither takes precedence. In *Harmony in Red* (1908), for example, wallpaper and tablecloth repeat the same pattern to create tension between our habit of reading the table and wall on separate planes and the artist's insistence on placing them on a single plane. Matisse's portraits simplify details with elemental brush strokes that express emotion rather than try to achieve lifelikeness. Who is to say, for example, that his 1905 *Portrait de Madame Matisse* (often called *Green Stripe*) is not more lifelike or at least more expressive of feeling than a photograph would be, even though Mme Matisse did not wear a green stripe down the middle of her face?

After Cézanne, cubist artists sought to convey an object from different points of view at once. Duchamp sought as well to convey different time frames simultaneously. His *Nude Descending a Staircase* (1912) illustrates cubist reductions of the female body to basic geometric shapes (without verisimilitude and certainly without the titillation most nudes arouse). It also conveys movement and simultaneity on a flat surface. In *Les demoiselles d'Avignon* (1907) Picasso similarly reduced female nudes to geometric shapes. In their analytical cubist period, Picasso and Braque so fragmented subjects (which they often teasingly named in their titles) that the subject matters became almost unrecognizable. The interest of these paintings lies in the way a motif taken from an object like a violin or vase can be repeated or faceted with almost infinite variations, like the surface of a cut diamond. The artists also pasted commonplace materials (tickets, newsprint, even mirrors) onto their canvases to ask fundamental questions about reality, representation, and the nature of art. For instance, if a subway ticket is pasted onto a canvas, is the ticket more real than the canvas? Do people look at it to see where it might take them or do they contemplate its place in a harmonious design? Does the canvas represent something or is it simply itself?

All these attempts to, in Ezra Pound's phrase, "make it new" insisted that a painting was done with brush and paint on a flat surface. Artists no longer pretended that the canvas was a window looking onto something else. They accepted the physical properties of their medium and demonstrated how their personal visions could create works of art independent of the world people saw as they passed through it. What people see, of course, is never simply objective reality. Twentieth-century scientists and artists alike have discovered how much perceptions are shaped by the observer's sensibilities and assumptions and by the structure of the brain itself.

After showing a series of slides and making these explanations, I ask the students to draw parallels between postimpressionist art and *The Sound and the Fury*. With encouragement, they point out the flattening of past and present in the Benjy, Quentin, and even Jason sections and the way Faulkner flattens both inside and outside reflections in these sections. They can see Faulkner's typographical experiments with punctuation and capitalization as further leveling or flattening. Often some mention the eye in the fourth section as an example of collage technique.

With coaxing, students can usually reflect on the way motifs are repeated or faceted in the novel. They often mention that Benjy and Quentin keep returning to the same recollections. They see how the Compson brothers associate dirt with sex, death with sex, water with sexlessness, trees with sexlessness, and time or some irresistible power with impotence. I encourage them also to see how Faulkner's faceting invites readers to make similar associations as he moves the narrative between Damuddy's death and Caddy's wedding, Benjy's name change and his castration, Quentin's failure and Julio's apparent success as brother-protector, Jason's loss of money and his feeling of impotence, and Mrs. Compson's inability to love and Mr. Compson's inability to inspire. The students see that Herbert Head, Gerald Bland, and Dalton Ames are virtually indistinguishable to Quentin, as womanizers who have no sisters and thus cannot understand protecting a woman's chastity as an imperative. That connection is visually reinforced (in the corrected text) by the lack of paragraphing when Quentin remembers scenes concerning these men.

I also point out that each of the four sections of the novel ends on a minimalist note: Benjy sees bright colors passing in his mind before he sleeps, Quentin paints his cut and brushes his hat before committing suicide, Jason invites "all Beale street and all bedlam [prostitution and insanity] in here" (264) after he leaves, and finally "cornice and façade [flow] smoothly once more from left to right, post and tree, window and doorway and signboard each in its ordered place" (321) so that Benjy no longer bellows in distress. Faulkner facets the four sections to make their ends suggest that life seems, as Macbeth says, but "a tale / Told by an idiot, full of sound and fury, / Signifying nothing" (5.5.26–28).

I then ask students how the fourth section differs from the other three. They note its narrative method, the impersonal voice that describes from the outside (showing graphically what the characters actually look like), the clarification of details that were unclear before, and its linear progression. They also note the different tone in the church scene. I call to their attention the motif of lifting and surmounting that predominates in the beginning description of Dilsey. Then we turn to Faulkner's descriptions of the church and its visiting minister. Both are unimposing, disappointing. (One could even compare the church's flattened and broken exterior to an early cubist painting.) But when the minister speaks, all thoughts of his being undersized or insignificant vanish. He transcends his "shabbiness and insignificance and [makes] it of no moment" (295). And the congregation's members transcend their separateness and their insignificance until "their hearts [are] speaking to one another in chanting measures beyond the need for words" (294).

Among the cubist shatterings, in which all things have become shadowy and paradoxical, this scene, like Dilsey's and Caddy's ability to love, suggests possibilities for human meaning and communion. Mr. Compson's nihilistic words only served to reinforce Quentin's suicidal determination; but had this African American religious experience—or any experience of faith and hope (see *"Are You Walking with Me?"*)—been available, the juxtaposition of this scene with the novel's fragmented structure suggests that other options could have opened for Quentin. Thus Faulkner appears to exhibit the dazzling pyrotechnics of modernist fragmentation partly to suggest, by contrast, the holistic order and meaning the modern age has lost. It may even be worthwhile pondering whether, in the midst of the novel's broken structure, the coherence and clarity of the last section may not affect readers with longing for a bygone age of artistic and communal straightforwardness.

Comparisons between art forms are fraught with danger, particularly when a key term means different things in different media. Words like "depth," "plane," "surface," "thickness," and "color" have fairly precise meanings in the visual arts, whereas in the verbal arts they are used metaphorically, without clear designations. If one falls into the trap of equating the illusion of depth in a painting with depth of characterization in a novel, the comparison says little. I try not to suggest a literal correspondence of technique across different media but instead to illustrate aspects of probable influence of visual and plastic arts on Faulkner's writing. Faulkner's Parisian experience establishes his knowledge of postimpressionist painting. His use of terms like "vortex" and "cubist" confirms his awareness of contemporary artistic movements. His method of composition, as he turned almost exclusively to prose writing in 1925, became a matter of shifting and arranging narrative segments in ways analogous to the procedures of fragmenting and reassembling practiced by cubist painters. Fragmentation came to typify modernism, but Faulkner's peculiar method of cutting and pasting, disassembling and reassembling, developed not when he read Eliot's poetry but, rather, after he had seen Picasso's paintings. Faulkner's ordering of narrative by motif rather than by linear plot could have been derived from either music or painting—though his exposure and interest suggest that painting was the primary source of inspiration and insight. It is clear in any case that examining the interface between method and meaning in the visual arts illuminates that same interface in the verbal arts, and especially in *The Sound and the Fury*.

APPENDIX
GUIDE TO READING
THE SOUND AND THE FURY

The Compson children

Quentin III (1891–1910)
Candace (Caddy) (1892–?): marries Herbert Head, April 1910;
   one daughter, Quentin, born November 1910 (Herbert is not the father)
Jason IV (1893/94–?)
Benjamin (first named Maury) (1895–?)

Compson servants: the Gibson family

Roskus and Dilsey have three children: Versh, Frony, and T. P.
(T. P. is born in 1894.) Versh is Benjy's first nurse, T. P. his second,
Luster his third. Luster is Frony's son, about the age of Miss Quentin.

The four sections of *The Sound and the Fury*

1. Saturday, 7 April 1928: Benjy's point of view
2. Thursday, 2 June 1910: Quentin III's point of view
3. Friday, 6 April 1928: Jason's point of view
4. Sunday, 8 April 1928 (Easter): omniscient narrator

Chronology of scenes recalled and relived by Benjy and Quentin
in sections 1 and 2

SECTION 1

The identity of Benjy's caretaker places events in section 1 from
childhood (Versh), adolescence (T. P.), or the present (Luster).

Events	*Dates*	*Caretakers*
Damuddy's death; getting wet at the branch; taking off the dress, the muddy drawers, the pear tree; Quentin sulking, trouble between Quentin and Versh	1898	Versh
Benjy's name changed; rain on the roof, firelight reflected on satin cushion; Quentin has been fighting	1900 (Nov.)	Versh
Uncle Maury–Mrs. Patterson affair; two messages delivered, one by Benjy and Caddy, 23 December, after Benjy was waiting for Caddy at the gate, one in the spring by Benjy and Versh (?); Uncle Maury appears with black eye; affair ends	1900–01? (Dec.–?)	Versh

Chronology of scenes (*cont.*)

Events	Dates	Caretakers
Caddy in swing with Charlie	1906	Versh, T. P.
Caddy uses perfume	1906	T. P.
Benjy, now 13, must sleep alone	1908	T. P.
Caddy's loss of virginity; Benjy's knowing	1909 (Aug.?)	T. P.
Caddy's wedding, Benjy and T. P. drunk	1910 (24 Apr.)	T. P.
Benjy attacks Burgess girl; is castrated	1910 (Apr.–May)	T. P.
Quentin III commits suicide	1910 (2 June)	T. P.
Mr. Compson dies; Dan (dog) howls; trips to cemetery begin (every Saturday?)	1912	T. P.
Roskus dies; Luster sees his ghost; Blue howls	?	Luster
Golfers, the lost quarter, new carriage wheel, Benjy's birthday, Miss Quentin on swing with "man with the red tie" (the present)	1928 (7 Apr.)	Luster

SECTION 2

Events	Dates
Damuddy's death	1898
Benjy's name changed	1900
Natalie scene	1906?
Caddy kisses a boy	1907
Caddy's loss of virginity to Dalton Ames; Quentin tries to get her to say that Ames made her submit; she tries to get Quentin to understand her passion; scene with knife	1909 (Aug.?)
Quentin's conversation with Father about virginity; assertion that he has committed incest; Father's nihilistic replies	next day
Quentin tries to run Dalton Ames out of town; Caddy sends Ames away thinking he has shot Quentin	3 days later

Chronology of scenes (*cont.*)

Events	*Dates*
Caddy becomes scandalously promiscuous; Mrs. Compson sends Jason to spy on her	fall 1909
Mrs. Compson takes Caddy on vacation to escape rumors and find her a husband; Quentin thinks of their trunks as coffins; Caddy meets Herbert Head at French Lick	1910 (Feb. or Mar.?)
Wedding preliminaries—the car ride, dialogue about Harvard and Herbert's attempt to bribe Quentin regarding cheating; Quentin fantasizes about shooting Herbert; Quentin tries to dissuade Caddy from marrying Herbert	1910 (Apr. 22–23)
The wedding	1910 (24 Apr.)
Wedding announcement printed; Quentin receives announcement near end of his first year at Harvard	1910 (May)
Quentin's preparations for suicide—killing time, the letters, the trunk, arrangements with Deacon, buying flatirons, boys on bridge, Italian girl, picnic with Blands, fight with Gerald; recollections of previous events (conversations with Father, etc.) become frenzied; final manic preparations for suicide	1910 (2 June)

Text and Context: Teaching
The Sound and the Fury after Deconstruction
John T. Matthews

The Sound and the Fury is not a very difficult novel to teach. But it is a very difficult novel to learn. Enticed by the thematic, stylistic, and technical riches of what was Faulkner's own favorite novel, braced by a critical literature appealing to all tastes, and confident in the author's influence on writers around the globe, any well-prepared teacher may be forgiven for overteaching *The Sound and the Fury*. What I try to recall when I teach this work, whose complexities I have struggled to solve in the classroom and on the page for nearly twenty years, is the thrill of the outraged amazement that the first page produces in the first-time reader. I envy my students that surprise—with the labor it will demand—and I tell them so. Sometimes they come to believe me.

I begin with the premise that Faulkner sets out to devastate his reader. Yet his modernist virtuosity amounts to more than a refreshment of aesthetic fashion; the difficult novelty posed by him, like that of Eliot, Pound, Joyce, Picasso, Braque, Stravinsky, or Schoenberg, responds to major transformations of Western society that took place in the period around World War I. Deconstruction has helped me direct students to rhetorical contradictions and silences in a text. The method is especially suitable—as Derrida's homage to Mallarmé makes clear—to works of modernism. Seen as modernism's family resemblance, these textual features suggest reading the work for its efforts to manage turbulent cultural and social contexts.

I teach *The Sound and the Fury* regularly in an advanced undergraduate course on the modern American novel. Beginning graduate students may take the course for credit, but nearly all forty-five to sixty students each semester are juniors or seniors, with never more than half of them majoring in English. (*The Sound and the Fury* is not the best Faulkner novel to teach in courses that are more introductory. For a lower-level fiction course I prefer *As I Lay Dying* because of its manageable structure and length, fidelity to plot, humor, yet genuine Faulknerian subject matter and style; for an introductory course in American literature, I usually choose *Go Down, Moses* because of its more explicit historical concerns. Knowing when not to teach *The Sound and the Fury* is one key to teaching Faulkner successfully; I've had lots of students who weren't ready for it when it was assigned to them in high school or the first year of college.) Normally I run The Modern American Novel as a mix of short lectures and classroom discussion. The early sessions on *The Sound and the Fury*, however, invariably go a little differently.

As with all the literature I teach, I try to practice my conviction that what matters in classroom interpretation is the perceptions and (especially) the language of the students. With *The Sound and the Fury* I have trained myself to let confusion, frustration, and irritation build if they will. In our first session, I usually don't have a chance even to begin a formal presentation on the novel before questions boil over. I keep track of them on the chalkboard, being careful to preserve key words supplied by students. If I can, I arrange points by broad categories (but without so designating them): technique, theme, style, et cetera. In the first hour we may do little more than identify obstacles Faulkner puts in the reader's way in the first—possibly interminable!—section of the novel: more than one character having the same name, the abrupt shifts in time and space, the simple yet puzzling syntax, the nondescriptive style.

Rather than provide even preliminary explanations, I try to intensify the readerly vertigo Faulkner induces by asking for examples of especially problematic moments or techniques. I spend a lot of time drawing from the students precise ways to describe what confuses them in the passages at hand, still resisting the temptation to interpret and connect. If someone refers to the first page, I normally don't explain (away) the play on "caddie," for example, since that would require me to name Benjy's problem as his sorrow over his missing sister, to detail the family relations, to fill in the Compson history that resulted in the sale of the pasture, and so on. Teachers must avoid serving as Faulkner's 1946 appendix, which was designed originally to introduce the novel when it was reprinted in the Viking *Portable Faulkner* but which was then expanded into a continuing narrative in a postface to a subsequent edition of the novel. We concentrate on what the novel itself looks at (and what it does not), how it describes its world (concretely, sensually, not abstractly), and what types of disturbances are created by the form and arrangement of the sentences. What does "hitting little" mean when Benjy describes the golfers (3)? Does it mean that they are far away (little hitters), or does it mean, as one of my students suggested, that they are putting (little hits)?

Students must try to generalize naively. Benjy seems to remember scenes of discomfort, scenes often associated with the sensation of loss or absence. What are the common elements in them? What triggers the move from one to another? If the narrative does not proceed chronologically, what are the principles of its organization? Benjy's world impinges on his consciousness in certain distinctive registers. Touch, sound, smell, and sight matter to him almost equally. Why? How do sensory images combine to create repeated moods or patterns of feeling? What powers of reasoning or abstraction does Benjy display? If those powers are absent, what takes their place? How do Benjy's flat, simple sentences, shorn of most modifiers, express his situation? Is it accurate to call this a first-person narration? Where and when does the narration take place? Or are we in some artificial zone of intersected narration? Is Benjy innocent author or Faulkner's ventriloquized dummy? How might Benjy's section be taken as a radical effort to unmask the distortions produced by conventional realist narration: the assumption that the author knows and can render the mental states of the characters; the conviction that the language of social interaction is the same as one's private language of sensations, associations, and memories; the confidence that linear plot reflects the linearity of real time?

After thorough discussion of such problems as problems, the class begins to shape answers for Benjy's section. I try to make the students do the work of connecting observations about content to observations about form: that Benjy's inability to reason, for example, produces a world (and a writing) organized by mnemonics and a syntax of contiguity and association. I point to the first time Benjy gets stuck on the nail as he climbs under the fence to the neighboring Pattersons' place (4) as the reader's initiation into the procedures of time travel through spatial memories. It is through "the broken place"—a gate, a hinge, a snare, a gap—that the reader finds her or his way into and around the text. All the issues we identify in Benjy's section carry us through the remaining three sections of the novel. Students pick up on Quentin's preoccupation with Caddy as a symbol, on his linguistic strategies for expressing and dodging his problems, on Faulkner's experimental depiction of consciousness, and so forth, once they have come to trust the novel's ability to teach them how to read it.

In the classes on the first two sections particularly, I invite questions about things we haven't touched on, especially details that don't make sense even within the patterns we have established. This is a little like facing a firing squad, I admit, but it does allow me to help students distinguish between what they simply need to know ("Agnes Mabel Becky" refers to the Merry Widows on a pack of condoms; that wire coming across Benjy's shoulder is the rod that opens the oven door, etc.), what they should figure out (Quentin's incest is a lie; gasoline gives Jason a headache), and what no one knows or I can't recall (who is Luster's father?). These occasions may require more humility than a teacher can comfortably muster, but students are emboldened by the realization that they don't need to dispel every confusion in order to grasp this novel quite well.

Once students gain confidence that they can read the novel from section to section by looking for the novel's overt (if at first incoherent) preoccupations, it is time to reverse the direction. *The Sound and the Fury* teaches the patient reader how to suffer the passage into social identity—that is, the formation of oneself as a subject at the price of an at least remembered oneness with the maternalized world. To the extent that the novel is organized around cultural processes that fuse selfhood, language, and loss, the reader may see the various crises of each section as different takes on a few problems—Quentin's phobias about sexuality and mortality in a world no longer founded on "stable things" (170); Jason's fears of becoming an impotent, displaced authority; Dilsey's efforts to carve out a present dignity and future betterment under a social regime designed to oppress her.

In other words, if the style challenges representational realism, it may also be seen as motivated by Faulkner's interest in how social realities in the modern South were being challenged. Like the style of Gertrude Stein's "Melanctha" (in *Three Lives*), Faulkner's style struggles to convey the language sphere that demarcates social identity. It stresses the way both the individual's and the society's linguistic possibilities structure reality—from Benjy's nondiscriminatory innocence to Jason's bigoted paranoia. The flexibility of the novel's voice from section to section aims at psychologically realistic effects; it tells the truth of consciousness rather than the truth of the shared outward world of action and revelation. The reader begins to appreciate the interpenetration of social and private language, of convention and immediacy. Even Benjy's innocence is a product of ways of speaking, memories, cultural history. The characters' having the same name might lead the class to a discussion of developments in modern philosophy or physics, developments that have destabilized the unities of time and space. Moreover, the ambiguity produced by male and female characters sharing names, when set in the context of Quentin's preoccupation with proper masculine and feminine behavior, makes sense as a marker of alterations in gender roles in modern American society.

To get at the contexts suggested by all that is left out of the text of *The Sound and the Fury*, one needs to subject the novel to a kind of reading between the lines. I describe this process to my students as "reading against the grain" (after Terry Eagleton). It is the strategy of looking for moments when broader social and historical material may be glimpsed beyond this deliberately myopic narrative. Given the deformation of fundamental social and economic absolutes in the decades bracketing World War I, *The Sound and the Fury* compels the reader to experience the bewildering upheavals of authority and identity suffered by the dominant classes. What do the novel's four fixated sections neglect? Students today will not accept Faulkner's explanation why a novel devoted to the absent nurturing female never permits her to tell her own story. She was, Faulkner remarked, "too beautiful" to "reduce her to telling" (Gwynn and Blotner 3). Students, after they have gauged Jason's character, may appreciate how Quentin's exaltation of feminine purity complements his brother's misogyny—as flip sides of Western habits of objectifying woman as a symbol of cultural needs (truth, virtue; falsehood, evil).

The Compson brothers try to ensure Caddy's and Miss Quentin's immobility. But the disruptive rebellions of mother and daughter (not to mention Mrs. Compson's exercise in noncompliance through hypochondria) point to the upheaval of gender relations in America around World War I. Birth control, new household technology, job opportunities during the war, women's suffragism (leading to their enfranchisement in 1920), and the southern abandonment of agrarian patriarchalism compose the background for Quentin's vague sense that all he's known has grown "shadowy paradoxical" (170). For this small-town Hamlet and his brother, the time is out of joint. A string of seemingly isolated remarks brings women's insubordination to the surface: Caddy's insistence on her own desire (92); her control of her passion (151); her accusation of Jason's lying (205–06) and her daughter's denunciation of his thieving (213); the contradiction of the values of virginity and maternity (102–04, 199); the need for Miss Quentin to lie, forge, and play out her longing for freedom (184); the oddly feminized yet impersonal room the youngest Compson inhabits (282). But the novel's minor key of race relations in the South, so expected a part of any work set in Mississippi in the first quarter of the twentieth century, is heard

only in off moments in the first three sections. Dilsey's tearful acceptance of
her lot marks a silence in the narratives of suffering. Like Caddy, she does not
tell her own story. Most of the African Americans in the novel have outsmarted
their white superiors—from Deacon's fleecing of his Harvard charges to Luster's comic service to his idiot master. They are poised to inherit a greater por-
tion of the modern South.

By forcing the novel away from its own terms (moaning, missing, incest,
love, pride, endurance), a reader may unearth what its narrators seek to repress
(inequality, authority, exploitation, history). The silencing of race can be observed when Quentin's memory of daydreaming in class interrupts two ex-
changes with blacks (86–89); in his many passing remarks about "niggers" as
lazy, comforting, stupid, sly, or immoral (86, 89, 92); and in Jason's even cruder
bigotry (189, 191, 231). Of course, one must be careful not to reduce so capa-
cious a fiction to an allegory of liberal democratic verities. Today's students
must be helped to see both that the novel is not prejudiced in ways leading to
simple-minded dismissal by political orthodoxies (since it works to show the
production and effects of its world's ideologies), and that it does not wholly
transcend its historical moment (any more than does any other work), although
like other classic texts it exhibits those questions and possibilities that enlarge
our thinking in categories felt to be universal.

Reading *The Sound and the Fury* with the grain psychologically but against
it historically, with the grain stylistically but against it mimetically, with the
grain of its voices but against them semantically—such reading constitutes a
deconstructive rendering of the text. The reader's inability to close the gap between interpretations makes the most of modernist difficulties. Theories that
describe modernism's repression of historical material are useful in understanding the novel's personalization of crisis. (In lectures introducing the
course, I rely on Andreas Huyssen's list of modernist attributes [in *After the
Great Divide*] and Fredric Jameson's hypothesis about the ideology of modernist form [in *The Political Unconscious*].) Derridean deconstruction teaches
readers to read for repressed power relations in binarisms. An awareness of
historical context enables readers to map such textual formations onto the social field that attracts an individual work's repressions. As readers vainly try to
cover figure and ground in the novel simultaneously, they may come to appreciate Faulkner's accomplishment in letting them experience the way aesthetic
expression attempts to solve or mediate social contradictions.

Since I usually teach other modern fiction with *The Sound and the Fury*, I
construct a representative literary context. I acknowledge the familiar orbits of
"high modernism" (using, say, Stein and early Hemingway as examples), but I've
also taken to questioning the dominance of this strain of modernism in received
literary history. If one pairs *The Sound and the Fury* with Tate's *The Fathers* or
with Hurston's *Their Eyes Were Watching God*, one can discern different inno-
vative approaches to changing mores and customs. Tate's nostalgia recondi-
tions southern plantocracy's paternalism by converting it from outdated economic

practices to renovated social and cultural forms. Janie Crawford's famous sexual awakening under the apple tree in Hurston's novel provides a productive contrast to Quentin's recollection of Caddy climbing a pear tree to see Damuddy's funeral. Autonomous eroticism versus the fear of pollution; sustained mounting significance versus fragmentary denial; fertility versus morality; and a black woman's subjectivity versus that of a white male—all these dichotomies set *The Sound and the Fury* within such other traditions or movements of the period as the Harlem Renaissance and the Southern Renaissance.

By moving between text and context, readers can draw on recent developments in critical methodology. *The Sound and the Fury* illustrates today's possibilities for a cultural criticism that has absorbed the countermetaphysical practice of deconstruction. Both Gregory Ulmer (in *Applied Grammatology*) and Patrick Brantlinger (in *Crusoe's Footprints*) have outlined projects in cultural studies emerging from a poststructuralist renovation of the study between base and superstructure, artwork and society, subject and genre, and so on. Whether or not teachers acknowledge the theoretical revolution in our teaching practices, we miss a genuine opportunity if—in a time when passive culture consumption is the norm—we fail to allow a book like *The Sound and the Fury* to produce all the disseminative, playful, puzzling, devastating effects of which it is capable.

"Barn Burning" and *The Sound and the Fury* as an Introduction to Faulknerian Style and Themes

Gail L. Mortimer

William Faulkner's "Barn Burning" is an excellent text for helping students learn how to read his often elusive prose. I usually have them read the short story before *The Sound and the Fury* because the experience gives them confidence in approaching the more formidable and longer text. Moreover, when a specific course allows only the briefest introduction to Faulkner's world, this story in itself can serve as a paradigmatic text. It is representative because it contains several basic Faulknerian concerns; at the same time, it is accessible because most students, recalling their childhood, can understand the confusion and divided loyalty of the story's protagonist, Sarty Snopes.

In their initial reading, students at times have difficulty understanding what takes place in "Barn Burning" because of its frequent narrative shifts between present and past (in the form of memories or summaries) and between Sarty's interior reactions and level of comprehension and the perspective of the omniscient narrator. By clarifying how and when the point of view shifts, an instructor can help students see the logic of Faulkner's narrative decisions, a logic that is central to the three Compson brothers' sections of *The Sound and the Fury*. These shifts in the story, as in the novel, are readily understood when one points out that they are triggered by specific events whose relevance to Sarty the narrator takes care to make evident. Faulkner uses them to show how Sarty's interpretations are based on his experiences with his father, Abner, experiences such as their appearances before a justice of the peace. Through the narrator Faulkner also provides facts (such as Abner's theft of Confederate horses during the Civil War) that Sarty has no way of knowing. The use of italics to signal Sarty's thoughts and hopes as they coexist alongside his perceptions of what is taking place is typical of Faulkner. Understanding the function of typography here prepares students to understand the juxtapositions based on free association so crucial to both Benjy's and Quentin's sections of *The Sound and the Fury*. Similarly, Sarty's turmoil (reflected in the urgency of his thinking) prepares students to grasp the psychological implications of the accelerating fluidity of language in Quentin's interior monologue.

Faulkner uses the pronoun "he" ambiguously throughout the story, and this confusing of Sarty and Abner contributes to students' bewilderment. I tell them that the ambiguity is deliberate, intended to express Faulkner's sense of how irrevocably people are entangled in the history of their families, so that sometimes they seem to have lived through the events of earlier generations. The pronoun confusion helps convey the idea that various experiences and perspectives are passed from father to son, from Abner to Sarty, in this tale that chronicles a boy's struggle to free himself from precisely the paternal worldview. The difficulty of extricating oneself from family legacies of guilt and distortion is, of course, basic to *The Sound and the Fury*, and it is signaled in the novel by the use of the names Jason and Quentin for more than one character. Caddy escapes the Compson home only at a terrible emotional cost, Quentin does so only through suicide, and Jason, who does not escape, succumbs to a bitter self-destructiveness.

Beyond clarifying what is taking place and how Faulkner structures the sequence of events in "Barn Burning," I take care to show why he chooses the narrative strategies he does. For example, he prepares the reader to understand simultaneously two aspects of Sarty's experience. First, by repeated references to Sarty's immediate experience of sounds and smells and of the fact that he cannot see either literally or figuratively what is happening around him, Faulkner establishes Sarty's immersion in the bitter perspective of his father, who divides the entire world into us and them. There is kindness in the judge's face and justice in the minds of the onlookers, but Sarty has yet to know that such things exist. Sarty's perceptual limitations set the stage for Faulkner's depiction of events whose convergence will bring about the boy's sudden understanding of a world with different values from those of his father. The employment here of a traditional third-person narrator focusing closely on Sarty, interspersed with direct glimpses of his thoughts, prepares students for the perceptual and conceptual limitations that are implicit in the first-person narratives of *The Sound and the Fury*, particularly Benjy's section, where color, sound, and smell are so closely associated with Benjy's feelings of comfort or dismay.

The second aspect of Sarty's experience that Faulkner highlights is his future, which the narrator repeatedly foreshadows by suggesting that although Sarty does not understand a particular event now, he will. "[T]wenty years later" he will remember and recognize, for example, that de Spain "wanted only truth, justice" ("Barn" 8). This strategy of referring to Sarty's future comprehension of events in his present childhood prepares the reader to accept Sarty's departure at the end of the story as admirable. His leaving his family is the act that confirms his new moral stature.

The events of the story, then, are temporally situated between the limited knowledge of Sarty's youth, emphasized in the opening scenes, and the indications of his later maturity, shown as being initiated by these very events. Two specific incidents—two vividly experienced disjunctions—trigger Sarty's crisis of awareness and lead him beyond his circumscribed understanding. His father strikes him and then (for the first time) gives an explanation for the blow in his "calm, outrageous voice" (9). The reason Abner offers, however, does not correspond in the least with Sarty's perception of what has happened. Shortly thereafter, father and son first see the de Spain mansion, and while Sarty feels awe and admiration, Abner reacts with surprising anger and bitterness, which jolts Sarty into the suspicion that his father's way of seeing may be distorted. The italicized passages record Sarty's private thoughts, including his hopes that his father will change: "*Maybe* [seeing the mansion] *will even change him now from what maybe he couldn't help but be*" (11). But Abner's deliberate defacement of the white rug in the de Spain entrance hall and his fury at the insult he finds in the very existence of de Spain's prosperity make Sarty's hopes poignantly irrelevant.

"Barn Burning" provides Faulkner with an occasion to foreground several of his basic concerns. Like many other American writers, he is particularly interested in the relation between childhood innocence and adult values, in that moment in a child's life when a choice is made to become a particular kind of human being. Sarty's consideration of the values he sees in the adults around him allows Faulkner to ponder the possibilities that exist before children are absorbed (apparently once and for all) into some configuration of adult values. Clear throughout the story is Faulkner's esteem for the dignity, honesty, and integrity represented by de Spain, shown in striking contrast to their absence in the figure of Abner Snopes. Sarty struggles to deny this disparity, trying until the very end of the story to think of his father in terms of such values as bravery. Like so many other sons in Faulkner's fiction, he struggles with the identity prescribed for him by his father. The story thus prepares the students for the dilemmas of Quentin Compson in *The Sound and the Fury* as he tries to extricate himself from his father's nihilism, of Caddy as she rebels against the stultifying myths her family perpetuates for its women, and of the younger Jason as he is hopelessly entangled, quite apart from his own angry penchant for evil, in the frantic mythologizing of his mother.

Teaching "Barn Burning" introduces students to the dichotomous values attributed in Faulkner's world to the aristocratic families and to such families as the Snopeses. Abner Snopes's lack of higher principles, his utter self-centeredness, can lead to a class discussion of the ethical qualities Faulkner most admired—

courage, honesty, integrity. Faulkner nostalgically ascribes these qualities to various members of his fictional aristocratic families, although not exclusively to them. Faulkner gives the virtues of honesty and industry to Byron Bunch in *Light in August* and Cash Bundren in *As I Lay Dying* and the virtues of compassion and fidelity to Dilsey in *The Sound and the Fury*. The relentless amorality of many of the Snopeses, however, remains associated with a rootless, inhumane, and at times rapacious way of living that Faulkner sees as characteristic of the twentieth century and that he persistently deplores.

Yet it is crucial to note that despite Abner's villainy and de Spain's virtue in "Barn Burning," Faulkner in most of his work shows himself well aware of the ambiguous nature of those traits the South had long associated with antebellum life and tended to see now as surviving only in the remnant aristocratic families of the new South. Faulkner provides contradictory versions of Civil War heroism, depicting in *Flags in the Dust*, for example, a moment of bravery both as an example of courage and as an instance of adolescent folly. And his treatment of once aristocratic families in the early twentieth century characteristically emphasizes their decadence. In *The Sound and the Fury*, the Compson family degenerates into feeblemindedness, suicide, and neurosis. Faulkner's honesty in detailing both sides of his ambivalence toward the past—his nostalgia for the Old South and for the values it claimed to embody and his recognition, at the same time, of the self-deception of its memories of former glory—is one of his strengths as a writer. Class differences are much more than a sociological phenomenon in Faulkner's South; they are the basis of an ethical discourse.

As events in "Barn Burning" transpire, the foreshadowing offered by the omniscient narrator prepares the reader to accept Faulkner's moral interpretation of the end of the story, Sarty's abandonment of his family. The reader is shown that Sarty will turn out to be the sort of honorable human being Faulkner admires, one who believes in and acts on ideas of justice and honesty. After he hears the gunshots, Sarty mourns openly for all he had wanted to believe his father was: ". . . the grief and despair now no longer terror and fear but just grief and despair. *Father. My father*, he thought. 'He was brave . . . he was! He was in the war!'" (24). The story's final paragraph, however, immediately following this passage, implies that everything will turn out well, that Sarty's decision was the right one. The image of a lonely child on a dark road is accompanied by suggestions of the difficulties Sarty will face, but each of them is quickly softened by narrative commentary:

> It would be dawn and then sun-up after a while and he would be hungry. But that would be to-morrow and now he was only cold, and walking would cure that. . . . He got up. He was a little stiff, but walking would cure that too as it would the cold, and soon there would be the sun. (25)

At the same time, Sarty is surrounded by the "silver voices" of birds, voices that make up "the urgent and quiring heart of the late spring night" (25). He has been welcomed into the harmonies of nature, into a serenity that is the antithesis of the tension and fear he has felt so long within his family.

To ensure that the reader does not condemn Sarty's departure, Faulkner has the narrator describe the women of the family, for whom the reader might otherwise have felt sympathy, as near caricatures, both bovine and ineffectual. When I teach this story in the context of other American short stories, I ask my students to notice that the ending is somewhat atypical, since writers tend to emphasize the difficulties or complexities of breaking free of one's family. I argue that an ending like this is virtually never to be found in the work of women writers, whose protagonists, even if they succeed in physically removing themselves from family entanglements and even if their departure is objectively justified, remain ambivalent, guilty, and torn about having left. I refer to other writers whose work features young protagonists and the initiation theme (Katherine Anne Porter, for one) and suggest that the students keep the following questions in mind as they explore other stories: How does the factor of gender affect an author's valuation of the autonomy sought by a character? Are there gender differences in authors' perceptions of the nature of adventure? How do various authors depict the families from which characters work to free themselves? What are the results for characters of attempting such a break?

Since in many of his texts Faulkner writes about the difficulty of freeing oneself from one's family, "Barn Burning" constitutes a fascinating exception. Moreover, when students realize that the author himself felt heavily burdened by family responsibilities and longed at times to abandon them, Sarty's story begins to seem like wish fulfillment. After all, Faulkner once said (somewhat notoriously) that he knew why there would always be war: "[I]t's the only condition under which a man who is not a scoundrel can escape for a while from his female kin" (Blotner, *Faulkner* [1974] 2: 1106). Textual fantasies of successful separation seem plausible only for male protagonists, possibly because with female protagonists such stories would strain belief. American culture, indeed, never condones what it sees as a woman's abandonment of family, whereas male autonomy may be justified on a variety of grounds. Yet American culture has always embraced the freeing of the individual from familial claims that lies at the heart of such tales as Washington Irving's "Rip Van Winkle" and Nathaniel Hawthorne's "Wakefield," as well as that paradigmatic American text *Adventures of Huckleberry Finn*. The favorable terms in which Faulkner couches Sarty's striking out on his own may be compensatory (given the realities of Faulkner's own family life), but the story is nevertheless plausible and it provides an opportunity to consider why particular types of plot may be associated with gender and, ultimately, with the expectations that American culture has long placed on its men and women.

While my strategies for teaching Faulkner's story (and all his work) begin with careful, close analysis and show students that there are sound reasons for his authorial decisions, I try to address the thematic issues with which he is concerned in ways that emphasize not only his unique treatment of them but also the implications about class, region, and gender that constitute threads linking his issues to all the American fiction students read. I attempt both to prepare students to tackle Faulkner's larger works and to understand how his concerns remain deeply connected with the realities of American culture.

Caddy and Nancy: Race, Gender, and Personal Identity in "That Evening Sun" and *The Sound and the Fury*

Louise K. Barnett

When I teach "That Evening Sun" with *The Sound and the Fury*, it is easy enough to get a class to discuss similarities between the characters of the short story and the novel. But if the categories of race, gender, and personal identity are brought into the discussion, more telling insights about the characters and about the larger implications of their behavior are apt to emerge. At every point in the examination of the two texts, a discussion of representations of race, gender, and sexual behavior and their relevance to social status is not only appropriate but often crucial to understanding. While my essay is necessarily restricted to this topic, I should say that class discussion ordinarily includes a great many other matters as well. My guiding principle in teaching any text is to suggest possibilities but not enforce a reading. The most successful teaching, for me, consists in encouraging students to think for themselves—and applauding their efforts when they make a strong case for a point of view.

To introduce the idea of a gender paradigm—a heuristic model for understanding representations of social behavior—in the discussion of both novel and short story, I begin with the Mississippi novelist Ellen Douglas's provocative assertion that "for women circumstances are always the same, always sexual. Women can impinge on the world and on men only through their sexuality" (163). This premise helps us draw together the superficially dissimilar characters of Caddy and Nancy, providing a critical link between the two texts. Approaching these characters through an analysis of gender roles leads students to realize that the child Caddy in "That Evening Sun" becomes, in the novel, the woman who is both promiscuous and pregnant with a child of uncertain paternity, like the black woman of the short story (Slabey 179). I also invite students to compare Quentin and Caddy in "That Evening Sun." They notice that while Quentin narrates the events of the story dispassionately, giving readers a seemingly neutral presentation of what happens, Caddy asks probing questions, and her questions have a particularly female dimension. Students can relate her curiosity to the world that Faulkner associates with women: matters of birth, sexuality, death —the life cycle of the natural being, the terrain on which Caddy's own life must be lived. Discussing the two texts with this particular focus opens up numerous topics that students can productively pursue. First of all, the lesson that the story contains—the attempts of the children to make meaning—can serve as a basic investigative technique for the class. Do Caddy and Quentin, or for that matter the story's adults, ask the right questions? And what are the answers?

Evaluating the questions asked in the short story provides a way of differentiating Caddy from other characters. Only Caddy "asks the right questions"

(Reed 32), that is, the questions that probe fundamental issues of human relationship. Jason, in keeping with his age, tends to ask obvious questions that require yes-or-no answers. Quentin asks only two questions ("That Evening Sun"
293, 309); as the narrator, he presents what happens more than he speculates
on it. Pursuing this investigation, I ask the class to consider how Caddy's questions in "That Evening Sun" relate not only to the truth of situations in the text
but also to the story of her adult life in *The Sound and the Fury*. The action behind "What have you done that made Jesus mad?" (300), for example, is the
very thing that Caddy herself will do, with the same result of making her husband mad. Caddy's questioning of the unlikely juxtaposition of the queen with
the unregal setting of the ditch in Nancy's story reverberates ironically with her
own later history as a woman of the respectable class who behaves "like a nigger wench" (*Sound* 189), a pattern that will be repeated by her daughter. Finally, the ditch is a literal and metaphoric space that dissolves social status and
other distinctions in its darkness and natural fecundity. Students might be re-
minded that when Jason pursues his niece and her boyfriend in *The Sound and
the Fury*, he encounters "a ditch full of briers" that become "thicker and
thicker" until he loses his sense of direction (240).

By examining such connections between texts, the class comes to understand how the text itself reflects Caddy's concerns through its multiple perspectives on identity. Students must pose and answer questions of identity
raised by the story: what it means to be black or white, male or female. These
critical distinctions connect the short story to the novel, where Caddy will
struggle to assert herself and to escape Nancy's hopelessness. Whether the
common destiny or definition of women is determinative in spite of the differences of class and race that separate Nancy and Caddy should be left to the
class to decide. There will be no dearth of opinions, since students—still defining themselves and their place in the world—consider these matters significant
both in and out of literary texts. In some fashion most students already understand that in a hierarchical society based on sharply differentiated roles the
placing of people according to race and sex is profoundly consequential. And
while such large issues sometimes make it difficult to keep the discussion focused, the time is well spent in allowing students to contribute examples of
their own that illuminate the characters' experiences.

When I ask students for their reactions to Nancy's iteration that she "aint
nothing but a nigger" ("That Evening Sun" 297), we are usually able to move
from the obvious personal level, where the statement functions as an apology
or excuse, to the broader explanation of what courses of action are open or
closed to Nancy because she is black. A similar process is at work with Jason's
counterpart refrain, "I aint a nigger" (297). Students can readily perceive a
number of meaningful differences between the two characters. As a white
child, Jason is safe from both Nancy's fear and Nancy's reality. Whether or not
Jesus will come to kill her, Nancy has a legitimate basis for her fear, whereas
Jason is afraid of Halloween phantoms. And, as a white male, he automatically

inherits a position of privilege that keeps both Nancy's fear and Jesus's frustration at a distance. Hence his being "scairder than a nigger" (309), as Caddy maintains, can be seen as a measure of his failure to live up to the expectations of white male identity.

The way the white males in the story exhibit institutionally authorized power, a power that the black males explicitly lack and that is repeatedly associated with the mistreatment of women, is one of the key discoveries of class discussion. Mr. Stovall, whose respectability is overdetermined by association with both church and bank, is always identified as the most flagrant example. He exploits Nancy— using her sexually, then abusing her financially and physically—without any negative consequences to himself. I typically need to draw the class's attention to a minor figure who is part of this paradigm, the mysterious and ironically named Mr. Lovelady, who may be implicated in a sinister way in the suicide of his wife and disappearance of his daughter. He, too, escapes accountability. (Faulkner subtly stresses the child's disappearance in the change he makes from the *American Mercury* version of the story to the final version in *These Thirteen*. In the earlier version he writes: "After his wife committed suicide Mr. Lovelady and the child went away. After a while Mr. Lovelady came back" ["That Evening Sun Go Down" 267]. In the final version he adds the word "alone" at the end of the second sentence ["That Evening Sun" 208].)

Mr. Compson evokes a more complicated response from students. Because they perceive him as sympathetic in both the story and the novel, they often do not look at his role closely. When their attention is directed to his repeated interjection of "nonsense" (307–08), however, they are apt to see that there is a link between his ineffectuality in "That Evening Sun" and in *The Sound and the Fury*: for all his concern, he can help neither Nancy nor his children. In the novel, his commitment to rationality precludes action; in the short story, it inhibits his crediting of Nancy's intuition-based fears. Mr. Compson's life contains no terrors or violent upheavals of emotion (his wife is nagging rather than unfaithful); as a result, in spite of his sympathy, he cannot fully imagine or respond to the world that Nancy lives in. His inability suggests once again the importance of race, class, and gender in determining relationships, without eclipsing the meaning that the text foregrounds: the impossibility of anyone's truly helping Nancy. Students who have read Melville's "Bartleby the Scrivener"—and usually many have—often see a thematic parallel between the two stories because they implicitly raise the question "Am I my brother's keeper?"

To explore the story systematically as a representation of the condition of black people in early twentieth-century Mississippi, a milieu alien to many students, I ask the class to list the black characters in the story and write what they can about their lives. They find that as a group blacks cannot protect themselves or their own: Dilsey, Rachel, and Roskus can no more do anything about Jesus's threat than Jesus himself can protect Nancy against white men. Both Nancy and Jesus chafe against their socially circumscribed identity as blacks, oscillating between passive resignation and an activity that, given the institutional limitations imposed on black self-actualization, can only be destructive, either of themselves or of other blacks. Although as a male he has more power than Nancy, as a black, Jesus—whose name ironically suggests transcendent power within a white tradition—is impotent against white males. (There is a suggestion that he is sexually impotent, since Nancy denies that he can be the father of her unborn child.) Whites can violate his domain—his kitchen, his house, his wife—but he cannot reciprocate; he is ordered out of the Compsons' kitchen. While Nancy protests her powerlessness with verbal violence, both in jail and in her fantasy of what she would do to any other woman she found with Jesus, his razor represents a real violence that can be directed only self-reflexively against his own people, and in particular against his wife.

On the basis of these typical observations, I ask students to describe the difference between the way blacks and whites are defined in "That Evening Sun," an assignment that invariably reveals a precise and stable definition for whites and an unstable, vague definition for blacks. (Analysis of *The Sound and the Fury* shows the same dichotomy, but it is easier to make the point with the simpler and shorter text.) For the dominant white culture, the general rubric of "nigger" seems to be sufficient. Whether Jesus is or is not Aunt Rachel's son, for instance, or who fathered Nancy's baby, are fundamental questions of identity that contrast with the clearly established identity of whites.

The importance of place to identity and the relation of place to race and sex need to be part of the discussion of social (i.e., legitimate) power. Displacement and interchangeability of place characterize people of low status. White characters in the story have not only well-established identities but also well-defined roles and places in society, however modest. Blacks are menials of one sort or another—temporary and interchangeable—or, like Jesus, they are troublemakers who occupy no specific place. The slot of cook in the Compson household is filled by a black woman—at one time Dilsey; at another, Nancy. Similarly, the story is framed by the procession of black laundresses at the beginning, one of whom is Nancy, and by Quentin's question at the end, "Who will do our washing now, Father?" (309). The flatness of the question's practicality suggests, after the overcharged atmosphere of the cabin, that Nancy can be matter-of-factly replaced with some other black woman. Jesus's exclusion from the Compson kitchen and from his own bed are emblematic of his exclusion from society, from the collective ascription of place.

Students readily see that placing Nancy and clarifying her identity is the underlying problem of the text. How to solve the matter of her placement usually generates a lively discussion since Nancy is both wife and prostitute—unfaithful to her husband, even taunting him for not fathering her child, yet fiercely possessive of him. Moreover, she is seriously displaced, literally and figuratively. Because the places where she truly belongs—her marriage, her house—offer no refuge, she attempts to find safety in places where she does not belong and cannot remain: the physical spaces of the Compsons' kitchen, whose rightful occupant is Dilsey; the children's bedroom; and the imaginary secure space created by her efforts to transform reality. Temporarily, Nancy even usurps Mrs. Compson's place by requiring the attention of Mr. Compson that his wife believes should rightly be devoted to herself.

Approaching the final movement of the short story, our discussion fruitfully compares Nancy's fear with the assertiveness of her earlier challenges to patriarchal authority. The class must assess the evidence here. Nancy has made a scene with Mr. Stovall, been physically attacked by him, and been taken to jail. In jail she is at first aggressively noisy and uncontrollable; then she withdraws into silence and attempts suicide, bringing on more physical punishment at the hands of another white man, the jailer. In this episode Nancy's violation of the stereotype of docility or passivity, a stereotype applied to both blacks and women, is given a pat explanation, one that satisfies another stereotype. According to the jailer, "no nigger would try to commit suicide unless he was full of cocaine, because a nigger full of cocaine wasn't a nigger any longer" (291). It should be noted, however, in a text containing many ambiguities, that the jailer's opinion is the only evidence that Nancy has taken cocaine, just as Mr. Compson's opinion that she is drunk is the only evidence of her drinking. These judgments, representing common negative stereotypes of black people, are open to question.

Once the class has placed Nancy, we can examine what she and Caddy have in common in spite of their obvious differences. We discover several prominent similarities: assertiveness in the face of risk and retribution is one; another is a pattern of self-destruction marked by sexual promiscuity, disrupted marriages, fatherless children, displacement, and a final, stoical acceptance of doom. Caddy's assertiveness usually seems admirable to students because it is directed toward ascertaining or demonstrating truth. Nancy's assertiveness is more problematic for them; it may be equally truthful, but students often conclude that, given her circumstances, she is more reckless than brave, more enigmatically motivated than the straightforward Caddy.

Having observed these character traits through the lens of the gender paradigm, we now examine an area that offers the richest vein of intertextuality in the comparison between Nancy and Caddy: the verbal isolation that the two women share. As Deborah Clarke observes generally, "Faulkner's women are not silenced but marginalized in a fictional world controlled by men and their language" ("Gender" 398). Students who have read other Faulkner texts—and most have read one or more—are often aware that women in his fiction do not engage in the meaningful verbal communication that helps establish the identity of men (Weinstein, "Meditations" 84–85). If we look specifically at speech in the story, we find that Nancy is defined by male versions of who and what she is—Mr. Stovall's, the jailer's, Mr. Compson's, her husband's, and Quentin's—and that all her attempts to convince others that she is in danger are ineffective. Her communications are rejected by Mr. Compson and inaccessible to the children. Caddy also lacks power as a speaker but for different reasons. Both as a child and as an adult she is preoccupied with acquiring and expressing truth, a characteristic that makes it particularly difficult for her to ratify her identity through speech. When I ask students how other members of the Compson family talk, they realize that Caddy shares no language with them. Eventually Caddy falls silent in *The Sound and the Fury* because she has no worthy or understanding partner for dialogue, either within or outside her family. Her direct utterances meet first with Quentin's ineffectual rhetoric and later with Jason's vindictiveness and sarcasm. She ends as she begins—an image. In the appendix to the novel, for instance, she appears as a photograph in a magazine, an image of displacement that embodies stasis and hopelessness just as the presumed originating image of the novel—the little girl climbing the tree to satisfy her curiosity— projects active engagement and confidence. Here, too, the class may see a parallel with Nancy, who begins as an image of harmonious balance and control but ends in a posture of fear of and resignation to being murdered by her husband. In both women the assertion of identity in opposition to the gender paradigm not only incurs a patriarchal punishment but also is self-destructive rather than liberating.

Teaching Narrative as Meaning in "A Justice" and *The Sound and the Fury*

Arthur F. Kinney

Elisabeth Muhlenfeld has remarked that she finds it beneficial to introduce *The Sound and the Fury* by way of one of Faulkner's short stories to rid classes of "Faulknerphobia." The brevity of a story allows students to keep all of it in mind and to refer to details throughout it. They are therefore able to see how the whole work is structured and how each part functions within the whole. Of the stories I have used to introduce *The Sound and the Fury*, "A Justice" works especially well. It prepares students for both the themes and the techniques of the novel. The story introduces Quentin, Caddy, Jason, and Roskus, but, generating ideas implicitly about their relationships and the layering of narrative, it does so in a ruptured and episodic form, like *The Sound and the Fury*. The story and the novel were conceived simultaneously, and the ending of the story on the word "twilight"—as the end of the day and the end of an age, or of childhood innocence—helps to explain why "Twilight" was the title of an early draft of the novel.

"A Justice" is presented in five apparently disjunctive sections. Quentin participates in and narrates the first and last; Sam Fathers does not participate in but narrates the middle three. The first question we address in class, then, is why there are two narrators. Why does Quentin ask for this kind of story? Why does Sam choose to tell the story he does? I suggest that in this split focus with two narrators, understanding the relation between them may help us anneal the work, give it continuous and unified meaning, and discover its purpose and point.

Almost at once, in our discussion, a student will remark that Sam Fathers is not really telling a story but only repeating to a child what he heard as a child from the older Herman Basket, cousin to Ikkemotubbe. Others may note further splitting—that the story, apparently about Ikkemotubbe in its early parts, is really about a man who calls himself David Callicoat (to set himself apart from Indian society), and then Doom (to become head of that society). The story later splits its focus between Craw-ford (Sam's "pappy") and an unnamed black slave whose wife Craw-ford wishes for himself. Such splittings and implied pairings bring us to discuss the opening and closing paragraphs of the story.

I read these paragraphs aloud and ask students to comment on their relation. The paragraphs, remarkably different in diction and tone, suggest two different Quentin Compsons. The Quentin of the opening paragraph is twelve years old, jammed into the family surrey but kept out of the conversation between Roskus and Quentin's grandfather; isolated, he masks his nervous energy by noting that this brief and passing time of childhood innocence and joy (of the smokehouse, the barn, and the blacksmith's shop) will end with the death of his grandfather. The second Quentin, already maturing, is full of abstract ideas that wrestle with the deeper significance of this particular trip, with the abstract meanings of

justice. He is restless because his mind is now inquiring and he has more questions than answers. The questions for class discussion come naturally: Does the
older Quentin know something the younger Quentin did not? If so, what took
place to produce that knowledge?

As we begin to peel back layers of the story, like approaching the center of
an onion, we ask what arouses Quentin's curiosity and why Sam responds with
the story he does. The younger Quentin—who appears naive and open—is
puzzled because Sam is called a nigger but does not look like one and does not
use "words like niggers do" ("Justice" 344). He asks Sam who he is; Sam responds quickly, wanting through narrative to explain to Quentin, and perhaps
to understand better himself, his own identity and history. (If the class also
reads "That Evening Sun," I point out that the other story introduces Quentin
as someone who knows things and ends with his increasing ignorance about
Nancy's insinuations, while "A Justice" works in the opposite way.)

"A Justice" recedes in planes of time, beginning with an implied present
(when the older Quentin will reflect on this incident), moving into the past
when he hears Sam's narrative, and moving further into the past, from Sam's
adult recollections of what Herman told him to the events themselves, happening at Sam's birth and before. The story, then, is about stories. It asks
whether stories are themselves events or selective and shaped narrations or,
later, reflections on what has taken place—just as *The Sound and the Fury* is
composed of different narrative perspectives that both reshape events and reflect on them, often to shield or hide memories at the twilight time of the
Compson family. Both story and novel raise comparable issues: Where does the
truth lie? Who is the best narrator, the participant with first-hand authority
(but with a biased perspective) or the distant listener who can judge more im-
partially (but is limited to what is told and how it is told)? If all the stories in
"A Justice" are shaped either by selective presentation (Sam) or motivated reflection (Quentin), does Faulkner ever provide the reader with any fully reliable account? Sam quite openly admits that Indians had slaves, but he does not
talk about the enslavement of his biological mother and nominal father or
about the inadequacy of both his fathers and the absence of his mother. It is
clear, however, that he locates his identity in a father—so that the story is a
search for the self by attempting to identify the father. Sam's story is also
Quentin's. In class, we return to the beginning of "A Justice," observing that
Quentin is not accompanied in the surrey by either of his parents.

We further measure the significance of Sam's story, for him and for Quentin,
by listing on the board its chief incidents, which I solicit from the class (partly
to initiate terms with which to talk about each of them): (1) the story of David
Callicoat going to New Orleans and returning as The Man, as Doom, with
slaves, a gold coat, and cyanide (346–50); (2) the story of Doom seizing the
steamboat as another act of pride and despotism (350–52); (3) the story of the
obedient Herman and the rebellious, self-indulgent Craw-ford, who seeks time
alone with the black woman (352–53); (4) the cockfight between Craw-ford

and the black slave over honor and the possession of the black slave's wife, a fight that is clearly a device by which Doom publicly distances himself from his seduction of the woman (354–58); and (5) the judgment of Doom on Craw-ford that orders Craw-ford to build a fence around the black slave's and slave woman's house—for now that she has a light-colored baby, which by the process of elimination must be Doom's, Doom wants to be rid of her (358–59). I ask a beginning class to figure out Doom's motivation in each episode; I ask an advanced class what similarities these episodes have, what Sam is clearly wrestling with and that will instruct Quentin, causing him to mature in the course of "A Justice." Students are usually fairly quick to see that each episode revolves around selfishness revealed; innocence corrupted; dreams, hopes, or plans short-circuited by outside forces; and deceptions exposed. Sooner or later they see that Doom works by manipulating others, by sheer heavy-handed dominance but also by shrewd canniness. Even when he does not poison pup-pies and men, he poisons the atmosphere with his narrow focus on lineage, pri-mogeniture, and inheritance. As the poison becomes literal, so does the enslavement, and both begin to shape the meaning, the possibility, of justice. We then examine other ways justice becomes restricted and we see that justice as an overarching principle becomes *a* justice, one kind among many.

At appropriate moments in classroom discussion, I insert two facts: that Chickasaws and Choctaws were matrilineal societies and that they passed laws forbidding marriage between Indians and blacks (Dabney 77–78, 86). Doom acts against both when he seizes power and creates a patrilineal society and when he impregnates the slave woman. But the greater significance, finally, is in using these facts not to judge Doom but to identify Sam. Sam Had-Two-Fathers actually has none, since his true father refuses to recognize him and the father who rears him is not his biological father. By the time of "A Justice," moreover, Sam has been sold to Grandfather Compson (in *Go Down, Moses*, he is sold to L. Q. C. McCaslin), so that his Indian blood has been denied and his matrilineal black blood made the basis for his identity. Justice, then, is se-lective and biased. *A* justice approaches the condition of injustice.

All these matters are serious and potentially or actually tragic, yet much of the story is told, like tall tales and the oral traditions of southern and southwestern humor, as high comedy: for instance, the lazy Sometimes-Wakeup with a blan-ket over his head; Craw-ford's sitting for days with his feet in a bucket; and the black slave trampling Craw-ford's cock in a one-sided cockfight. In our discus-sion we address the function of humor—as distraction, as cover-up, and as self-defense. Why is humor used to convey a story of moral corruption, materialism, arrogance, seduction, betrayal, and other forms of injustice? Is it to preserve the idea or hope of justice as an overarching and constant possibility? Is it an at-tempt to make light of injustice so as to weaken its force? Is it an attempt to mock justice so as to have fun without risking the validity of justice? Sam's sto-ries do not explain much of the past. In fact, Sam's confessions are clearer to us than they seem to be to Sam—or possibly even to Quentin. Perhaps this is because Faulkner is not interested in what happened to Sam's heritage because of the cost of his losing his parents. Rather, this cost that Sam reveals in the story functions to help Quentin sense his own loss and realize that he, like Sam, needs to fill the lack, to replace his absent father.

In the end, the reader must return to Quentin. Quentin learns through stories, including humorous ones. He learns ways in which people can more adequately face themselves. The cynicism at the heart of Sam's stories introduces my students to the cynicism that informs the character of Mr. Compson's story in *The Sound and the Fury*. The place accorded women in Sam's society helps students understand Mrs. Compson and Caddy and the limited roles available to them in their society. The use of sardonic humor to cover the sheer pathos that students sense in Doom helps them understand Jason Compson. But the whole sense of Doom as a corruption of "L'Homme"—of man—argues that people carry their own doom within them. In "A Justice," that is the justice Sam finally teaches Quentin; in *The Sound and the Fury*, it will be the "Nothing" ("Justice" 360) that is everything. Doom then will become Benjy's idiocy, Caddy's promiscuity, Quentin's death, Mr. Compson's alcoholism, Mrs. Compson's hypochondria, Dilsey's servitude, and "post and tree, window and doorway and signboard each in its ordered place" (*Sound* 321).

All the important conceptual seeds of *The Sound and the Fury* can be found in "A Justice." Students come to the novel from this story more fully aware of Faulkner's interest in the characters' individual consciousness, and of Faulkner's emphasis on their relationships, of the indirect ways in which fiction functions, and of some of the narrative strategies Faulkner enlists to make meaning in one of the greatest and most memorable of his novels.

"A Rose for Emily":
The Faulknerian Construction of Meaning

Claudia Clausius

William Faulkner's short story "A Rose for Emily" starts with the adverb "when." This beginning connects to two themes of the story. "When" locates the tale in the past; "when" also connects the past with the present. The story is about the past, about Miss Emily's tenacious clinging to the past and about the past of the Old South and the Confederacy. But the story is also a present narrative about historical events and the so-called facts that a contemporary reader interprets.

The following pedagogical approach to "A Rose for Emily" centers first on narrative unreliability and irony and second on meaning and significance as artificial constructs. Students' study of the short story is an exercise that will teach them to be aware of and to beware of the narrative voice; they will learn not to trust its veracity. The exercise will warn them of the susceptibility and vulnerability of readers at the hands of the author and the text, warn them that they should not rely too much on their assumptions and beliefs. This approach works well if one teaches "A Rose for Emily" by itself, but it also serves to introduce students to novels such as *The Sound and the Fury* and *Absalom, Absalom!* The exercise makes clear to the students that meaning does not reside in the text or even within the author; rather, it is produced in the dynamic that includes them as readers who interpret the text with and sometimes without the author's guidance.

We begin with an exploration of the story's events as if "A Rose for Emily" were both a Gothic tale and a detective story. Students are asked to consult a reputable literary dictionary and to come to class prepared to discuss characteristics of these two genres. The suspension of clarification eases the entry into a discussion of the difficult concept of narrative unreliability, irony, and the Gothic and detective genres. In this way students are invited to participate in Faulkner's narrative technique. The climactic structure of Faulkner's story is familiar to students. Although the story is a progression into the past, the narrative avoids a simple linear movement backward. Rather, the text moves along two parallel lines, one Miss Emily's real biography, the other the biography that the townspeople write for her. The real biography is progressive; moving forward, it is revealed only after the story's climax and is realized only through the participation of an interpreting reader.

Both Miss Emily and the townspeople work together to make her a symbol of the decline of the Old South. This collaboration includes, until almost the very end, the reader. The repetition of words and images, as well as the pervasive irony, illustrates how the meaning of a text is not so much an accumulative progression as it is a tapestry or network of significance, a fabric woven by the perceiver or reader of the text, whether the text is Miss Emily's life story from the perspective of the town or Faulkner's rendition of her story in his tale. In a wonderful blending of Victorian Gothic and Freudianism, the house itself, with its closed front door, its darkened upper story, and its dusty secrets, is an ironic representation of Miss Emily's mind. Although Miss Emily imprisons herself in her tomblike residence, the townspeople believe that they know her personal history and the reasons for her self-imposed isolation. The events of the story lead the reader not only into the past but also into the deranged recesses of Miss Emily's mind. Thus, the process of reading Faulkner's tale includes an exploration of the individual and collective unconscious of the South.

The classroom presentation of the story involves the students in narrative structure through the present activity of detection. As readers, they assume the role of detective to uncover the clues that point to the Gothic revelation at the end. The deeper purpose of the exercise is to introduce them into the ironic fabric of the story and its concomitant theme: personal and historical time as artificial constructs. Words and images function as clues for, on one level, a murder mystery (with the added twist that the townspeople and the reader are unaware of a death) and, on another level, the Gothic tale of a southern town's confrontation with its historical self-consciousness.

This hands-on approach to narrative structure and irony develops over three stages. Each stage asks students to read the story looking for different techniques. First, the instructor has the students make two lists of the events in the story. One list reflects the town's perception of Miss Emily's life; the other list gives the events as we can infer them in a rereading of the text in the light of the ending. The lists might read as follows:

Historical Perception	*Real Biography*
1. Funeral of a stubborn spinster, a relic	Funeral of a madwoman and murderess
2. Embarassing smell from Miss Emily's house	Rotting of Homer's body
3. Bereavement after father's death	Insanity after father's death
4. Liaison with pleasure-loving northern laborer	Hopeful courtship with Homer Barron
5. Scandal. Cousins sent for	Gossip. Visit from cousins
6. Wedding preparations	Purchase of silver toilet set, gentleman's clothing, and arsenic
7. Desertion	Murder
8. Aging and isolation	Vigilance over her house and her beloved
9. Occasional appearance at window	Occasional or possibly frequent visits upstairs
10. Death	Death
11. Discovery of body and gray hair on other pillow	Invasion of bridal chamber

The reason for the discrepancy between the two versions is not simply that one is a Gothic tale and the other a detective story; the discrepancy is also a demonstration of how reality, both historical (for the townspeople) and personal (for Miss Emily), is constructed. If Miss Emily creates her own world, so does the town. Students recognize that the story's irony is located between the two versions, in the fact that the townspeople are unaware that the senile old lady is actually a deranged murderess. The town's acceptance of Miss Emily's eccentricity and pride parallels the reader's faith in the narrative voice of the text, which, it turns out, also has sinister underpinnings.

The townspeople's ability to understand (read) the facts of Miss Emily's life is severely compromised by their indulgence of the anachronistic spinster and by their presuming to know the details of her private life. Into the gaps in their knowledge they inscribe a likely and conventional version of what they imagine happened. The opening paragraphs of part 4 express the certainty in the town's gossip: "We all said"; "Then we said"; "Then we were sure"; "later we learned . . . and we said"; "So we were not surprised"; "but we believed"; "as we had expected all along" ("Rose" 126–27). A close examination of the wording exposes the story's irony and lets students discover for themselves the unreliability of the narrator. It also warns them to suspect any authoritative historical or textual facts.

The second stage enlarges both on narrative uncertainty and unreliability and on how meaning is constructed. The teacher divides the class into small groups and asks them to reassess the story's events in the light of how the narrative uses foreshadowing and flashback to augment significance. Students, comparing their first uninformed reading of the following passages with later informed readings, begin to see how the townspeople have constructed the facts of Miss Emily's life from their assumptions about "the last Grierson":

> So the next night, after midnight, four men crossed Miss Emily's lawn and slunk about the house. . . . They broke open the cellar door and sprinkled lime there, and in all the outbuildings. . . . After a week or two the smell went away.   (122–23)

> That was when people began to really feel sorry for her. People in our town, remembering how old lady Wyatt, her great aunt, had gone completely crazy at last, believed that the Griersons held themselves a little too high for what they really were.   (123)

> She carried her head high enough. . . . It was as if she demanded more than ever the recognition of her dignity as the last Grierson; as if it had wanted that touch of earthiness to reaffirm her imperviousness. Like when she bought the rat poison, the arsenic.   (125)

> During the next few years [her hair] grew grayer and grayer until it attained an even pepper-and-salt iron-gray, when it ceased turning. Up to the day of her death at seventy-four it was still that vigorous iron-gray, like the hair of an active man.   (127–28)

In the last excerpt, three things merit mention: Emily's hair turns salt-and-pepper over a period of several years; this color remains constant until her death; and the description ends with a surprising simile. This focus on hair, together with the detection of the hair on the pillow, contributes to the Gothic horror at the end when the reader realizes that it has been Miss Emily's custom for over forty years to visit Homer's remains in the bridal chamber. Although her neighbors see her only in the downstairs windows and although she seems to have "shut up the top floor of the house" (128), the ending reveals that this top-floor room is a place of refuge and comfort. More important is the simile comparing Miss Emily to an active and virile man. "Iron-gray" has connotations not of vulnerability or decay but of purpose and determination. The text hints at a certain reserved admiration for Miss Emily despite her arrogance and poverty. In this regard Faulkner's mystery-tale structure supports the town's "cabal" (127) with the protagonist. Irony operates most forcefully in the arrangement of events, and their sequence maintains maximum narrative unreliability.

The third stage is to have students examine the text not with reference to events but in the light of the images and metaphors woven through the story. Here again the aim is for students to discover the degree to which the text is an artificial construct. History and characterization both are products of specific assumptions and fulfillments of expectations. The instructor may start by pointing out that the beginning of the tale aggrandizes both Miss Emily and her house. Even in decay, they are legendary, larger than life. Miss Emily is "a fallen monument," the house "an eyesore among eyesores" (119). Throughout, the text presents her almost entirely as icon, historical artifact, portrait. To illustrate this, the instructor asks the class to locate places in the text that describe Miss Emily (or those closest to her) as an object for viewing. The list should include the following instances:

On a tarnished gilt easel before the fireplace stood a crayon portrait of Miss Emily's father.   (120)

As they recrossed the lawn, a window that had been dark was lighted and Miss Emily sat in it, the light behind her, and her upright torso motionless as that of an idol.   (123)

We had long thought of them as a tableau, Miss Emily a slender figure in white in the background, her father a spraddled silhouette in the foreground, his back to her and clutching a horsewhip, the two of them framed by the back-flung door.   (123)

When we saw her again, her hair was cut short, making her look like a girl, with a vague resemblance to those angels in colored church windows—sort of tragic and serene.   (124)

She looked back at him, erect, her face like a strained flag.   (126)

Now and then we would see her in one of the downstairs windows . . .
like the carven torso of an idol in a niche, looking or not looking at us, we
could never tell which. Thus she passed from generation to generation—
dear, inescapable, impervious, tranquil, and perverse.   (128)

A thin acrid pall as of the tomb seemed to be everywhere upon this room
decked and furnished as for a bridal.   (129)

A discussion of these examples may focus on how the townspeople make an
icon and an artifact of Miss Emily, of her father, of Homer, of her entire life.
These iconographic metaphors sustain the irony of Faulkner's story by merg-
ing the two parallel narratives; they illustrate how Miss Emily and her fellow
southerners construct a lifetime and inscribe it with specific significance. Particularly noteworthy are words suggesting art, artifact, and therefore artifice.
Metaphors make clear how historical reality is captured (held still) by such
means as a portrait, an icon, a tableau, or a flag. Temporal imprisonment leads
to an assumption of fact or truth.

Death, usually the termination of life and of time, in this story is the vehicle
for suspending time and forestalling the end. Homer's death keeps him alive
for Miss Emily. Murder controls time by stopping it. In retrospect the reader
realizes that the bad smell comes from the rotting corpse of Homer Barron and
that Miss Emily's appearance at the window is her vigil over her beloved. After
transforming (at least in her mind) the pleasure-loving northern laborer into a
gentleman complete with silver toilet set and new wardrobe, Miss Emily en-
shrines him in a rose-colored bridal chamber. In murdering Homer, she marries him in an eternally present time. Dead, he cannot desert her. Ironically,
the townspeople, in their respect for Miss Emily, share similarities with her;
they ascribe a special status to Homer. Like her, they are unable to acknowledge the irrevocability of time. The town's deference to Miss Emily is a barely
sublimated desire to recapture some of its own historical exclusivity. In this
way, everyone shares in the production of personal and historical significance.

And so Miss Emily becomes associated with time, with history. Her unwillingness to abandon her noblesse oblige reflects the town's reluctance to confront
reality, which would mean abandoning its noblesse oblige. Notwithstanding rep-
resentatives of the "rising generation" (122), the town feels its "hereditary obligation" (119) to Miss Emily: "Thus she passed from generation to generation—dear,
inescapable, impervious, tranquil, and perverse" (128). Despite "more modern
ideas" (120), Miss Emily is the town's emblem of history. At her funeral the past
is momentarily re-created. Old men in Confederate uniforms imagine how they
might have courted Miss Emily. Her death is their avenue to a romantic and
chivalrous past. Only the horrible revelation at the end, the opening of the tomb,
restarts the clock.

Miss Emily vanquishes the tax collectors and her fastidious neighbors. The
surreptitious sprinkling of lime on her property involves her neighbors in an

ironic complicity with her macabre domestic charade. The well-meaning townspeople, by underwriting Miss Emily's mad scripting of her own story, are also collaborating to sustain her role and their own as the noble, aristocratic, defeated South. An investigation of the story from the perspectives of narrative, metaphor, and irony suggests how history, biography, autobiography, and even reading are processes that construct their own self-directed and self-serving meanings. In approaching the multiple voices of Faulkner's novels, particularly of *The Sound and the Fury*, students, familiarized with the approach outlined here, will better understand how those narratives construct and how they relate to and echo each other in the process of that construction.

Desires Become Words: A Formal and Thematic Approach to Teaching "Dry September" and *The Sound and the Fury*

Stephen Hahn

> If you's a good boy,
> The law will leave you 'lone.
> —Arthur Pettis, "Good Boy Blues"

"Dry September" is frequently taught with an emphasis on its documentary value as a story about racism in the deep South around 1930. Such an approach, however, begs the question of fiction as an accurate representation of social life. It also flattens the texture of the story, diverting attention from medium to message before readers have fully explored the turns taken by fiction away from literal representation and toward more complex forms of understanding. The documentary approach tends to imply, contrary to the usual thrust of Faulkner's fiction, that the antecedent social world is a complete and knowable totality rather than an incomplete, elusive aspect of becoming that is knowable only in retrospect and only through the fragile agency of words and stories. Moreover, such an approach to "Dry September" is now considerably complicated by the belated discovery of a letter published in the *Memphis Commercial Appeal*, 15 February 1931, under the title "Mob Sometimes Right," and signed "William Falkner [*sic*]/Oxford, Mississippi" (letter qtd. in McMillen and Polk 4–6). The letter challenges one's sense of Faulkner's presumed outrage about lynching, since it was written barely a month after "Dry September" was published in a national magazine (McMillen and Polk).

I teach "Dry September" with *The Sound and the Fury* to help students explore the signifying aspects of form that establish the complex relations between saying and knowing. One may ask, What is so significant about form compared to the brute sounds and ignominious fury of lynching in "Dry September" or to the more dispersed but also brutal and brutalizing events in *The Sound and the Fury*? I do not want to minimize the brutality of the things that are occurring behind Faulkner's representations; rather, I want to explore—first—how the short story form causes readers to focus on the social relations surrounding the events in the story.

Many students think of the poetic devices of fictional narrative—the manipulation of point of view, and tropes such as enigma, metaphor, and synecdoche—as elements in a game the author structures so that readers move in a more or less oedipal procession from darkness to light, to a crucial moment of illumination, revelation, or epiphany. By this model, a story is a detour on the way to knowledge and judgment, which are satisfactions provided to readers through a temporal conclusion and a thematic resolution (sometimes called a moral) to be drawn from the story. A story of this sort embodies summation of all we know and all we need to know; it is a self-enclosed artifact that resolves all the questions it raises. "A Rose for Emily" may initially seem to be a paradigmatic instance of this mode in Faulkner. On later critical readings, however, readers may find that the paradigm breaks down as the narrator vacillates about the town's presumed knowledge and as the action proceeds through its troubling achronicities. Like "A Rose for Emily," "Dry September" and *The Sound and the Fury* are narratives that play both with and against the model of linear progression toward recognition and revelation. But each leaves open a figurative space that is not filled with knowledge, since crucial events, presumed to have happened, are not represented to the reader. Into this space the reader's desire for knowledge and certainty may interpolate what may or may not have happened, completing, as is sometimes said, the story behind the narrative. Because "Dry September" at first feels to readers as though it does progress linearly toward a resolution, it is useful to examine the story closely to understand the functions and implications of its form. If students can begin to grasp the significance of form here, they will be better prepared to accept the idea that the formal eccentricity of *The Sound and the Fury* is significant—not merely as an artifact of the author's perverse will to play with the reader or as a necessary detour on the way to certain knowing but also as an acknowledgment of the reader's role in constructing the story. Reading "Dry September," students will also have learned something about the stories people tell themselves and how the telling of stories relates to dominant themes of Faulkner's work.

Introducing "Dry September," I explain some historical background. I tell students that lynching was epidemic in the South in the first third of the twentieth century; that Faulkner was writing in the South but that his story was published in a national magazine for middle-class readers (*Scribner's* Jan. 1931) during a time of national media attention and opposition to lynching; that racial ideology was closely related to sexual ideology at the time; that Faulkner's attitudes about race may have been partly influenced by the knowledge of his great-grandfather's probable siring of a black family (a situation mirrored in Faulkner's story "There Was a Queen"). For historical sources, teachers may want to refer to Joel Williamson's *William Faulkner and Southern History* and James McGovern's *Anatomy of a Lynching: The Killing of Claude Neal*, among others. I sometimes also introduce into our reading Faulkner's 15 February 1931 letter, asking students to comment on how it affects their perception of the story. With respect to literary form, I point out that American short stories, most of them written for magazine publication, consistently establish a theme through the use of a word or phrase early in the story and present the reader with an enigma to be resolved. I explain the terms *theme* and *enigma*. I indicate that early drafts of the story focused on Minnie Cooper and roles available to women in the South but that at some point Faulkner chose to reorder the narrative in its present sequence. (For the early drafts, see *William Faulkner Manuscripts* 9: 258–92.) Depending on the time available and the level of the course, we may look at typescript passages of those drafts and contrast them with the published work.

When the students have read the whole story once, we focus in class on the first paragraph. What, I ask, is the key word relating to theme in this paragraph? For some it is "bloody" or "fire"—words that signify qualities of both the physical and psychological environments. (In a survey or period course we will have already examined such devices, having read Frank Norris's "A Deal in Wheat," Jack London's "The Law of Life," or similar naturalistic fiction. We talk about whether this story works like those examples.) Other students suggest the word "rumor," the phrase "whatever it was" or "exactly what had happened," or even "it" in the clause "it had gone like a fire in the grass" ("Dry September" 169). We talk about the use of descriptive metaphor to suggest motive and causation—an idea the class will return to—and about what the words, phrases, and portions of the dialogue tell us, at the outset, that the characters lack. They lack certain knowledge that anything at all happened.

We proceed like country lawyers to examine the question, What do we know and how do we know we know it? From class to class, the question plays out a little differently, but the following is typical. We know, a student suggests, that something happened to Minnie Cooper. As we explore the question of how we know it, we begin to suspect that we do not know any more than the two barbers on the street or Minnie's intrusive friends, who wonder, "Do you suppose anything really happened?" (182). We examine other possible avenues to certainty, such as that we know Will Mayes is innocent (but do we? or do we only infer that he is from his behavior?) and that we know he is lynched (but do we? or do we only infer that he is from the description of his abduction, the ominous mention of the "brick kiln" and the "vats" in which the farmer reportedly lost his mules [179], and the number of passengers returning in the car [180]?). The point is not to dispute the interpretation but to understand it as an interpretation. We discuss the means by which readers draw inferences from incomplete information. For instance, the metonymy of the mention of the vats indicates how the murder, supposing it happened, happened, following the principle of narrative economy, whereby an author neither mentions nor represents things that are not important to the story. But students are cannily aware that the author might also suggest something contrary to fact. Readers enter into a quandary in which they find that they do not know more than the characters. They are on a level with the characters, both trying to make sense of what they have heard.

I ask the students, What do we lack that a country lawyer would try to secure? Students observe that we lack physical evidence and the means to obtain it, that we lack the ability to cross-examine, and that we lack eyewitness testimony about important alleged events. I ask, What do we have that the lawyer would be interested in? "Incomplete and conflicting reports" is a typical answer. We reenter the narrative to see again how we go about constructing the story, retelling it according to our interpretations, inferring certainties from probabilities. We compare our method of constructing the story with the methods the characters use to construct their various stories.

Central to this approach is the fact that something is not represented. No correspondence between word and image issues forth on the classical model of

Oedipus's scene of recognition, that moment in *Oedipus Tyrannus* when the conflicting testimony of the characters coalesces. The totality of the story provides, instead, a representation of partiality afforded by conflicting testimony and point of view. Between the abduction of Will and the return of McLendon's car, for instance, is a gap in which readers are restricted to Hawkshaw's point of view—and Faulkner clearly could have used another narrative strategy. We consider the effect of the omission of a description of the lynching. (In some courses, I assign chapters of McGovern's *Anatomy of a Lynching*, and students report on the details of Claude Neal's murder [80]. The descriptions make difficult reading, and instructors may want to avoid this approach, but it also makes one obvious case for Faulkner's omission: describing a lynching even for fictional purposes would be cruel.) A student might argue that an account of the lynching would make what happened to Will the focus of the story. We consider why Faulkner, given the historical context, would want only to suggest rather than describe, and we discuss how readers would have been likely to receive a story about a lynching. Why is the lynching not the focus? Why are readers left, clearly by design, with uncertainty about so many events in the story? If readers do not come to a recognition, a resolution of the enigma, in the form of a correspondence between their inferences and the descriptions of actualities, how is this reading experience significant? Students will reply, at the very least, that "Dry September" shows how hearing or reading a story can predispose us to believe in its literal truth, can lead us to wrong conclusions, can "make us" (without our realizing it?) complete the story by supplying missing elements (who did it? did what?) according to our previous assumptions about what is likely to occur.

We are led finally to an examination of how the rumor of sexual assault spreads and how it is sustained in the face of doubt cast on it throughout the opening colloquy, through Will's denial, and through the description of Minnie's breakdown, following the paths of various desires for a coherent narrative and its presumed moral. We consider whether the heat wave is an adequate explanation of the events that unfold or whether there are other explanations. For some students, Minnie Cooper appears to be a causal agent, but as we try to determine her role, we find that she has never really said anything coherent. The rumor therefore may have arisen anywhere, as rumors do—in a gesture, a look, a malicious remark or from a deliberate vendetta. The reader simply does not know. Minnie's hysteria may be more the result of the rumor than its cause. Rumor itself seems to be the cause, and we look again at the opening metaphor of "fire in dry grass" (169) to consider its aptness in describing rumor as an impersonal force that consumes what it touches, leaving its fuel lifeless and unable to fuel further fire.

In this intensive reading of "Dry September," we begin by pursuing the implications of form, observing relations between the how of the telling and the effects of the telling; we see that the lack of description of the two central events—the lynching and the alleged sexual assault—leads us to reflect on the social and psychological processes of character and community and on our own process of making meaning as we read. We see, too, that the story highlights its status as literary artifice through its incompleteness. With this experience behind us, we turn to *The Sound and the Fury*, which, I suggest to the class, we may explore as a series of incomplete and conflicting reports, looking both for what is represented and for what is only rumored or suggested. To illustrate what we have learned about incomplete and conflicting reports, I quote a passage from the episode of Quentin's encounter with the boys fishing on the bridge: "They all talked at once, their voices insistent and contradictory and impatient, making of unreality a possibility, then a probability, then an incontrovertible fact, as people will when their desires become words" (117). I suggest that the narrative procedures and the effects of narrative form we have observed in the short story imply some skepticism on Faulkner's part about the ability of any story to speak, as the familiar courtroom saying has it, "the truth, the whole truth, and nothing but the truth."

Our exploration of the divagations of the narrative as we enter the verbal world of *The Sound and the Fury* will be guided by an enhanced sense of the gap between words and what, in Addie Bundren's phrase, "they are trying to say at" (*As I Lay Dying* 171). The complex relation between saying and knowing, our susceptibility to rumor, and our need to complete the stories we tell are aspects of a social and mental world we can neither entirely integrate nor fully transcend. Having explored these themes in our reading of "Dry September," we are better prepared to find our way among the conflicting and incomplete reports of *The Sound and the Fury*, attending to the gaps in narration that chasten our readerly hubris, making more critically alert readers of us all.

To frame our discussion and bring into play the contemporaneous voices of African American men on themes related to the story, I begin our class sessions by playing a recording of Arthur Pettis singing "Good Boy Blues" (recorded in the Delta town of Tunica in 1930) and end by playing that song again and then Sam Collins singing the obscure and haunting "Lonesome Road Blues" (recorded in 1931). I ask how we might interpret the lines in "Good Boy Blues," which serve as an epigraph for this essay. Are they innocent or are they ironically subversive? How might we interpret the voice of Will Mayes, given what we know of Faulkner and of the social conditions that legitimized lynching for some of the population of Faulkner's South (and for some elsewhere)? We replay Collins's performance of "Lonesome Road Blues" and ask why some of its lines are inaudible. Is it purely the deficiency of the recording equipment, or is the vocalist deliberately evasive? We compare the mixture of tones in these two blues songs with the dispassionate case-study tones of Faulkner's story. As we move to reading *The Sound and the Fury*, I ask students to consider what we hear or do not hear in the voices, which are like these recorded sounds—in the fragmented recollections of Benjy (not Benjy's voice but the voices for which he is the medium) and in the following sections of the novel. The songs as well as Faulkner's short story become part of our exploration of the complex relations of desiring, knowing, telling, and listening.

CONTRIBUTORS AND SURVEY PARTICIPANTS

Ann J. Abadie, *University of Mississippi*
Louise K. Barnett, *Rutgers University, New Brunswick*
Anthony Barthelemy, *University of Miami*
Margaret D. Bauer, *University of Tennessee, Knoxville*
Harry M. Bayne, *Brewton-Parker College*
James D. Bloom, *Muhlenberg University*
Sr. Anne Denise Brennan, *College of Mount Saint Vincent*
Stacy Burton, *University of Nevada, Reno*
Mary Ellen Byrne, *Ocean County College, NJ*
Hilda Carey, *Boston College*
Claudia Clausius, *Concordia University, Loyola Campus*
Philip Cohen, *University of Texas, Arlington*
Thomas D. Cohen, *University of North Carolina, Chapel Hill*
Charles Davis, *University of North Carolina, Greensboro*
John F. Desmond, *Whitman College*
Sally Ann Drucker, *North Carolina State University*
John N. Duvall, *Memphis University*
Catarina Edinger, *William Paterson College*
Leonard Engel, *Quinnipiac College*
Doreen Fowler, *University of Kansas*
Mark Frisch, *Duquesne University*
Henry Louis Gates, *Harvard University*
Donald B. Gibson, *Rutgers University, New Brunswick*
Mimi R. Gladstein, *University of Texas, El Paso*
Norma W. Goldstein, *Mississippi State University*
Joan Wylie Hall, *University of Mississippi*
Peter Hayes, *University of California, Davis*
Daniel J. Holtz, *Peru State University*
Nicholas Howe, *Ohio State University, Columbus*
Donald M. Kartiganer, *University of Mississippi*
Bruce Kawin, *University of Colorado, Boulder*
Pamela E. Knights, *University of Durham*
Martin Kreiswirth, *University of Western Ontario*
Deborah Kuhlmann, *Galveston College*
Jun Liu, *California State University, Los Angeles*
Reginald Martin, *Memphis University*
John T. Matthews, *Boston University*
Thomas McHaney, *Georgia State University*
Toni J. Morris, *University of Indianapolis*
Gail L. Mortimer, *University of Texas, El Paso*
Elisabeth S. Muhlenfeld, *Florida State University*
Robert Dale Parker, *University of Illinois, Urbana*
Charles Peek, *University of Nebraska, Kearney*

Alice Hall Petry, *Rhode Island School of Design*
Robert L. Philips, *Mississippi State University*
Noel Polk, *University of Southern Mississippi*
Panthea Reid, *Louisiana State University, Baton Rouge*
Thomas Samet, *Northwestern State University of Louisiana*
Pamela S. Saur, *Lamar University*
Evelyn Jaffee Schreiber, *George Washington University*
Dorothy M. Scura, *University of Tennessee, Knoxville*
Rajini Srinkanth, *Tufts University*
Walter Taylor, *University of Texas, El Paso*
Terrell L. Tebbetts, *Lyons College*
William Vesterman, *Rutgers University, New Brunswick*
Clyde Wade, *University of Missouri, Rolla*
William Walling, *Rutgers University, New Brunswick*
James G. Watson, *University of Tulsa*
Jay Watson, *University of Mississippi*
Arnold Weinstein, *Brown University*
Philip M. Weinstein, *Swarthmore College*
Mary Ann Wimsatt, *University of South Carolina, Columbia*
Joel Wingaard, *Moravian College*
Judith Bryant Wittenberg, *Simmons College*

WORKS CITED

Books and Articles

Adams, Richard P. *Faulkner: Myth and Motion*. Princeton: Princeton UP, 1968.

Aiken, Charles S. "Faulkner's Yoknapatawpha County: A Place in the American South." *Geographical Review* July 1979: 331–48.

———. "Faulkner's Yoknapatawpha County: Geographical Fact into Fiction." *Geographical Review* Jan. 1977: 1–21.

———. "A Geographical Approach to Faulkner's 'The Bear.'" *Geographical Review* Oct. 1981: 446–59.

Akin, Edward N. *Mississippi: An Illustrated History*. Northridge: Windsor, 1987.

Allard, William Albert, and Willie Morris. "Faulkner's Mississippi." *National Geographic* Mar. 1989: 312–39.

Arrington, Philip K. "Contentious Forms: Trope and the Study of Composition." *Farther Along: Transforming Dichotomies in Rhetoric and Composition*. Ed. Kate Ronald and Hephzibah Roskelly. Portsmouth: Boynton/Cook, 1990. 149–67.

Ayers, Edward L. *The Promise of the New South: Life after Reconstruction*. New York: Oxford UP, 1992.

———. *Southern Crossing: A History of the American South, 1877–1906*. New York: Oxford UP, 1995.

Backman, Melvin. *Faulkner: The Major Years: A Critical Study*. Bloomington: Indiana UP, 1966.

Barthes, Roland. *The Pleasure of the Text*. Trans. Richard Miller. New York: Farrar, 1975.

———. *S/Z*. Trans. Richard Miller. New York: Farrar, 1974.

Bassett, John [Earl]. *Faulkner: An Annotated Checklist of Recent Criticism*. Kent: Kent State UP, 1983.

———. *Faulkner in the Eighties: An Annotated Critical Bibliography*. Metuchen: Scarecrow, 1991.

———. *William Faulkner: An Annotated Checklist of Criticism*. New York: Lewis, 1972.

———. *William Faulkner: The Critical Heritage*. London: Routledge, 1975.

Belsey, Catherine. *Critical Practice*. London: Methuen, 1980.

Bennett, E. A. *What Jung Really Said*. New York: Schocken, 1967.

Bleikasten, André. *The Ink of Melancholy: Faulkner's Novels from* The Sound and the Fury *to* Light in August. Bloomington: Indiana UP, 1990.

———. *The Most Splendid Failure: Faulkner's* The Sound and the Fury. Bloomington: Indiana UP, 1976.

———, ed. *William Faulkner's* The Sound and the Fury: *A Critical Casebook*. New York: Garland, 1982.

Bloom, Harold, ed. *William Faulkner's* The Sound and the Fury: *Modern Critical Interpretations*. New York: Chelsea, 1988.

Blotner, Joseph. *Faulkner: A Biography*. 2 vols. New York: Random, 1974.

———. *Faulkner: A Biography*. 1 vol. New York: Random, 1984.

———. *William Faulkner's Library: A Catalogue*. Charlottesville: UP of Virginia, 1964.

Brantlinger, Patrick. *Crusoe's Footprints: Cultural Studies in Britain and America*. New York: Routledge, 1990.

Brodhead, Richard H. *Faulkner (New Perspectives)*. Twentieth Century Views. Englewood Cliffs: Prentice, 1983.

Brodsky, Louis Daniel, and Robert W. Hamblin. *Faulkner: A Comprehensive Guide to the Brodsky Collection, Volume 2: The Letters*. Jackson: UP of Mississippi, 1984.

Brooks, Cleanth. *William Faulkner: First Encounters*. New Haven: Yale UP, 1983.

———. *William Faulkner: The Yoknapatawpha Country*. 1963. New Haven: Yale UP, 1966.

Broughton, Panthea Reid [Panthea Reid]. "The Cubist Novel: Toward Defining a Genre." Fowler and Abadie, *"Cosmos"* 36–58.

———. "Faulkner's Cubist Novels." Fowler and Abadie, *"Cosmos"* 59–94.

———. *William Faulkner: The Abstract and the Actual*. Baton Rouge: Louisiana State UP, 1974.

Brown, Calvin S. *A Glossary of Faulkner's South*. New Haven: Yale UP, 1976.

Buckley, G. T. "Is Oxford the Original of Jefferson in William Faulkner's Novels?" *PMLA* 76 (1961): 447–54.

Budd, Louis J., and Edwin H. Cady. *On Faulkner: The Best from* American Literature. Durham: Duke UP, 1989.

Butler, Judith. *Gender Trouble: Feminism and the Subversion of Identity*. New York: Routledge, 1990.

Campbell, Harry Modean, and Ruel E. Foster. *William Faulkner: A Critical Appraisal*. Norman: U of Oklahoma P, 1951.

Carothers, James B. *William Faulkner's Short Stories*. Ann Arbor: UMI Research, 1985.

Cash, W. J. *The Mind of the South*. New York: Knopf, 1941.

Cather, Willa. *O Pioneers!* Boston: Houghton, 1916.

Cecil, L. Moffit. "A Rhetoric for Benjy." *Southern Literary Journal* 3.1 (1970): 32–46.

Cheuse, Alan. *"Candace" and Other Stories*. Cambridge: Apple-wood, 1980.

Clarke, Deborah. "Gender, Race, and Language in *Light in August*." *American Literature* 61 (1989): 398–413.

———. *Robbing the Mother: Women in Faulkner*. Jackson: UP of Mississippi, 1994.

Cofield, Jack. *William Faulkner: The Cofield Collection*. Introd. Carvel Collins. Oxford: Yoknapatawpha, 1978.

Cohen, Philip, and Doreen Fowler. "Faulkner's Introduction to *The Sound and the Fury*." *American Literature* 62 (1990): 262–83.

Coindreau, Maurice Edgar. "Preface to *The Sound and the Fury*." Trans. George M. Reeves. *Mississippi Quarterly* 19 (1966): 107–15.

Collins, Carvel. "The Interior Monologues of *The Sound and the Fury*." 1952. *Psychoanalysis and American Fiction*. Ed. Irving Malin. New York: Dutton, 1965. 223–43.

Connolly, Thomas E. *Faulkner's World*. Lanham: UP of America, 1988.

Coughlan, Robert. *The Private World of William Faulkner*. New York: Harper, 1954.

Cowan, Michael H. *Twentieth Century Interpretations of* The Sound and the Fury. Twentieth Century Views. Englewood Cliffs: Prentice, 1968.

Cowley, Malcolm. *The Faulkner-Cowley File: Letters and Memories, 1944–1962*. New York: Viking, 1966.

——, ed. *The Portable Faulkner*. New York: Viking, 1946.

Cox, Leland H. *William Faulkner: A Biographical and Reference Guide*. Detroit: Gale, 1982.

Creighton, Joanne V. *William Faulkner's Craft of Revision*. Detroit: Wayne State UP, 1977.

Cross, Ralph D., Robert W. Wales, and Charles T. Traylor, eds. *Atlas of Mississippi*. Jackson: UP of Mississippi, 1974.

Cullen, John B., with Floyd C. Watkins. *Old Times in the Faulkner Country*. Chapel Hill: U of North Carolina P, 1961.

Dabney, Lewis M. *The Indians of Yoknapatawpha: A Study in Literature and History*. Baton Rouge: Louisiana State UP, 1974.

Dain, Martin J. *Faulkner's Country: Yoknapatawpha*. New York: Random, 1964.

Dasher, Thomas E. *William Faulkner's Characters: An Index to the Published and Un-published Fiction*. New York: Garland, 1981.

Davenport, Basil. "Tragic Frustration." Rev. of *The Sound and the Fury*, by William Faulkner. *Saturday Review of Literature* 28 Dec. 1929: 601–02.

Davenport, F. Garvin, Jr. *The Myth of Southern History: Historical Consciousness in Twentieth-Century Southern Literature*. Nashville: Vanderbilt UP, 1970.

Davis, Thadious M. *Faulkner's "Negro": Art and the Southern Context*. Baton Rouge: Louisiana State UP, 1983.

Deleuze, Gilles. *Nietzsche and Philosophy*. Trans. Hugh Tomlin. New York: Columbia UP, 1983.

Desvergnes, Alain, and Regis Durand. *Yoknapatawpha: The Land of William Faulkner*. Trans. William Wheeler. Paris: Marval, 1980.

Dollard, John. *Caste and Class in a Southern Town*. New Haven: Yale UP, 1937.

Douglas, Ellen. "Faulkner's Women." Fowler and Abadie, *"Cosmos"* 149–67.

Duvall, John N. *Faulkner's Marginal Couple: Invisible, Outlaw, and Unspeakable Com-munities*. Austin: U of Texas P, 1990.

Eagleton, Terry. *Against the Grain: Essays, 1975–1985*. London: Verso, 1986.

Edinger, Edward. *Ego and Archetype: Individuation and the Religious Function of the Psyche*. Baltimore: Penguin, 1973.

Eggleston, William, and Willie Morris. *Faulkner's Mississippi*. Birmingham: Oxmoor, 1990.

Eliot, T. S. *The Waste Land*. New York: Boni, 1922.

England, Martha Winburn. "Teaching *The Sound and the Fury*." *College English* 18 (1957): 221–24.

Ermarth, Elizabeth. *Realism and Consensus in the English Novel*. Princeton: Princeton UP, 1983.

Everett, Walter K. *Faulkner's Art and Characters*. Woodbury: Barron's, 1969.

Falkner, Murray C. *The Falkners of Mississippi: A Memoir*. Baton Rouge: Louisiana State UP, 1967.

Fant, Joseph L., and Robert Ashley. *Faulkner at West Point*. New York: Random, 1964.

Faulkner, Jim. *Across the Creek: Faulkner Family Stories*. Jackson: UP of Mississippi, 1986.

Faulkner, John. *My Brother Bill: An Affectionate Reminiscence*. New York: Trident, 1963.

Faulkner, William. *Absalom, Absalom!* 1936. New York: Vintage, 1990.

———. "Appendix: Compson: 1699–1945." Cowley, *The Portable Faulkner* 737–56. Rpt. in Faulkner, *Sound* [Norton] 203–15.

———. *As I Lay Dying*. 1930. New York: Vintage, 1990.

———. "Barn Burning." Faulkner, *Collected Stories* 3–26.

———. *Collected Stories*. 1950. New York: Vintage, 1977.

———. "Dry September." Faulkner, *Collected Stories* 169–84.

———. *Essays, Speeches, and Public Letters by William Faulkner*. Ed. James Meriwether. New York: Random, 1968.

———. *Faulkner on Love: A Letter to Marjorie Lyons*. Ed. Richard Lyons. Fargo: Merrykit, 1974.

———. *Flags in the Dust*. Ed. Douglas Day. New York: Random, 1973.

———. *Go Down, Moses*. New York: Vintage, 1990.

———. *Helen: A Courtship and Mississippi Poems*. Ed. Carvel Collins and Joseph Blotner. New Orleans: Tulane UP and Yoknapatawpha, 1981.

———. "Interview with Jean Stein vanden Heuvel." *Paris Review* 12 (1956): 28–52. Meriwether and Millgate 237–56.

———. Introduction. *Sanctuary*. 1931. New York: Modern Library, 1932. iii–vi. Rpt. in *Sanctuary*. Ed. Noel Polk. New York: Random, 1987: 337–39.

———. "An Introduction to *The Sound and the Fury*." [1st.] Ed. James B. Meriwether. *Southern Review* 8 (1972): 705–10.

———. "An Introduction to *The Sound and the Fury*." [2nd.] Meriwether 156–61.

———. "A Justice." Faulkner, *Collected Stories* 343–60.

———. "The Kid Learns." [New Orleans] *Times-Picayune* 31 May 1925. Rpt. in Faulkner, *William Faulkner: New Orleans Sketches* 86–91.

———. "The Kingdom of God." [New Orleans] *Times-Picayune* 26 Apr. 1925. Rpt. in Faulkner, *William Faulkner: New Orleans Sketches* 55–60.

———. *Light in August*. 1932. New York: Vintage, 1990.

———. *Mayday*. 1926. Ed. Carvel Collins. Notre Dame: U of Notre Dame P, 1978.

———. "Mississippi." *Holiday* Apr. 1954: 33–47. Rpt. in Faulkner, *Essays* 11–43.

———. "Mob Sometimes Right." Letter. *Memphis Commercial Appeal* 15 Feb. 1931. Rpt. McMillen and Polk 4–6.

———. *Mosquitoes*. New York: Liveright, 1927.

———. *Requiem for a Nun*. New York: Random, 1951.

———. "A Rose for Emily." Faulkner, *Collected Stories* 119–30.

———. *Selected Letters of William Faulkner*. Ed. Joseph Blotner. New York: Random, 1977.

———. *Selected Short Stories of William Faulkner*. New York: Modern Library, 1962.

———. *The Sound and the Fury*. 1929. Introd. Richard Hughes. Hammondsworth: Penguin, 1962.

———. *The Sound and the Fury*. New York: Vintage, 1990.

———. *The Sound and the Fury*. Norton Critical Edition. 2nd ed. Ed. David Minter. New York: Norton, 1994.

———. The Sound and the Fury *and* As I Lay Dying. New York: Modern Library, 1956.

———. "That Evening Sun." Faulkner, *Collected Stories* 289–309.

———. "That Evening Sun Go Down." *American Mercury* 22 (1931): 257–67.

———. *These Thirteen*. New York: Cape, 1931.

———. *Thinking of Home: William Faulkner's Letters to His Mother and Father, 1918–1925*. Ed. James G. Watson. New York: Norton, 1992.

———. *William Faulkner Manuscripts*. 44 vols. Ed. Joseph Blotner et al. New York: Garland, 1986–88.

———. *William Faulkner: New Orleans Sketches*. Ed. Carvel Collins. New York: Random, 1958.

———. *William Faulkner: Uncollected Stories*. Ed. Joseph Blotner. New York: Random, 1979.

Ferguson, James. *Faulkner's Short Fiction*. Knoxville: U of Tennessee P, 1991.

Fitts, Dudley. "Two Aspects of Telemachus." Rev. of *The Sound and the Fury*, by William Faulkner. *Hound and Horn* Apr.–June 1930: 445–47. Rpt. Bassett, *Critical Heritage* 87–89.

Ford, Margaret Patricia, and Suzanne Kincaid. *Who's Who in Faulkner*. Baton Rouge: Louisiana State UP, 1963.

Fowler, Doreen, and Ann J. Abadie, eds. *"A Cosmos of My Own": Faulkner and Yoknapatawpha, 1980*. Jackson: UP of Mississippi, 1981.

———, eds. *Faulkner and Race: Faulkner and Yoknapatawpha, 1986*. Jackson: UP of Mississippi, 1987.

———, eds. *Faulkner and Women: Faulkner and Yoknapatawpha, 1985*. Jackson: UP of Mississippi, 1986.

———, eds. *Faulkner: International Perspectives: Faulkner and Yoknapatawpha, 1982*. Jackson: UP of Mississippi, 1984.

Franklin, Malcolm. *Bitterweeds: Life with William Faulkner at Rowan Oak*. Irving: Soc. for the Study of Traditional Culture, 1963.

Freud, Sigmund. *Beyond the Pleasure Principle*. 1920. Trans. and ed. James Strachey. New York: Norton, 1961.

———. *The Ego and the Id*. 1923. Trans. Joan Riviere. Ed. James Strachey. New York: Norton, 1962.

Genovese, Eugene D. *The Southern Tradition: The Achievement and Limitations of an American Conservatism*. Cambridge: Harvard UP, 1994.

Gilbert, Sandra M., and Susan Gubar. *No Man's Land: The Place of the Woman Writer in the Twentieth Century.* Vol. 1. New Haven: Yale UP, 1988.

Grantham, Dewey W. *The South in Modern America: A Region at Odds.* New York: Harper, 1994.

Gray, Richard. *The Life of William Faulkner.* Cambridge: Blackwell, 1994.

———. *The Literature of Memory: Modern Writers of the American South.* Baltimore: Johns Hopkins UP, 1977.

———. *Writing the South: Ideas of an American Region.* Cambridge: Cambridge UP, 1986.

Gresset, Michel. *Fascination: Faulkner's Fiction, 1919–1936.* Adapt. Thomas West. Durham: Duke UP, 1989.

———. *A Faulkner Chronology.* Jackson: UP of Mississippi, 1985.

———. *Faulkner: Œuvres romanesques.* Paris: Gallimard, 1977.

Grimwood, Michael. *Heart in Conflict: Faulkner's Struggles with Vocation.* Athens: U of Georgia P, 1987.

Grossman, James. *Land of Hope: Chicago, Black Southerners, and the Great Migration.* Chicago: U of Chicago P, 1989.

Gutting, Gabriele. *Yoknapatawpha: The Function of Geographical and Historical Facts in William Faulkner's Fictional Picture of the Deep South.* New York: Lang, 1992.

Gwin, Minrose C. *The Feminine and Faulkner: Reading (beyond) Sexual Difference.* Knoxville: U of Tennessee P, 1990.

Gwynn, Frederick L., and Joseph L. Blotner, eds. *Faulkner in the University: Class Conferences at the University of Virginia, 1957–1958.* New York: Random, 1959. New York: Vintage, 1975.

Harrington, Evans, and Ann J. Abadie, eds. *Faulkner and the Short Story: Faulkner and Yoknapatawpha, 1990.* Jackson: UP of Mississippi, 1992.

———. *Faulkner, Modernism, and Film: Faulkner and Yoknapatawpha, 1978.* Jackson: UP of Mississippi, 1979.

Haynes, Jane Isbell. *William Faulkner: His Lafayette County Heritage: Lands, Houses, and Businesses, Oxford, Mississippi.* Ripley: Tippah County Historical and Genealogical Soc., 1992.

———. *William Faulkner: His Tippah County Heritage: Lands, Houses, and Businesses, Ripley, Mississippi.* Columbia: Sejay, 1985.

Hemingway, Ernest. *The Sun Also Rises.* New York: Scribner's, 1926.

Hines, Thomas. "Architecture and the Tangible Past: The Built Environment of Faulkner's Yoknapatawpha." *Places: A Quarterly Journal of Environmental Design* 5.8 (1988): 40–55.

Hoffman, Frederick J. *Freudianism and the Literary Mind.* 2nd ed. Baton Rouge: Louisiana State UP, 1957.

———. *William Faulkner.* New York: Twayne, 1961.

Hoffman, Frederick J., and Olga W. Vickery, eds. *William Faulkner: Three Decades of Criticism.* East Lansing: Michigan State UP, 1960.

———, eds. *William Faulkner: Two Decades of Criticism.* East Lansing: Michigan State Coll. P, 1951.

Howe, Irving. *William Faulkner: A Critical Study*. New York: Random, 1952. Rev. ed. Chicago: U of Chicago P, 1975.

Hunt, John W. *William Faulkner: Art in Theological Tension*. Syracuse: Syracuse UP, 1965.

Hurston, Zora Neale. *Their Eyes Were Watching God*. 1937. Greenwich: Fawcett, 1969.

Huyssen, Andreas. *After the Great Divide: Modernism, Mass Culture, Postmodernism*. Bloomington: Indiana UP, 1986.

Irwin, John T. *Doubling and Incest / Repetition and Revenge: A Speculative Reading of Faulkner*. Baltimore: Johns Hopkins UP, 1975.

Jameson, Fredric. *The Political Unconscious: Narrative as a Socially Symbolic Act*. Ithaca: Cornell UP, 1981.

Jehlen, Myra. *Class and Character in Faulkner's South*. New York: Columbia UP, 1976.

———. "Gender." *Critical Terms for Literary Study*. Ed. Frank Lentricchia and Thomas McLaughlin. Chicago: U of Chicago P, 1990. 263–73.

Jenkins, Lee C. *Faulkner and Black-White Relations: A Psychoanalytic Approach*. New York: Columbia UP, 1981.

Jones, Diane Brown. *A Reader's Guide to the Short Stories of William Faulkner*. New York: Twayne, 1994.

Joyce, James. *Dubliners*. 1914. New York: Viking, 1969.

———. *A Portrait of the Artist as a Young Man*. 1916. New York: Viking, 1968.

———. *Ulysses: The Corrected Text*. New York: Random, 1986.

Jung, C. G. *Contributions to Analytical Psychology*. Trans. H. G. and Cary Baynes. New York: Harcourt, 1928.

Karl, Frederick R. *William Faulkner: American Writer*. New York: Weidenfeld, 1989.

Kartiganer, Donald M. *The Fragile Thread: The Meaning of Form in Faulkner's Novels*. Amherst: U of Massachusetts P, 1979.

Kawin, Bruce F. *Faulkner and Film*. New York: Ungar, 1977.

Keating, Bern, and Franke Keating. *Mississippi*. Jackson: UP of Mississippi, 1982.

Kerr, Elizabeth M. *Yoknapatawpha: Faulkner's "Little Postage Stamp of Native Soil."* New York: Fordham UP, 1969.

Kierkegaard, Søren. Fear and Trembling *and* The Sickness unto Death. Trans. and introd. Walter Lowrie. Garden City: Doubleday, 1941.

King, Richard H. *A Southern Renaissance: The Cultural Awakening of the American South, 1930–1955*. New York: Oxford UP, 1980.

Kinney, Arthur F., ed. *Critical Essays on William Faulkner: The Compson Family*. New York: Garland, 1982.

———. *Faulkner's Narrative Poetics: Style as Vision*. Amherst: U of Massachusetts P, 1978.

Kirk, Robert W., and Marvin Klotz. *Faulkner's People: A Complete Guide and Index to the Characters in the Fiction of William Faulkner*. Berkeley: U of California P, 1963.

Kreiswirth, Martin. *William Faulkner: The Making of a Novelist*. Athens: U of Georgia P, 1983.

Lester, Cheryl. "Racial Awareness and Arrested Development: *The Sound and the Fury* and the Great Migration." Weinstein, *Cambridge Companion* 123–45.

Lind, Ilse Dusoir. "The Teachable Faulkner." *College English* 16 (1955): 284–87, 302.

Lockyer, Judith. *Ordered by Words: Language and Narration in the Novels of William Faulkner.* Carbondale: U of Southern Illinois P, 1991.

Matthews, John T. *The Play of Faulkner's Language.* Ithaca: Cornell UP, 1982.

———. *The Sound and the Fury: Faulkner and the Lost Cause.* Boston: Hall, 1991.

"*McCall's* Visits 'Miss Maud.'" *McCall's* Oct. 1956: 21+.

McGovern, James. *Anatomy of a Lynching: The Killing of Claude Neal.* Baton Rouge: Louisiana State UP, 1982.

McMillen, Neil. *Dark Journey: Black Mississippians in the Age of Jim Crow.* Urbana: U of Illinois P, 1989.

McMillen, Neil, and Noel Polk. "Faulkner on Lynching." *Faulkner Journal* 8.1 (1994): 3–14.

Mellard, James M. *Using Lacan / Reading Fiction.* Urbana: U of Illinois P, 1991.

Meriwether, James B., ed. *A Faulkner Miscellany.* Jackson: UP of Mississippi, 1974.

———. "A Prefatory Note by Faulkner for the Compson Appendix." *American Literature* 43 (1971): 281–84.

Meriwether, James B., and Michael Millgate, eds. *Lion in the Garden: Interviews with William Faulkner, 1926–1962.* New York: Random, 1968. Lincoln: U of Nebraska P, 1980.

Millgate, Michael. *The Achievement of William Faulkner.* 1966. Lincoln: U of Nebraska P, 1978.

Miner, Ward L. *The World of William Faulkner.* Durham: Duke UP, 1952.

Minter, David. "Faulkner, Childhood, and the Making of *The Sound and the Fury.*" *American Literature* 51 (1979): 376–93.

———. *William Faulkner: His Life and Work.* Baltimore: Johns Hopkins UP, 1980.

Mississippi: The WPA Guide to the Magnolia State. 1938. Introd. Robert S. McElvaine. Jackson: UP of Mississippi, 1988.

Mitchell, Juliet. *Psychoanalysis and Feminism.* New York: Random, 1974.

Moreland, Richard. *Faulkner and Modernism: Rereading and Rewriting.* Madison: U of Wisconsin P, 1990.

Morris, Willie. *North toward Home.* 1967. Oxford: Yoknapatawpha, 1982.

Morrison, Gail M. "William Faulkner's *The Sound and the Fury*: A Critical and Textual Study." Diss. U of South Carolina, 1980.

Morrison, Toni. *Playing in the Dark: Whiteness and the Literary Imagination.* Cambridge: Harvard UP, 1992.

Mortimer, Gail L. *Faulkner's Rhetoric of Loss: A Study in Perception and Meaning.* Austin: U of Texas P, 1983.

Muhlenfeld, Elisabeth. "Teaching Faulkner Today." Teaching the Major Writers Today: Shakespeare, Joyce, Faulkner. MLA Convention. New York Hilton. 28 Dec. 1983.

Murfin, Ross C. "What Is Psychoanalytic Criticism?" *The House of Mirth.* By Edith Wharton. Ed. Murfin. New York: Bedford–St. Martin's, 1994. 447–59.

Nathanson, Nicholas. *The Black Image in the New Deal: The Politics of FSA Photography*. Knoxville: U of Tennessee P, 1992.

Nietzsche, Friedrich. The Birth of Tragedy *and* The Case of Wagner. Trans. Walter Kaufman. New York: Vintage-Random, 1967.

———. On the Genealogy of Morals *and* Ecce Homo. Ed. and trans. Walter Kaufman. New York: Vintage-Random, 1967.

———. *Twilight of the Idols*. *The Portable Nietzsche*. Ed. and trans. Walter Kaufman. New York: Random, 1954. 463–563.

———. *The Will to Power*. Trans. Walter Kaufman and R. J. Hollingdale. Ed. Kaufman. New York: Vintage-Random, 1968.

Oakes, James. *The Ruling Race: A History of American Slaveholders*. New York: Vintage, 1983.

O'Connor, William Van. *The Tangled Fire of William Faulkner*. Minneapolis: U of Minnesota P, 1954.

Olney, James. "Autobiography and the Cultural Moment: A Thematic, Historical, and Biographical Introduction." *Autobiography: Essays Theoretical and Critical*. Ed. James Olney. Princeton: Princeton UP, 1980. 3–27.

Parker, Robert Dale. *Faulkner and the Novelistic Imagination*. Urbana: U of Illinois P, 1985.

Percy, Walker. "Stoicism in the South." *Commonweal* 6 July 1956: 342–44.

Phillips, Gene D. *Fiction, Film, and Faulkner: The Art of Adaptation*. Knoxville: U of Tennessee P, 1988.

Pilkington, John. *The Heart of Yoknapatawpha*. Jackson: UP of Mississippi, 1981.

Polk, Noel. *An Editorial Handbook for William Faulkner's* The Sound and the Fury. New York: Garland, 1985.

———, ed. *New Essays on Faulkner's* The Sound and the Fury. Cambridge: Cambridge UP, 1993.

Proust, Marcel. *Remembrance of Things Past*. Trans. C. K. Montcrieff and Terence Kilmartin. 3 vols. New York: Random, 1981.

Raboteau, Albert J. *Slave Religion: The "Invisible Institution" in the Antebellum South*. New York: Oxford UP, 1978.

Reed, Joseph W., Jr. *Faulkner's Narrative*. New Haven: Yale UP, 1973.

Reid, Panthea [Panthea Reid Broughton]. "The Scene of Writing and the Shape of Language for Faulkner When 'Matisse and Picasso Yet Painted.'" *Faulkner and the Artist: Faulkner and Yoknapatawpha, 1993*. Ed. Donald Kartiganer and Ann J. Abadie. Jackson: UP of Mississippi, 1996. 82–109.

Roberts, Diane. *Faulkner and Southern Womanhood*. Athens: U of Georgia P, 1994.

Rosenblatt, Louise. *Literature as Exploration*. 1938. New York: MLA, 1995.

Rubin, Louis D., Jr., et al. *The History of Southern Literature*. Baton Rouge: Louisiana State UP, 1985.

Runyan, Harry. *A Faulkner Glossary*. New York: Citadel, 1964.

Saxon, Lyle. "A Family Breaks Up." Rev. of *The Sound and the Fury*, by William Faulkner. *New York Herald Tribune Books* 13 Oct. 1929: 3. Rpt. in Kinney, *Critical Essays* 81–82.

Schwartz, Lawrence H. *Creating Faulkner's Reputation: The Politics of Modern Literary Criticism*. Knoxville: U of Tennessee P, 1988.

Senn, Fritz. "Book of Many Turns." *Fifty Years: Ulysses*. Ed. Thomas F. Staley. Bloomington: U of Indiana P, 1974. 29–46.

Sensibar, Judith L. *The Origins of Faulkner's Art*. Austin: U of Texas P, 1984.

Shakespeare, William. *The Tragedy of Hamlet, Prince of Denmark*. *The Riverside Shakespeare*. Boston: Houghton, 1974. 1135–97.

———. *The Tragedy of Macbeth*. *The Riverside Shakespeare*. Boston: Houghton, 1974. 1306–42.

Silver, James W. *Mississippi: The Closed Society*. New York: Harcourt, 1963.

Simpson, Lewis P. *The Brazen Face of History: Studies in the Literary Consciousness of America*. Baton Rouge: Louisiana State UP, 1980.

Singal, Daniel J. *The War Within: From Victorian to Modernist Thought in the South, 1919–1945*. Chapel Hill: U of North Carolina P, 1982.

Skei, Hans H. *William Faulkner: The Short Story Career: An Outline of Faulkner's Short Story Writing from 1919 to 1962*. Oslo: Universitelaget, 1981.

Slabey, Robert M. "Quentin Compson's 'Lost Childhood.'" *Studies in Short Fiction* 1 (1964): 173–83.

Slatoff, Walter. *Quest for Failure: A Study of William Faulkner*. Ithaca: Cornell UP, 1960.

Smith-Rosenberg, Carroll. *Disorderly Conduct*. New York: Knopf, 1985.

Snead, James A. *Figures of Division: William Faulkner's Major Novels*. New York: Methuen, 1986.

Snell, Susan. *Phil Stone of Oxford: A Vicarious Life*. Athens: U of Georgia P, 1991.

Stein, Gertrude. *Three Lives*. 1933. New York: Penguin, 1990.

Stevens, Wallace. "The Snow Man." *Collected Poems of Wallace Stevens*. New York: Knopf, 1957. 9–10.

Stonum, Gary Lee. *Faulkner's Career: An Internal Literary History*. Ithaca: Cornell UP, 1979.

Strandberg, Victor. *A Faulkner Overview: Six Perspectives*. New York: Kennikat, 1981.

Styron, William. "William Faulkner." *"This Quiet Dust" and Other Writings*. New York: Random, 1982. 257–63.

Sundquist, Eric J. *Faulkner: The House Divided*. Baltimore: Johns Hopkins UP, 1983.

———. *To Wake the Nations: Race in the Making of American Literature*. Cambridge: Harvard UP, 1993.

Sweeney, Patricia E. *William Faulkner's Women Characters*. Santa Barbara: ABC-CLIO Information Services, 1985.

Tate, Allen. *The Fathers*. 1938. Chicago: Swallow, 1970.

———. "Religion and the Old South." *Essays of Four Decades*. Chicago: Swallow, 1968. 558–76.

Taylor, Walter. *Faulkner's Search for a South*. Urbana: U of Illinois P, 1983.

Taylor, William R. *Cavalier and Yankee: The Old South and the American National Character*. New York: Braziller, 1961.

————. *William Faulkner: An Introduction and Interpretation*. New York: Holt, Rinehart, 1967.

Townsend, Kim. *Sherwood Anderson*. Boston: Houghton, 1987.

Tuck, Dorothy. *Crowell's Handbook of Faulkner*. Introd. Lewis Leary. 1964. Rpt. as *The Apollo Handbook of Faulkner*. New York: Crowell, 1969.

Ulmer, Gregory L. *Applied Grammatology: Post(e)-Pedagogy from Jacques Derrida to Joseph Beuys*. Baltimore: Johns Hopkins UP, 1985.

Vickery, Olga W. *The Novels of William Faulkner: A Critical Interpretation*. Rev. ed. Louisiana State UP, 1964.

Volpe, Edmond L. "Appendix: Chronology and Scene Shifts in Benjy's and Quentin's Sections." *A Reader's Guide to William Faulkner*. New York: Farrar, 1968. 353–77.

von Franz, M. L. "The Process of Individuation." *Man and His Symbols*. Ed. C. G. Jung and von Franz. Garden City: Doubleday, 1964. 158–229.

Wadlington, Warwick. *Reading Faulknerian Tragedy*. Ithaca: Cornell UP, 1987.

Waggoner, Hyatt. *William Faulkner: From Jefferson to the World*. Lexington: U of Kentucky P, 1959.

Wagner, Linda Welsheimer, ed. *William Faulkner: Four Decades of Criticism*. East Lansing: Michigan State UP, 1973.

Walton, Anthony. *Mississippi: An American Journey*. New York: Knopf, 1996.

Warren, Robert Penn, ed. *Faulkner: A Collection of Critical Essays*. Twentieth Century Views. Englewood Cliffs: Prentice, 1966.

Wasson, Ben. *Count No 'Count: Flashbacks to Faulkner*. Jackson: UP of Mississippi, 1983.

Watson, James G. *William Faulkner: Letters and Fictions*. Austin: U of Texas P, 1987.

Wayne, Michael. *The Reshaping of Plantation Society: The Natchez District, 1860–1880*. Baton Rouge: Louisiana State UP, 1983.

Webb, James W., and A. Wigfall Green. *William Faulkner of Oxford*. Baton Rouge: Louisiana State UP, 1965.

Weinstein, Philip M., ed. *The Cambridge Companion to William Faulkner*. New York: Cambridge UP, 1995.

————. *Faulkner's Subject: A Cosmos No One Owns*. New York: Cambridge UP, 1992.

————. "Meditations on the Other: Faulkner's Rendering of Women." Fowler and Abadie, *Faulkner and Women* 81–99.

Wells, Dean Faulkner, ed. *The Ghosts of Rowan Oak: William Faulkner's Ghost Stories for Children*. Oxford: Yoknapatawpha, 1980.

Welty, Eudora. *Eudora Welty: Photographs*. Jackson: UP of Mississippi, 1989.

————. *One Time, One Place: Mississippi in the Depression: A Snapshot Album*. New York: Random, 1971.

Williams, Joan. "In Defense of Caroline Compson." Kinney, *Critical Essays* 402–07.

Williams, Tennessee. *A Streetcar Named Desire*. 1947. New York: New Directions, 1980.

Williamson, Joel. *A Rage for Order: Black-White Relations in the American South since Emancipation*. New York: Oxford UP, 1986.

———. *William Faulkner and Southern History*. New York: Oxford UP, 1993.

Wilson, Charles Reagan, and William Ferris, eds. *Encyclopedia of Southern Culture*. Chapel Hill: U of North Carolina P, 1989.

Wilson, Jack Case. *Faulkners, Fortunes, and Flames*. Nashville: Annandale, 1984.

Wittenberg, Judith Bryant. *Faulkner: The Transfiguration of Biography*. Lincoln: U of Nebraska P, 1979.

———. "William Faulkner: A Feminist Consideration." *American Novelists Revisited: Essays in Feminist Criticism*. Ed. Fritz Fleischmann. Boston: Hall, 1982. 325–38.

Woodward, C. Vann. *The Burden of Southern History*. 1960. 3rd ed. Rev. Baton Rouge: Louisiana State UP, 1993.

Wright, Elizabeth. *Psychoanalytic Criticism*. London: Methuen, 1984.

Wyatt-Brown, Bertram. *The Literary Percys: Family History, Gender, and the Southern Imagination*. Athens: U of Georgia P, 1994.

———. *Southern Honor: Ethics and Behavior in the Old South*. New York: Oxford UP, 1982.

Audiovisual Materials

"Are You Walking with Me?" Sister Thea Bowman, William Faulkner, and African American Culture. Prod. Lisa N. Howorth. Videocassette. Center for the Study of Southern Culture, 1989.

Cleanth Brooks: An Introduction to William Faulkner's Fiction. Eminent Scholar / Teachers Modern Amer. Lit. Ser. Videocassette. Omnigraphics, 1988.

Collins, Sam. "Lonesome Road Blues." 1931. *Lonesome Road Blues*.

Duchamp, Marcel. *Nude Descending a Staircase*. Philadelphia Museum of Art.

Faulkner's Mississippi: Land into Legend. Video. Prod. Robert D. Oesterling. Script by Evans Harrington. Univ. of Mississippi Center for Public Service and Continuing Studies, 1965.

Intruder in the Dust. Film. Prod. Clarence Brown. Dir. Clarence Brown. MGM, 1949.

Lonesome Road Blues: Fifteen Years in the Mississippi Delta, 1926–1941. Audiocassette. Yazoo 1038; Shanachie Records, 1991.

Matisse, Henri. *La chambre rouge (Harmony in red)*. Hermitage Museum, Leningrad.

———. *Portrait de Madame Matisse (La raie verte)*. Statens Museum for Kunst, Copenhagen.

Pettis, Arthur. "Good Boy Blues." 1930. *Lonesome Road Blues*.

Picasso, Pablo. *Les desmoiselles d'Avignon*. Museum of Modern Art, New York.

———. *La vie*. Cleveland Museum of Art.

The Reivers. Film. Dir. Mark Rydell. National General Films, 1969.

A Rose for Emily. Videocassette. Dir. John Huston. PBS, 1982.

The Sound and the Fury. Film. Prod. Jerry Wald. Dir. Martin Ritt. Twentieth Century Fox, 1959.

A Sound Portrait of William Faulkner. Narr. Colleen Dewhurst and Tennessee Williams. National Public Radio, 1980.

Tomorrow. Film. Screenplay by Horton Foote. Prod. Gilbert Pearlman and Paul Roebling. Dir. Joseph Anthony. 1971.

Two Black Churches. Dir. William Ferris. Videocassette. Yale University Films and Center for Southern Folklore, 1975.

Two Soldiers. Videocassette. Prod. Jacob Bertucci. Dir. Christopher LaPalm. Amer. Film Inst., 1985.

William Faulkner: A Life on Paper. Videocassette. Script by A. I. "Buzz" Bezzerides. Mississippi Authority for Educ. Television and PBS, 1979.

William Faulkner of Oxford. IQ Films, n.d. (in the 1950s).

William Faulkner Reads. 1954. (Selections from *As I Lay Dying*, "Old Man," "Nobel Prize Speech.") Caedmon Records. LP and videocassette. LC RA55-2.

William Faulkner Reads Selections from Light in August *and* The Sound and the Fury. 1957. Listening Library AA3336. LP. LC 79-751884.

William Faulkner's "Barn Burning." Videocassette. Screenplay by Horton Foote. Prod. Cal Skaggs. Dir. Peter Werner. Learning in Focus, 1980.

William Faulkner's Mississippi. Videocassette. Benchmark, 1965.

William Faulkner's "The Bear." Videocassette. BFA Educ. Media, 1980.

INDEX

Modern Language Association of America
Approaches to Teaching World Literature
Joseph Gibaldi, series editor

Achebe's Things Fall Apart. Ed. Bernth Lindfors. 1991.
Arthurian Tradition. Ed. Maureen Fries and Jeanie Watson. 1992.
Austen's Pride and Prejudice. Ed. Marcia McClintock Folsom. 1993.
Beckett's Waiting for Godot. Ed. June Schlueter and Enoch Brater. 1991.
Beowulf. Ed. Jess B. Bessinger, Jr., and Robert F. Yeager. 1984.
Blake's Songs of Innocence and of Experience. Ed. Robert F. Gleckner and
  Mark L. Greenberg. 1989.
Brontë's Jane Eyre. Ed. Diane Long Hoeveler and Beth Lau. 1993.
Byron's Poetry. Ed. Frederick W. Shilstone. 1991.
Camus's The Plague. Ed. Steven G. Kellman. 1985.
Cather's My Ántonia. Ed. Susan J. Rosowski. 1989.
Cervantes' Don Quixote. Ed. Richard Bjornson. 1984.
Chaucer's Canterbury Tales. Ed. Joseph Gibaldi. 1980.
Chopin's The Awakening. Ed. Bernard Koloski. 1988.
Coleridge's Poetry and Prose. Ed. Richard E. Matlak. 1991.
Dante's Divine Comedy. Ed. Carole Slade. 1982.
Dickens' David Copperfield. Ed. Richard J. Dunn. 1984.
Dickinson's Poetry. Ed. Robin Riley Fast and Christine Mack Gordon. 1989.
Eliot's Middlemarch. Ed. Kathleen Blake. 1990.
Eliot's Poetry and Plays. Ed. Jewel Spears Brooker. 1988.
Ellison's Invisible Man. Ed. Susan Resneck Parr and Pancho Savery. 1989.
Faulkner's The Sound and the Fury. Ed. Stephen Hahn and Arthur F. Kinney. 1996.
Flaubert's Madame Bovary. Ed. Laurence M. Porter and Eugene F. Gray. 1995.
García Márquez's One Hundred Years of Solitude. Ed. María Elena de Valdés and
  Mario J. Valdés. 1990.
Goethe's Faust. Ed. Douglas J. McMillan. 1987.
Hebrew Bible as Literature in Translation. Ed. Barry N. Olshen and
  Yael S. Feldman. 1989.
Homer's Iliad *and* Odyssey. Ed. Kostas Myrsiades. 1987.
Ibsen's A Doll House. Ed. Yvonne Shafer. 1985.
Works of Samuel Johnson. Ed. David R. Anderson and Gwin J. Kolb. 1993.
Joyce's Ulysses. Ed. Kathleen McCormick and Erwin R. Steinberg. 1993.
Kafka's Short Fiction. Ed. Richard T. Gray. 1995.
Keats's Poetry. Ed. Walter H. Evert and Jack W. Rhodes. 1991.
Kingston's The Woman Warrior. Ed. Shirley Geok-lin Lim. 1991.
Lessing's The Golden Notebook. Ed. Carey Kaplan and Ellen Cronan Rose. 1989.
Mann's Death in Venice *and Other Short Fiction.* Ed. Jeffrey B. Berlin. 1992.
Medieval English Drama. Ed. Richard K. Emmerson. 1990.
Melville's Moby-Dick. Ed. Martin Bickman. 1985.
Metaphysical Poets. Ed. Sidney Gottlieb. 1990.
Miller's Death of a Salesman. Ed. Matthew C. Roudané. 1995.

Milton's Paradise Lost. Ed. Galbraith M. Crump. 1986.

Molière's Tartuffe *and Other Plays*. Ed. James F. Gaines and
    Michael S. Koppisch. 1995.

Momaday's The Way to Rainy Mountain. Ed. Kenneth M. Roemer. 1988.

Montaigne's Essays. Ed. Patrick Henry. 1994.

Murasaki Shikibu's The Tale of Genji. Ed. Edward Kamens. 1993.

Pope's Poetry. Ed. Wallace Jackson and R. Paul Yoder. 1993.

Shakespeare's King Lear. Ed. Robert H. Ray. 1986.

Shakespeare's The Tempest *and Other Late Romances*. Ed. Maurice Hunt. 1992.

Shelley's Frankenstein. Ed. Stephen C. Behrendt. 1990.

Shelley's Poetry. Ed. Spencer Hall. 1990.

Sir Gawain and the Green Knight. Ed. Miriam Youngerman Miller and
    Jane Chance. 1986.

Spenser's Faerie Queene. Ed. David Lee Miller and Alexander Dunlop. 1994.

Sterne's Tristram Shandy. Ed. Melvyn New. 1989.

Swift's Gulliver's Travels. Ed. Edward J. Rielly. 1988.

Thoreau's Walden *and Other Works*. Ed. Richard J. Schneider. 1996.

Voltaire's Candide. Ed. Renée Waldinger. 1987.

Whitman's Leaves of Grass. Ed. Donald D. Kummings. 1990.

Wordsworth's Poetry. Ed. Spencer Hall, with Jonathan Ramsey. 1986.

3 5282 00448 4179